Kennedy's
New Latin Pri

ALSO FROM TIGER XENOPHON

Grammaire Élémentaire de l'Ancien Français
Joseph Anglade

From Latin to Italian
Charles H. Grandgent

Grammar of the Gothic Language
Joseph Wright

A Greek Grammar
William W. Goodwin

ALSO FROM TIGER OF THE STRIPE

The Student's Dictionary of Anglo-Saxon
Henry Sweet

**The History of English Handwriting
A.D. 700–1400**
Sir Edward Maunde Thompson

Kennedy's New Latin Primer

A New Edition by

GERRISH GRAY

TIGER ◢ XENOPHON

TIGER XENOPHON
is an imprint of
TIGER OF THE STRIPE
50 Albert Road
Richmond
Surrey TW10 1DP
United Kingdom

first edition in this form
© 2008 Tiger of the Stripe
all rights reserved

ISBN 978-1-904799-18-4

typeset in the United Kingdom by
Tiger of the Stripe

printed in the United States
and the United Kingdom by
Lightning Source

Contents

Publisher's Foreword

The book usually known as *Kennedy's Revised Latin Primer* has remained, with good reason, the pre-eminent Latin reference grammar in British schools and universities for many decades. *Kennedy's New Latin Primer* from Tiger Xenophon is the first entirely new edition in two generations.

As well as clearer and more legible typography, this new edition has been modernised for today's readers. In earlier editions the English was occasionally almost as alien to the novice as the Latin – with, for instance, *quōcumque* being translated as *whithersoever*. This and many other relics of a bygone age have been revised without the 'dumbing down' which afflicts so many modern textbooks.

The sections on pronunciation have been revised to reflect modern scholarship. Readers wishing to learn more about this subject, and particularly the fascinating detective work which allows us to know with reasonable accuracy how Latin was pronounced in the Classical period, are encouraged to consult W. Sidney Allen's *Vox Latina* (2nd edn, Cambridge University Press, 1978).

One of the most vexed questions facing the editors and publishers of modern Latin grammars is whether to spell consonantal **u** as **u** or **v**. James Moorwood in his excellent *Latin Grammar* (Oxford University Press, 1999) rejoiced in producing 'the first Latin grammar in English to have banished the letter "v" from the Latin alphabet. It was never there.' It might be more accurate to say that **u** was never there, but that **v** represented both English **u** and **w** pronunciations and never English **v**. Because there is a distinction in pronunciation, albeit a subtle one, we have chosen to retain **v** in this edition. The only disadvantage is the danger that English-speaking students will be tempted to pronounce it in the English manner. All we can say is *don't!*

A US edition of this book is also available. It differs only in a few spellings and the order in which substantives and adjectives are declined.

Peter Danckwerts
Richmond, 2008

The Latin Language

1 Latin was the dialect of the Latini, or people of Latium in Italy. It was spoken by the ancient Romans, and, as their poets and prose-writers all used this dialect, the language was called Latin, not Roman.

Latin belongs to the family of languages known as Indo-European; among the many languages in this group are sanskrit, Hindi, Urdu, Bengali, the Germanic languages (such as German, English, Swedish, etc.), Russian, Polish, Greek, Farsi, Welsh and Irish. The imperial power of Rome made Latin the general speech of much of Western Europe, and from it are derived the modern Italian, French, Spanish, Portuguese, Romansch and Romanian, hence called Romance languages.

Note: In England, after its conquest by the Angles and Saxons, a Germanic language, called Old English, was spoken. After the Norman Conquest (A.D. 1066), this became mixed with Norman French, a Romance dialect, an off-shoot of Latin. After the revival of Classical learning in the sixteenth century, a large number of words were brought into English direct from Latin, and more have been added since, so that to understand the English language thoroughly it is necessary to have a knowledge of Latin.

The influence of Greek civilisation on Latin was very great; it was chiefly exerted at two distinct eras. The first of these began about 550 B.C., through the commerce of the Romans with the Greek colonies in Southern Italy. The second may be dated from the third century B.C., when literary activity began at Rome. This influence was further developed through the conquest of Greece by Rome, which was completed 146 B.C.

Nearly all Latin literature, except the satiric writings of Horace, Persius, and Juvenal, is formed on Greek models. The earliest specimens of Latin we possess are inscriptions, laws, annals, and fragment's of songs.

The credit of authorship is first ascribed to Livius Andronicus, who is said to have exhibited plays at Rome 240 B.C. The works of the poets who followed soon after this date have mostly perished, except the comedies of Plautus and Terence, about 200 to 140 B.C., and a prose fragment of the elder Cato.

The ages regarded as classical may be said to begin about 80 B.C., lasting about 200 years.

The so-called Golden Age ended with the death of Augustus, A.D. 14, when the Silver Age began, ending about 120 A.D. The authors most studied are, in prose, Cicero, Caesar, Livy, Tacitus; in poetry, Lucretius, Virgil, Horace, Ovid, and Juvenal.

LETTERS AND LAWS OF SOUND

2   **The Latin Alphabet** contains twenty-three letters, with the following signs:-

A B C D E F G H I K L M N O P Q R S T V X Y Z
a b c d e f g h i k l m n o p q r s t u x y z

Note: In early times C was written to represent the sounds of both C and G, which were probably not clearly distinguished in speaking. Afterwards G was made out of C, and K, becoming superfluous, went out of use. Y and Z were added in Cicero's time, being borrowed directly from the Greek alphabet, but they are only found in words taken from the Greek.

Although the Romans had cursive scripts, as well as the monumental capitals for which they are well known, small letters of the form we use today were only introduced in medieval times.

The letters are divided into:
1. **Vowels** (sounding by themselves);
2. **Consonants** (sounding with a vowel).

VOWELS

3   The vowels are **a, e, i, o, u** and **y. i** and **u** were also used as consonant (see below). The most open sound is **a**; the closest sharp sound is **i** ; and the closest flat sound is **u**; **e** is intermediate between **a** and **i**, and **o** is intermediate between **a** and **u**.

```
              a
          e       o
        i       u
```

Y is always a vowel, as in *lyra,* and was sounded as French *u.*

4   QUANTITY OF VOWELS

Each of the six vowels, except **y**, which is always short, can be either short or long: short when pronounced quickly, like English *a* in *man*; long when the voice dwells on the sound, as in *far.* A short vowel is sometimes distinguished by the *breve* sign ˘, a long one by the *macron* sign ˉ: *ămō.* However, in this book, we will rarely mark short vowels (an unmarked vowel being understood to be short). Thus the six vowels stand for eleven different sounds:

a ā e ē i ī o ō u ū y

There were, no doubt, many finer shades of sound for each vowel, which cannot be exactly ascertained, but the following ten English words may give an approximate idea of their pronunciation.

a	ā	e	ē	i	ī	o	ō	u	ū
cut	cart	met	mate	kip	keep	cop	cope	foot	boot

5   DIPHTHONGS

A diphthong (double sound) is formed by two vowels meeting in one syllable. The diphthongs commonly found in Latin are **ae** (pronounced like the **y** in English *my*), **au** (like the **ow** in *cow*), **ei** (approximating to the **a** in *race*), **eu** (a short **e** sound gliding into a **u**), **oe** (probably like the **oy** in *boy*), **ui** (like the french word *oui*).

Note: In the oldest Latin there were six diphthongs: **ai, au, ei, eo, ai, au.** Of these, **ai** passes in classical Latin into **ae**, *mensae* for *mensai;* **au** remains unchanged; **ei** is found in old inscriptions, but in the literary language its place is taken by **ē** or by **ī**, as in *dīco,* except in the exclamation *ei;* **eu** is found in *ceu, heu, neu, seu,* and in many words of Greek origin; **oi** passes into **oe,** and sometimes into later **u:** *poena, punio;* ou becomes **ū,** as in **dūco.**

The diphthongs are always long (see § 474 ff.).

CONSONANTS

6   (i) velar stops, **c, k, qu** and **g**.
     (ii) dental stops (teeth sounds) **t, d**.
     (iii) labial stops (lip sounds) **p, b**.
     (iv) the unvoiced alveolar fricative, **s**.
     (v) the unvoiced labio-dental fricative, **f**.
     (vi) consonant **u**, (written **v** in this book).
     (vii) the glottal fricative, **h**.
     (viii) consonant **i**, the palatal approximant.
     (ix) nasals, **n, m**.
     (x) liquids, **l, r**.

> **Note: x** is really a double letter, standing for **cs, gs**. The letters **y** and **z** and the three Greek aspirates, **ch, ph, th,** are only found in Greek words, as *zōna, chlamys, phalanx, theātrum.*

Table of Latin Consonants

	STOPS (plosives)		FRICATIVES		LIQUIDS	NASALS	APPROXIMANTS
	unvoiced	voiced	unvoiced	voiced	voiced	voiced	voiced
LABIAL	p	b				m	
LABIO-DENTAL			f				
DENTAL	t	d			l, r		
ALVEOLAR			s	z		n	
LABIO-VELAR							u (v)
VELAR	c, k, q	g					
PALATAL						[ng]	i (j)
GLOTTAL			h				

7   PRONUNCIATION OF CONSONANTS

b   was pronounced much as it is in English, except before **t** or **s**, when it became unvoiced, sounding like **p**.

c   was similar to English **c** in *cat* but never like English **c** in *cite* or Italian **c** as in *cello*. Originally, Latin had no separate letter for the voiced sound, **g**, hence the abbreviation **C.** for *Gaius*.

d was usually similar to English **d**. However, it is clear from such spellings as *afferō* for *adferō*, that it was often assimilated into a following consonant.

f was like English **f**.

g was pronounced like English **g** in *goat*, never like **g** in *gin*. The combination **gn** appears to have been pronounced like **gn-n** in the English *wing-nut*.

h was like English **h**, though it was very lightly pronounced and sometimes disappeared, as happens in some English dialects (e.g., Cockney), witness *Adria* for *Hadria*, Adriatic. Also as in Cockney, those who were prone to drop **h**, often added it to words which had no call for it. Between two vowels, **h** often failed to prevent the vowels eliding.

i as a consonant is sometimes written **j** and was pronounced like English **y** is *yes* and German **j** as in *ja*. In classical times, it was never pronounced as the English **j** as in *judge* or the French **j** in *juge*, although both words derive from Latin *iūdex*.

k was rarely used, except for *Kalendae* and a few other words. It was pronounced as Latin **c**, English **k**.

l was similar to English **l** in all positions.

m was similar to English **m**. At the end of words, it tended to be reduced to simply nasalizing the preceding vowel.

n was like English **n**. It is possible that it was more generally dental (created by contact between the tongue and teeth) rather than alveolar (contact between the tongue and gum ridge) as is more common in English. In come positions, such as before **s**, it was usually only pronounced as a nasalization of the preceding vowel.

p was similar to English **p** but less aspirated, like Greek **π**.

qu is thought to have been pronounced as a **k** with rounded lips rather than the English **qu** in *quick*.

r may have been pronounced in Latin rather as in modern Italian. It was certainly more than a vowel-modifier as it is in some modern English pronunciations.

s is always unvoiced in classical Latin, as in English *sip*, not English *wise*.

> **Note:** As W. Sidney Allen rather charmingly puts it in *Vox Italia, causae* should be pronounced *cow-sigh*, not *cow's eye*.

t is generally believed to have been created by touching the tongue to the back of the top teeth, although it may also have been articulated in the same way as in most English dialects, with the tongue touching the gum ridge.

v (**consonant u**) was pronounced as English **w** in *water*.

x was simply a sign for **cs**, pronounced as English **x** in tax.

z is a late borrowing from the Greek **ζ** and is used to represent a voiced fricative, like the English **z** in *zoo*, in foreign words.

8a   **Syllables:** A syllable consists of one or more letters which can be sounded with a single accent or tone of the voice: *īlex* is thus two syllables, *ī* and *lex*.

When a consonant comes between two vowels, it belongs to the same syllable as the vowel which follows it: *pa-ter*.

When two or more consonants come between two vowels, at least one of them belongs to the preceding syllable: *mēn-sa, victrix*, with the exception that a plosive (**b, c, d, g, p, t**) followed by a liquid (**l, r**) can belong to the following syllable: *pa-trēs*. However, they are sometimes split between the two syllables: *pat-rēs*.

8b   The quantity of syllables (that is their weight) is the basis of Latin metre (see § 474 ff.). This is unlike English verse which relies on stress.

A syllable is **heavy** if:

1. it contains a long vowel or diphthong;

2. it ends in two consonants (including **x**, which is really **cs**);

3. it ends in a consonant and the next syllable begins with a consonant.

It can be seen from the above simple rules that the first syllable of *victor* is heavy, although the vowel is short, because the syllable ends in a consonant and the next begins with one: *vic-tor*.

Note 1: The last syllable of a word is called **ultimate**; the last but one **penultimate**; the last but two **ante-penultimate**.

Note 2: A syllable ending in a vowel is called **open**. One ending in a consonant is called **closed**.

---

9 **Accent:** The accent or tone falls on some one syllable in every word. The accented syllable was pronounced with greater force and also in a higher key than the other syllables. In Latin the rule is to throw the accent back; therefore in words of two or more syllables, the last syllable is never accented.

In words of more than two syllables the accent always falls on the last but one (penultimate), if it is long.

If the penultimate is short, the accent falls on the last but two (ante-penultimate).

The accents are not usually printed in Latin.

VOWEL CHANGE

10 ## I. CHANGE IN ACCENTED SYLLABLES

1. Original **e** may become **i**: *simul* (cf. *semel*), *venia* (cf. *vindex*).
2. **e** becomes **o** before **l**: *solvō* (*se-luō*).
3. **ou** becomes **ū**: *doucō* (later *dūcō*).
4. **i** becomes **e** before **r**: *serō* (for *sisō*).
5. **o** sometimes becomes **u**: *huc* (for *ho-ce*).

11 ## II. CHANGE IN UNACCENTED SYLLABLES

(A) In final syllables

1. **o** becomes **u**: *corpus* (stem *corpos-*).
2. **i** becomes **e**: *mare* (stem *mari-*), or is lost altogether: *animal* (for *animale*, stem *animali-*).

(B) In medial syllables the vowel is commonly affected by the next consonant

1. **e** appears before **r**: *cinis, cineris.*

2. **o** becomes **u** before **l** or a labial: as in *cultus* (*colō*), *epistula* (earlier *epistola*). But when **i** or **e** precedes, the vowel remains **o**: as *filiolus, alveolus.*

3. **i** appears before any other single consonant: as in *meritus, monitus* (*moneō*). (For exception see **13**.)

12
(C) In Compounds

Here the principle is the same, and generally the rules are the same as in (B), but the examples are much more numerous.

a to **e** in closed syllables and before **r**: *cōnsecrō* from *sacer; dēscendō* from *scandō; trādere from dare.*

a to **i** in most open syllables and before **ng**: *difficilis* from *facilis; attingō* from *tangō.*

a to **u** or **i** before labials: *occupō* and *accipiō* from *capiō;* and before **l**: *īnsultō, īnsiliō,* from *saltō, saliō.*

e to **i** often in open syllables, but never before **r**: *diligō* from *legō;* but *ferō, auferō.*

ae to **ī**: *collīdō* from *laedō.*

au to **ū** or **ō**: *inclūdō* from *claudō; explōdō* from *plaudō.*

o and **u** are generally unchanged in compounds.

Note: There is a vowel variation often seen in Latin inflection which is not due to change in the Latin language itself, but came down to it from the Indo-European language. Thus the same noun can have two or more stems, as *homo;* older stem *homon-,* later weak stem, *homin-; agmen-, agmln-; pater, patr-; genus* (orig. *genos*), *gener-.*

In these words the vowel of the strong stem is preserved in the nom. sing., while the weak stem appears in the other cases.

---

13   **Vowel Assimilation and Dissimilation:** The vowels of two following syllables tend to become alike in sound: *vegeō, vegetus* (*vigeō*), *pupugī* (for *pepugī*), nihil (for *nē-hil*), *mihi, tibi*.

On the other hand, two vowels coming together are sometimes dissimilated: **ii** becomes **ie** in *pietās, societās, abietis*.

14   **Vowel Contraction:** When two similar vowels are separated by consonant **i** or **u**, or by **h**, they commonly throw out the letter between them, and unite in a long vowel: *rēs* is contracted from *re-i-es, nēmō* from *nē-h-emō, nīl* from *ni-h-il, audīsse* from *audīvisse*.

Two dissimilar vowels sometimes unite in the same manner: *amāre* from *ama-i-ere; āmō* from *ama-i-ō; amāstī* from *amā-v-istī*.

Two vowels placed next each other often contract: *dēgō* from *dē-agō; nullus* from *nē-ullus; prōmō* from *prō-emō*.

15   **Syncope:** Dropping of an unaccented vowel between two consonants: *dextra* for *dextera; valdē* for *validē*. It often takes place in compounds: *calfaciō* for *calefaciō*. The vowel of the reduplicating syllable sometimes drops; *reppulī* for *repepulī*.

> **Note:** Sometimes when any one of the letters **l, r, m,** or **n** follows a consonant, a vowel not found in the stem springs up before it because of the semi-vocalic character of the sound; *ager,* stem *agro-; populus,* original stem *poplo-; asinus* (*asno-*); *volumus* (contrast *vul-tis*).

16   **Apocope:** Dropping of a final vowel: **e** is dropped in *quīn* for *quī-nē; dīc* for *dīce;* **i** falls off in *ut* for *uti, quot, tot* (*totidem*).

17   **Changes of Quantity:** A vowel generally shortens before another vowel: thus *rēī* became *rĕī*. A long vowel often becomes short through effect of the accent on the preceding or following syllable: *iūrō* becomes *periŭrō*, afterwards weakening to *pēierō; lŭcerna* from *lūceō*. In flectional endings, a vowel originally final is sometimes shortened. But when a final consonant is lost (as final **d** in the ablative), the length of the vowel seems to be preserved: *Gnaeō* (earlier *Gnaivōd*).

Vowel lengthening is often due to **compensation**. When two consonants follow an accented vowel the first of the two is often dropped, and the vowel lengthened, so that the syllable keeps its length: *nīdus* for *nisdus* (English nest retains the **s**).

CONSONANT CHANGE

18 **Consonants at the beginning of a word:** Two unvoiced consonants at the beginning of a word were avoided. Thus we find *locus* for original *stlocus, tīlia* for *ptīlia*. Sometimes a fricative preceding a stop is dropped: *caveō* for *scaveō*, but generally it is retained: *scandō, sternō, spērō*. A stop followed by a liquid is generally unchanged: as *crescō, trēs, plaudō;* but **g** before **n** is lost in *nōtus* for *gnōtus* (cf. *ignōtus*), and in *nōdus*, knot. The unvoiced fricative **f** remains before a liquid *flos, frons;* but **sm** becomes **m**, as in *mīrus, memor;* **sn** becomes **n** in *nix* (snow), *nurus* (Old English *snoru*), daughter-in-law.

19 **Consonants in the middle of a word:** In the middle of a word if two consonants come next each other which cannot be easily sounded together, either one drops out, *quālus* for *quas-lus*, basket, or one is assimilated to the other, as in *sella* for *sedla*, a seat. A stop often drops out before a nasal or liquid, with lengthening of the preceding vowel, as in *exāmen* for *exagmen*.

Other cases in which a letter is dropped are *quīntus* for older *quīnctus; ascrībō* for *ad-scrībō; asportō* for *abs-portō; bimēstris* from stem *bi-menstri-; iūdex* from *iūs-dic-*.

20 **Consonant Assimilation** is of two kinds:

(a) **Complete assimilation,** when the first letter becomes the same as the following one: *alloquor* for *ad-loquor; arrogō* for *ad-rogō; summus* for *supmus* (*suprēmus*); *assentiō* for *ad-sentiō, offerō* for *ob-ferō; suggerō* for *sub-gerō; accidō* for *ad-cadō; succumbō* for *sub-cumbō; differō* for *dis-ferō*.

(b) **Partial assimilation,** when the first letter changes to one which combines more easily with the following one: *rēxī* (*rēc-sī*), *rēctum* from *regō; scrīpsī, scrīptum*, from *scrībō*.

m becomes **n** (**ng**) before a guttural and **n** hefore a dental: *congruō* (sounded *cong-gruō*), *condūcō, constō*. **n** becomes **m**

before a labial: *impotēns, imbibō.* An unvoiced stop becomes voiced between vowels or between a vowel and a semi-vowel: *trīgintā* for *trīcentā; pūblicus,* stem *poplico-.*

> **Note:** **tt** and **dt** change to **ss**: hence the supines in *-sum* and past partciples in *-sus* are formed: *dēfend-to-* becomes *dēfensso-, dēfensum; claudto-, clausso-, clausum, pat-to-* becomes *passo-, passus.*
>
> Occasionally a following consonant is assimilated to the preceding one: *collum* for *colsum; ferre* for *ferse.*

20a **Dissimlilation** is seen in *caeruleus* from *caelum, merīdiēs* for *medīdiēs;* and in adjectives in *-āris* and *-ālis, familiāris, nātūrālis.* **s** between two vowels usually changes to **r**: *flōrēs, honōrēs,* from *flōs, honōs; quaesō* becomes *quaerō.*

21 **Metathesis:** Interchange of position between a vowel and liquid in the same syllable. This is chiefly seen in the case of **r**: *ter, trēs; spernō, sprēvī; terō, trīvī.*

> **Note:** When the vowel becomes the last letter of the stem by this change of position, it is always lengthened.

22 **Consonants at the end of a word:** A Latin word never ends in a double consonant: *mell-, farr-,* become *mel, far.*

A dental drops off after a guttural: *lac,* from stem *lact-.* The only exceptions are a labial stop or nasal followed by **s**: *urbs, stirps, dēns, hiems* (usually written *hiemps*).

c or **g** followed by **s** is written **x**: *dux, rēx.*

d falls off in *cor,* stem *cord-,* and in the ablative singular *extrā(d), intrā(d).*

n regularly falls off in the nominative of the n-stems : *leo.*

> **Note:** Both **m** and **n** were very lightly sounded at the end of a word, and a syllable ending in **m** is sometimes elided before a vowel: *animum advertere.* This elision takes place regularly in poetry. Final **d** and **t** were also lightly sounded and are sometimes interchanged: *haud, haut.*

23 **Dropping of Syllables:** When two syllables beginning with the same letter come together in the middle of a word, the first one is sometimes dropped. Thus *venēnī-ficium* becomes *venēficium, cōnsuētitūdō, cōnsuētūdō.*

INFLECTION

24 Inflection is a change made in the form of a word to show differences of meaning and use.

The **stem** is the simplest form of a word in any language before it undergoes changes of inflection. The **stem character** is the final letter of the stem. The **root** is the primitive element which the word has in common with kindred words in the same or in other languages. Every word has a stem and a root. They may be the same, but more often the stem is formed from the root. Thus in *agitāre*, *agita-* is the Stem and **a** the stem character, but *agis* the root, as shown by other words, *agere, agmen, agilis*.

Note 1: A language which expresses changes of meaning chiefly by inflection, and makes little use of help-words, is called synthetic. Latin is a synthetic language. A language which has little flection and uses many help-words is called analytic. English as now spoken is an analytic language. In analytic languages the place of the inflectional endings is often supplied by prepositions used with nouns: *Caesaris,* of Caesar; by auxiliaries used with verbs: *agitur,* it is being done. Analytic languages also use the article: *rēx* can be translated in English as *a* king or *the* king; and they use pronouns with verbs: *agō,* I do.

Note 2: Inflection sometimes takes place by letter-change in the root-syllable, *agi-mus, ēgi-mus,* or by an addition before it, which is called a prefix, as ***ce-**cin-ī* from *canō*. Most frequently, however, it consists in an addition made after the stem, which is called a suffix, In *agitāre,* *-re* is a suffix, and is also the ending; in *agitārēmus,* a second suffix, ***-mus***, is added and becomes the ending.

PARTS OF SPEECH

25 Words are divided into:

Nouns (substantives): names of persons, places, or things:

Caesar, Caesar; *Rōma,* Rome; *sōl,* sun; *virtus,* virtue.

Adjectives, which express the qualities of substantives:

*Roma **antiqua**,* ancient Rome; *sōl **clarus**,* the bright sun.

Pronouns, which stand for a substantive:

ego, I; *ille,* that, he.

Verbs, which express an action or state:

Sōl **dat** *lūcem,* the sun gives light; *Rōma* **manet,** Rome remains.

Adverbs, which qualify and limit verbs, adjectives, and sometimes other adverbs:

Rōma **diū** *flōruit; nunc* **minus** *potēns est.* Rome flourished long; now it
is less powerful.

Prepositions, which denote the relation of a noun to other
words in the sentence:

Per *Rōmam errō.* I wander through Rome.

Conjunctions, which connect words, phrases, and sentences:

Caelum suspiciō **ut** *lūnam* **et** *sīdera videam.*
I look up to the sky that I may see the moon and stars.

Interjections: words of exclamation: *heu, ēheu,* alas!

Nouns, adjectives, pronouns and **verbs** are inflected (see
§24).

26   There is no article in Latin. *Lūx* may be translated as *a light,* **the**
light, or simply *light.*

27   **Nouns** are:

(a) **Concrete:** *vir,* man; *mēnsa,* table. The names of persons or
places are called **proper names** (or proper nouns): *Caesar,*
Rōma.

(b) **Abstract:** *virtūs,* virtue.

(c) **Collective:** a word expressing a group or collection of persons or things of the same kind: *turba,* crowd.

DECLENSION DEFINED

28   **Declension** describes the change of form which nouns, adjectives and pronouns undergo to show changes of **number** and **case**.

29   There are **two numbers**:

Singular for one person or thing: *mēnsa*, a table; *gēns*, a nation.

Plural for more than one: *mēnsae*, tables; *gentēs*, nations.

30   **Case** is the form which a noun takes to show its relation to other words in the sentence.

There are **six cases**:

Nominative, used for the the subject of the sentence, and also the complement.

Vocative, the case of one addressed.

Accusative, used for the direct object of the sentence.

Genitive, usually expressing possession.

Dative, the case of the indirect object.

Ablative, often expressing *from*.

EXAMPLES OF THE CASES

Nominative: *Dominus dūcit*, the lord leads.
Vocative: *Ō domine*, O lord.
Accusative: *Dominum videō*, I see the lord.
Genitive: *Lūx sōlis*, the sun's light.
Dative: *Dominō librum dō*, I give the lord a book.
Ablative: *Sōle lūx ēditur*, light issues from the sun.

Note 1: The dative is also rendered *for* in English: *Senātus urbī cōnsulit,* the Senate consults for the city.

Note 2: The ablative is rendered by many English prepositions besides from: *in, by, with.* To express the person by whom an action is done, the ablative is used with the preposition *ā, ab: Remus ā Rōmulō interfectus est,* Remus was slain by Romulus. To express the instrument with which an action is done, the ablative is used alone: *Remus **gladiō** interfectus est,* Remus was slain with (or by) a sword.

Note 3: In ancient Latin there were two more cases, the **instrumental** answering the question With what? and the **locative** answering the question Where? The use of the instrumental passed entirely to the ablative, but the locative is often found in classical literature: *humī,* on the ground; *Romae,* at Rome; *Athēnīs,* at Athens.

RULES OF GENDER

31 There are **three genders**:
1, **masculine**; 2, **feminine**; 3, **neuter** (*neutrum,* neither of the two).
Gender is shown by the form of a word and by its meaning.

(A) FORM

(a) Masculine are most substantives in **-us** of the second and fourth declensions, and those in **-er** of the second declension.

(b) Feminine are nearly all nouns in **-a**, of the first declension and in **-es** of the fifth declension.

(c) Neuter are nouns in **-um** of the second declension, in **-ū** of the fourth declension, and indeclinable nouns, including the infinitive verb-noun (see §107).

For the third declension no general rule can be given.

(B) MEANING

(a) Masculine are all names of men, gods, months, and winds; also of most rivers and mountains: *Rōmulus, Mars, Octōber, Boreās,* north wind, *Tiberis, Olympus.*

Exceptions: Some mountains and a few rivers ending in **-a** or **-e** are feminine: *Allia, Lēthē, Aetna, Rhodopē, Alpēs* (plur,); neuter, *Pēlion, Sōracte.*

(b) Feminine are all names of women, goddesses, islands; and of most countries, cities, and trees: *Cornēlia, Iūnō, Lesbos, Asia, Rōma, pīnus.*

> Exceptions: Countries ending in **-um**, neuter: *Latium; Pontus* is masculine. Cities with plur. form in **-ī** are masculine: *Coriolī, Delphī;* those in **-um, -on, -a** (plur.) are neuter: *Tarentum, Īlion, Arbēla.*

Note 1: In the early ages people imagined natural objects as living beings, and made them masculine or feminine, according to their notions of their qualities: *ventus,* wind, *fluvius,* river, *mōns,* mountain, masculine ; *-regiō,* country, *urbs,* city, *arbor,* tree, feminine; and words belonging to these classes took the same genders.

Note 2: Many **o-** stems masc. (called **mobilia**) have a corresponding form in **-a** feminine:

fīlius, son	*deus,* god	*arbiter* ⎫
fīlia, daughter.	*dea,* goddess	*arbitra,* ⎭ umpire.

Other corresponding forms are used: *rēx,* king, *rēgīna,* queen; *victor, victrīx,* conqueror; *nepōs,* grandson, *neptis,* granddaughter; *socer, socrus,* father-, mother-in-law.

Note 3: Nouns which include both masculine and feminine are said to be of common gender: *sacerdōs,* priest or priestess, *vātēs,* seer, *parēns,* parent, *dux,* leader, *comes,* companion, *cīvis,* citizen, *custōs,* guardian, *iūdex,* judge, *hērēs,* heir, *āles,* bird, *canis,* dog, *serpēns,* serpent, *tigris,* tiger.

Many names of animals, though used of both sexes, have (in grammar) only one gender; they are called **epicene:** *aquila,* eagle, fem.; *lepus,* hare, masc.; *passer,* sparrow, masc. (For Memorial Lines on Gender, see § 503)

DECLENSION OF SUBSTANTIVES

32 Substantives are grouped in declensions according to the character or final letter of the stem as follows:

(1) First declension: a- stems, -ae genitive singular.

(2) Second declension: o- stems, -ī genitive singular.

(3) Third declension: consonant stems and i- stems, -is genitive singular.

(4) Fourth declension: u- stems, ūs genitive singular

(5) Fifth declension: e- stems, -eī or -ēī genitive singular.

TABLE OF CASE-ENDINGS

Decl.	1	2		3		4	5
stem char	a-	ō-		consonant	i-	u-	ē-
				SINGULAR			
	f. (m.)	m.	n.	m. f. n.	f. m. n.	m (f) n	f
Nom.	a	us	um	various	is, es ĕ, l, r	us ū	ēs
Voc.	a	e	um	various	is, es is, es	us ū	"
Acc.	am	um	um	em "	im " em	um ū	em
Gen.	ae	ī		is	is	ūs	eī (ēī)
Dat.	ae	ō		ī	ī	uī (ŭ)	eī (ēī)
Abl.	ā	ō		e	ī or e	ū	ē
				PLURAL			
Nom.	ae	ī a		ēs a	ēs ia	ūs ua	ēs
Voc.	ae	ī a		ēs a	ēs ia	ūs ua	ēs
Acc.	ās	ōs a		ēs a	ēs, īs ia	ūs ua	ēs
Gen.	ārum	ōrum		um	ium	uum	ērum
Dat.	īs	īs		ibus	ibus	ibus	ēbus
Abl.	īs	īs		ibus	ibus	ibus	ēbus

33 The character of the stem is most clearly seen before the ending
-**um** or -**rum** of the genitive plural.

The nominative, masculine and feminine, takes -**s**, except in **a**-
stems, some stems in **ro**- of the second declension, and stems in
s, l, r, n, of the third. The vocative is like the nominative, except
in the singular of nouns in -**us** of the second declension.

The accusative of neuter nouns is always the same as the
the nominative in both singular and plural; the nominative and
accusative plural always end in **a**.

FIRST DECLENSION

34   A- Stems

The nominative singular is the same as the stem, except that the final **a** of the nominative is short.

Stem mēnsā-, *table,* **f.**

	SINGULAR	PLURAL
Nom.	**mēnsa**, a table	**mēnsae**, tables
Voc.	**mēnsa**, o table	**mēnsae**, o tables
Acc.	**mēnsam**, a table	**mēnsās**, tables
Gen.	**mēnsae**, of a table	**mēnsārum**, of tables
Dat.	**mēnsae**, to a table	**mēnsīs**, to tables
Abl.	**mēnsā**, from a table	**mēnsīs**, from tables

Decline like mensa: **aquila**, *eagle;* **luna**, *moon;* **rēgina**, *queen;* **stella**, *star.*

First declension nouns are mostly feminine. A few are masculine, as *scrība*, a notary; *Hadria*, the Adriatic sea.

Note1: An old form of the gen. sing. -āī for -ae is sometimes used by poets, as *aulāī*. Also an old genitive of *familia* remains in compounds: *pater- (māter-) familiās*, father (mother) of a family.

Note 2: The locative (see §30, note 3) sing. ends in -ae; the plur. in -īs; *Rōmae*, at Rome; *mīlitiae*, at the war; *Athēnīs*, at Athens.

Note 3: The genitive plural is sometimes formed in **-um** instead of **-ārum**, by compounds with *-cola, -gena: agricola*, a farmer; and in some words borrowed from Greek: *amphora, drachma.*

Note 4: *Dea* and *fīlia* have dative and ablative plural **-ābus**, in order to distinguish them from the dative and ablative plural of *deus* and *fīlius*.

SECOND DECLENSION

35   O- Stems

The nominative is formed from the stem by adding **s**; in neuter nouns, **m**; the character **o** being weakened to **u**.

In the greater number of nouns whose stem ends in **-ero**, or in **-ro** preceded by a stop, the **-o** is dropped, and the nominative ends in **-er**.

Stem	anno- *year,* m.	puero- **boy,** m.	magistro- *master,* m.	bello- *war,* n.
	SINGULAR			
Nom.	annus, *a year*	puer	magister	bellum
Voc.	anne, *o year*	puer	magister	bellum
Acc.	annum, *a year*	puerum	magistrum	bellum
Gen.	annī, *year's*	puerī	magistrī	bellī
Dat.	annō, *to a year*	puerō	magistrō	bellō
Abl.	annō, *from a year*	puerō	magistrō	bellō
	PLURAL			
Nom.	annī, *years*	puerī	magistrī	bella
Voc.	annī, *o years*	puerī	magistrī	bella
Acc.	annōs, *years*	puerōs	magistrōs	bella
Gen.	annōrum, *years'*	puerōrum	magistrōrum	bellōrum
Dat.	annīs, *to years*	puerīs	magistrīs	bellīs
Abl.	annīs, *from years*	puerīs	magistrīs	bellīs

Decline like annus: **amīcus**, *friend;* **dominus**, *lord;* **servus**, *slave.*

Decline like puer: **gener**, *son-in-law;* **socer**, *father-in-law;* **līberī** (plur.), *children;* **lūcifer**, *light-bringer;* **armiger**, *armor-bearer.*

Decline like magister: **ager**, *field;* **cancer**, *crab;* **liber**, book. Decline like bellum: **rēgnum**, *kingdom;* **verbum**, *word.*

Nouns in **us, er,** are masculine; in **um** neuter.

As well as words feminine by meaning, the following **-us** words are feminine: **alvus**, *paunch;* **colus**, *distaff;* **humus**, *ground;* **vannus**, *winnowing-fan;* also several from the Greek: **arctus**, *the bear constellation;* **carbasus**, *linen;* plur. **carbasa**, n., *sails.*

Neuter in **us** (and used in the sing. only) are **pelagus**, *sea;* **virus**, *venom.*

Note: **Vulgus**, crowd, is generally neuter, rarely masculine.

35a The following have some exceptional forms:

Stem	fīlio-	viro-	deo-
	son, m.	man, m.	god, m.

	SINGULAR		
Nom.	fīlius	vir	deus
Voc.	fīlī	vir	deus
Acc.	fīlium	virum	deum
Gen.	fīliī or fīlī	virī	deī
D, Abl.	fīliō	virō	deō

	PLURAL		
N.V.	fīliī	virī	dī (deī)
Acc.	fīliōs	virōs	deōs
Gen.	fīliōrum	virōrum or virum	deōrum or deum
D. Abl.	fīliīs	virīs	dīs (deīs)

Note 1: Like *fīlius* are declined *genius*, guardian spirit, and many proper names in **-ius**: *Claudius, Virgilius;* like *vir*, its compounds, *decemvir, triumvir*, &c. The contracted gen. sing. in **-ī**, as *fīlī, ingenī*, is used by writers of the best age, especially poets.

Note 2: The **locative** singular ends in **ī**; the plural in **is**: *humī*, on the ground; *bellī*, at, the war; *Mīlētī*, at Miletus; *Philippīs*, at Philippi,

Note 3: The genitive plural in **-um** is often found; especially in words denoting coins, sums, weights, and measures: *nummus*, coin; *talentum*, talent. Some nouns have genitive plural in **-um** or **-ōrum**: *socius*, ally; *faber*, smith; *līberī*, children. Also *superī*, the gods, from adj. *superus* (§ 304),

THIRD DECLENSION

36   CONSONANT AND I- STEMS

The Third Declension contains:

A. Consonant Stems

Stops (plosives)

(1) Palatals,	**c, g**
(2) Dentals,	**t, d**
(3) Labials,	**p, b**
Fricative,	**s**

Nasals,	**n, m**
Liquids,	**l, r**

B. i- Stems

37 **Syllabus of consonant-stem nouns**

Stem-end	Nom. Sing.	Genitive Sing.	English

Stems in palatals with **x** in nom. for **cs** or **gs**

Stem-end	Nom. Sing.	Genitive Sing.	English
ac-	fax, f.	facis	torch
āc-	pāx, f.	pācis	peace
ec-	nex, f.	necis	death
ec-, ic-	apex, m.	apicis	peak
ēc-	vervēx, m.	vervēcis	wether
ic-	fornix, m.	fornicis	arch
ic-	iūdex, c.	iūdicis	judge
īc-	rādīx, f.	rādīcis	root
ōc-	vōx, f.	vōcis	voice
uc-	dux, c.	ducis	leader
ūc-	lūx, f.	lūcis	light
eg-	grex, m.	gregis	flock
ēg-	rēx, m.	rēgis	king
eg-, ig-	rēmex, m.	rēmigis	rower
ig-	strix, f.	strigis	screech-owl
ug-	conjunx, c.	conjugis	spouse
ūg-	frūx f.	frūgis, f.	fruit

Stems in dentals drop **t, d**, before **s** in the nom.

Stem-end	Nom. Sing.	Genitive Sing.	English
at-	anas, f.	anatis	duck
at-	aetās, f.	aetātis	age
et- s	seges, f.	segetis	corn-crop
et-	pariēs, m.	parietis	room-wall
ēt-	quiēs, f.	quiētis	rest
et-, it-	mīles, c.	mīlitis	soldier
it-	caput, n.	capitis	head
ōt-	nepōs, m.	nepōtis	grandson
ūt.	virtūs, f.	virtūtis	virtue, courage
ct-	lac, n.	lactis	milk
ad-	vas, m.	vadis	surety
ed-	pēs, m.	pedis	foot
ēd-	mērces, f.	mercēdis	hire
aed-	praes, m.	praedis	bondsman
ed-, id-	obses, c.	obsidis	hostage

id-	lapis, m.	lapidis	stone
ōd-	custōs, c.	custōdis	guardian
ud-	pecus, f.	pecudis	beast
ūd-	incūs, f.	incūdis	anvil
aud-	laus, f.	laudis	praise
rd-	cor. n.	cordis	heart

Stems in labials form nom. regularly with **s**

ap-	*wanting*	dapis, f.	banquet
ep- ip-	prīnceps, c.	prīncipis	chief
ip-	*wanting*	stipis, f.	dole (a coin)
op-	*wanting*	opis, f.	help
ep-, up-	auceps, m.	aucupis	fowler

Stems in the frivative **s**, which, except in **vās**, becomes **r**

ās-	vās, n.	vāsis	vessel
aes- aer-	aes, n.	aeris	copper, bronze
es- er-	Cerēs, f.	Cereris	Ceres
is- er-	cinis, m.	cineris	cinder
ōs- ōr-	honōs, m.	honōris	honour
os- or-	tempus, n.	temporis	time
us- er-	opus, n.	operis	work
ūs- ūr-	crūs, n.	crūris	leg

Stems in liquids

al-	sāl, m.	salis	salt
ell-	mel, n.	mellis	honey
il-	mūgil, m.	mūgilis	mullet
ōl-	sōl, m.	sōlis	sun
ul-	cōnsul, m.	cōnsulis	consul
ar-	iubar, n.	iubaris	sunbeam
arr-	fār, n.	farris	flour
er-	ānser, m.	ānseris	goose
ēr-	vēr, n.	vēris	spring
ter- tr-	māter, f.	mātris	mother
or-	aequor, n.	aequoris	sea
or-	ebur, n.	eboris	ivory
ōr-	soror, f.	sorōris	sister
ur-	vultur, m.	vulturis	vulture
ūr-	fūr, m.	fūris	thief

Stems in nasals

en- in-	nōmen, n.	nōminis	name
on- in-	homō, m.	hominis	man
ōn-	leō, m.	leōnis	lion
iōn-	ratiō, f.	ratiōnis	reason
rn-	carō, f.	carnis	flesh
in-	canis, c.	canis	dog
en-	iuvenis, c.	iuvenis	young person
em-	hiem(p)s, f.	hiemis	winter

A. CONSONANT STEMS

38   (1) Stems in palatals: c, g

Stem	iūdic- judge, c.		rādīc- root, f.	rēg- king, m.
SINGULAR				
Nom.	iūdex,	a judge	rādīx	rēx
Voc.	iūdex,	o judge	rādīx	rēx
Acc.	iūdĭcem,	a judge	rādĭcem	rēgem
Gen.	iūdicis,	of a judge	rādĭcis	rēgis
Dat.	iūdicī,	to a judge	rādīcī	rēgī
Abl.	iūdice,	from a judge	rādīce	rēge
PLURAL				
Nom.	iūdicēs,	judges	rādīces	rēgēs
Voc.	iūdicēs,	o judges	rādīces	rēgēs
Acc.	iūdicēs,	judges	rādīces	rēgēs
Gen.	iūdicum,	of judges	rādīcum	rēgum
Dat.	iūdicibus,	to judges	rādīcibus	rēgibus
Abl.	iūdicibus,	from judges	rādĭclbus	regibus

Decline also: f. vōx, vōc-, voice; c. dux, duc-, leader; m. grex, greg-, flock.

39   **(2) Stems in dentals: *t, d***

Stem	mīlit-	ped-	capit-
	soldier, c.	*foot*, m.	*head*, n.

SINGULAR

Nom.	mīles	pēs	caput
Voc.	mīles	pēs	caput
Acc.	mīlitem	pedem	caput
Gen.	mīlitis	pedis	capltis
Dat.	mīlitī	pedī	capitī
Abl.	mīlite	pede	capite

PLURAL

N.V.	mīlitēs	pedēs	capita
Acc.	mīlitēs	pedēs	capita
Gen.	mīlitum	pedum	capitum
Dat.	mīlitibus	pedibus	capitibus
Abl.	mīlitibus	pedibus	capitibus

Decline also: f. *virtūs, vlrtūt-* virtue; c. *seges,* **seget-**, corn; m. *lapis, lapld-*, stone.

40   **(3) Stems in labials: *p, b***

Stem	**prīncep-, prīncip-** *chief*, c.	
	SINGULAR	PLURAL
Nom	prīnceps	prīncipēs
Voc.	prīnceps	prīncipēs
Acc.	prīncipem	prīncipēs
Gen.	prīncipis	prīncipum
Dat.	prīncipī	prīncibus
Abl.	prīncipe	prīncibus

Decline also: c. *forceps,* **forclp-** , tongs; m. *auceps,* **aucup-**, fowler.

41   **(4) Stems in the fricative *s***

Stems in **s** do not add **s** in the nominative singular, and generally they change **s** into **r** in the other cases.

Stem	**flōs-**	**opus-**	**crūs-**
	flōr-	**oper-**	**crūr-**
	flower, m.	*work*, n.	*leg*, n.

SINGULAR

Nom.	**flōs**	**opus**	**crūs**
Voc.	**flōs**	**opus**	**crūs**
Acc.	**flōrem**	**opus**	**crūs**
Gen.	**flōris**	**operls**	**crūris**
Dat.	**flōrī**	**operī**	**crūrī**
Abl.	**flōre**	**opere**	**crūre**

PLURAL

Nom.	**flōrēs**	**opera**	**crūra**
Voc.	**flōrēs**	**opera**	**crūra**
Acc.	**flōrēs**	**opera**	**crūra**
Gen.	**flōrum**	**operum**	**crūrum**
Dat.	**flōribus**	**operibus**	**crūribus**
Abl.	**flōribus**	**operlbus**	**crūribus**

Decline also: m. *honōs, honour-,* honour; n. *tempus, tempor-,* time ; *corpus, corpor-,* body; *genus, gener-,* race; *iūs, iūr-,* law.

Note 1: Vās, *vas-,* n., a vessel, keeps **s** in all the cases, and has plural vāsa, vāsōrum, vāsīs. *Os, oss-,* n., bone; *ās, ass-,* m., a coin, keep **s** in all the cases, and have gen. plur. *ossium, assium.*

Note 2: *Honōs,* honour, *colōs,* colour, and other words changed in later classical Latin to *honor, color,* &c., in the nom. sing., with gen. *-ōris. Arbōs,* f., changed to *arbor, arboris,* tree.

42   **(5) Stems in liquids: *l, r***

Stems in **l, r,** do not take **s** in the nominative singular.

Stem	cōnsul- consul, m.	amōr- love, m.	pater-, patr- father, m.	aequor- sea, n.
SINGULAR				
N. V.	cōnsul	amŏr	pater	aequor
Acc.	cōnsulem	amōrem	patrem	aequor
Gen.	cōnsulis	amōrls	patrls	aequoris
Dat.	cōnsulī	amōrī	patrī	aequorī
Abl.	cōnsule	amōre	patre	aequore
PLURAL				
N. V.	cōnsulēs	amōrēs	patrēs	aequora
Acc.	cōnsulēs	amōrēs	patrēs	aequora
Gen.	cōnsulum	amōrum	patrum	aequorum
Dat,	cōnsulibus	amōribus	patribus	aequoribus
Abl.	cōnsulibus	amōribus	patribus	aequoribus

Decline also: m. *sōl, sōl-,* sun; *ōrātōr, ōrātōr-,* speaker; *carcer, carcer-,* prison; *frāter, frātr-,* brother; n. *ebur, ebor-,* ivory.

43   **(6) Stems in Nasals: *n, m***

Stems ending in **n** do not take **s** in the nominative singular. Stems in **ōn, on,** drop the **n.**

Stem	leōn- lion, m.	virgōn-, virgin- virgin, f.	nomen-, nomin- name, n.
SINGULAR			
N. V.	leō	virgō	nōmen
Acc.	leōnem	virginem	nōmen
Gen.	leōnis	virginis	nōminis
Dat.	leōnī	virginī	nōminī
Abl.	leōne	virgine	nōmine
PLURAL			
N.V.	leōnēs	virginēs	nōmina
Acc.	leōnēs	virginēs	nōmina
Gen.	leōnum	virginum	nōminum
Dat.	leōnibus	virginibus	nōminibus
Abl.	leōnibus	virginibus	nōminibus

Decline also: m. *latrō, latrōn-,* robber; f. *ratiō, ratlōn-,* reason; m. *ōrdō, ōrdin-,* order; *homō, homin-,* man; n. *carmen, carmin-,* song.

There is only one stem in **m**: *hiem(p)s,* winter; gen. *hiemis,* f.

B. I-STEMS.

44   **(1) Stems with nom. sing. in -*is,* and in -*er* from stem *ri*-**

	Stem	cīvi-	imbri-
		citizen, c.	*shower,* m.
	SINGULAR		
	N.V.	**cīvis**	**imber**
	Acc.	**cīvem**	**imbrem**
	Gen.	**cīvis**	**imbris**
	Dat.	**cīvī**	**imbrī**
	Abl.	**cīve, -ī**	**imbre, -ī**
	PLURAL		
	N.V.	**cīvēs**	**imbrēs**
	Acc.	**cīvēs**	**imbrēs, -īs**
	Gen.	**cīvium**	**imbrium**
	Dat.	**civibus**	**imbribus**
	Abl.	**cīvibus**	**imbribus**

Decline like **cīvis**: m. *amnis,* river; *ignis,* fire; f. *avis,* bird.

Decline like **imber**: f. *linter,* boat; m. *ūter,* leather bottle.

Note 1: Some words have acc. **-im**, abl. **ī**: f. *tussis,* cough; *sitis,* thirst; most rivers and towns, m. *Tiberis,* Tiber; f. *Neāpolis,* Naples. Sometimes f. *febris,* fever; *puppis,* stern; *turris,* tower; *clāvis,* key; *nāvis,* ship; *restis,* rope; *secūris,* axe; *sēmentis,* sowing. *Ignis* has usually abl. *ignī.* The acc. plur. is sometimes written **-īs**, which is the older form.

Note 2: **Vīs**, force, is the only long **ī**-stem. It has acc. sing. *vim,* abl. sing. *vī,* plur. *vīrēs, vīrium, vīribus.*

---

45   **(2) Stems with nom. sing. in -*ēs*:**

	Stem	nūbi-	*cloud,* f.
		SING.	PLUR.
	N.V.	**nūbēs**	**nūbēs**
	Acc.	**nūbem**	**nūbēs**
	Gen.	**nūbis**	**nūbium**
	Dat.	**nūbī**	**nūbibus**
	Abl.	**nūbe**	**nūbibus**

Decline also: *cautēs,* rock; *mōlēs,* pile; *rūpēs,* crag.

Note: Some have nom. sing. *-ēs* or *-is*: *vallēs* or *vallis,* valley; *vulpēs* or *vulpis,* fox. *Trabs,* beam, *plebs,* the common people, are often found for *trabēs,* *plebēs.* *Famēs,* hunger, and *tabēs,* corruption, have abl. sing. *famē, tabē.*

---

46   **(3) Stems with two consonants before i**
These generally drop **i** before the **s** in the nom. sing.

Stem	monti-	urbi-
	mountain, m.	*city*, f.
SINGULAR		
N. V.	**mons**	**urbs**
Acc.	**montem**	**urbem**
Gen.	**montis**	**urbis**
Dat.	**montī**	**urbī**
Abl.	**monte**	**urbe**
PLURAL		
N. V.	**montēs**	**urbēs**
Acc.	**montēs, -īs**	**urbēs, īs**
Gen.	**montium**	**urbium**
Dat.	**montlbus**	**urbibus**
Abl.	**montibus**	**urbibus**

Decline also: f. *arx, arci-*, citadel; *ars, arti-*, art; *stirps, stirpi-*, stem; *frons, fronti-*, forehead; *frōns, frondi-*, leaf; m. *dēns, denti-*, tooth.

47   **(4) Neuter stems with nom. sing. in -*e, -al, -ar***
These either change **i** into **e** in the nom. sing. or drop the vowel and shorten the final syllable.

Stem	cubili	animāli-	calcāri-
	couch	*animal*	*spur*
SINGULAR			
N. V. Acc.	**cubīle**	**animal**	**calcar**
Gen.	**cubīlis**	**animālis**	**calcāris**
Dat. Abl.	**cubīlī**	**animālī**	**calcārī**
PLURAL			
N. V. Acc.	**cubīlia**	**animālia**	**calcāria**
Gen.	**cubīlium**	**animālium**	**calcārium**
Dat. Abl.	**cubīlibus**	**animālibus**	**calcāribus**

Decline also: *conclāve*, room; *sedīle*, seat; *rēte*, net (abl. sing. -*e*); *tribūnal*, tribunal; *exemplar*, pattern.

Note: *Mare*, sea, has abl. sing. *marī*, or more rarely *mare;* the gen. plur. is only found once: *marum. Baccar*, an aromatic root, *fār*, flour, *iubar*, a sunbeam, *nectar*, nectar, have abl. sing. -**e**.

48   Consonant Stems and i-Stems

Consonant stems and i-stems are placed in one declension because of the difficulty of distinguishing their forms. I-stems are very rare in early Latin; they were being developed in the Classical period, and their forms are liable to uncertainty. The genitive plural (by which in other declension the stem is determined) often varies in the third declension between **-um** and **-ium**. In classing words as consonant or i-stems, the genitive plural must be considered, together with the accusative singular **-em** or **-im**, ablative singular **-ī**; accusative plural **-ēs** or **-īs**, and in neuters the nominative plural **-ia**; but often the classification remains doubtful, and rests chiefly on analogy with other Latin words, or on comparison with cognate words in other languages.

49   The following rule with regard to the form of the genitive plural may be given for practical convenience:

Nouns with a syllable more in the genitive singular than the nominative (**imparisyllabic nouns**) have genitive plural in **-um**.

Nouns with the same number of syllables in the nominative singular and genitive singular (**parisyllabic nouns**) have genitive plural in **-ium**. The chief exceptions to this rule are the following:

(a) Imparisyllabic nouns which have genitive plural in **-ium** are: *glīs, līs, mās, mūs, nox,* and nouns of one syllable of which the nominative singular ends in *-ns, -rs, -ps, -bs, -rx, -lx;*[*] and neuters in *-al, -ar*.

Often also *rēn, lār, dōs, fraus,* nouns of two syllables with nominative singular ending *-ns, -rs,* and most nouns in **-ās** (genitive **-ātis**). These latest and nouns in **-ns** are especially variable. Horace writes both *parentum* and *parentium,* but the latter is rare. Livy writes always *cīvitātium*.

---

[*] Nouns of one syllable of which the stem has two consonants before **i-**, are apparently only imparisyllabic because the nom. sing. originally ended in **-is** (§ 47), and some some are recorded with both forms,, e.g. *orbs* and *orbis.*

(b) Parisyllabic nouns which have genitive plural in **-um** are: *canis, iuvenis, senex, sēdēs, pater, māter, frāter, accipite.**

50   Nouns with exceptional forms
(1) **Iuppiter** (for *Dieus* + *piter*) and **bōs**, ox.

	SING.		PLUR.
N.V.	**Iuppiter**	**bōs**	**bovēs**
Acc.	**Iovem**	**bovem**	**bovēs**
Gen.	**Iovis**	**bovis**	**boum**
Dat.	**Iovī**	**bovī**	**bōbus or būbus**
Abl.	**Iove**	**bove**	**bōbus or būbus**

(2) Two stems in **-u**, declined like consonant nouns: **grūs**, crane, **sūs**, pig. These are the only uncontracted **u**- nouns.

	SING.	PLUR.	SING.	PLUR.
N.V.	**grūs**	**gruēs**	**sūs**	**suēs**
Acc.	**gruem**	**gruēs**	**suem**	**suēs**
Gen.	**gruis**	**gruum**	**suis**	**suum**
Dat.	**gruī**	**gruibus**	**suī**	**suibus (subus)**
Abl.	**grue**	**gruibus**	**sue**	**suibus (subus)**

Iter, journey, has gen. sing. *itineris* (and rarely *iteris*); *iecur,* liver, *iecoris,* and *iecinoris.*

Senex, old man, has sing. acc. *senem;* gen. *senis;* dat. *senī;* abl. *sene;* plur., n., acc. *senēs;* gen. *senum;* dat., abl. *senibus.*

Supellex, furniture, forms the other cases from stem *supellectili-.* *Iūsiūrandum,* oath, is declined in both parts: n., v., acc. *iūsiūrandum;* gen. *iūrisiūrandī;* dat. *iūriiūrandō;* abl. *iūreiūrandō.* No plural.

Paterfamiliās, māterfamiliās, father, mother of a family, have *pater, māter* fully declined in the sing. cases, but *familiās* remains unaltered. The plur. *patrēsfamiliārum* is sometimes found.

Note: The locative sing. of the third declension ends in **-ī** or **-e**; the plural in **-ibus: rurī, rure,** in the country; **vesperī, vespere,** in the evening ; **Carthāginī, Carthāgine,** at Carthage; **Gādibus,** at Gādes (Cadiz).

---

*   *Pater, māter, frāter, accipiter* are only apparently parisyllabic because the **e** of the nom. sing. has fallen out in the other cases.

GENDER IN THE THIRD DECLENSION

51 **Consonant Stems**

Nouns which end in **-ōs, -ō** (except **-dō, -gō, -iō**), **-or, -er,** and **imparisyllabic** nouns in **-is es, ēs** are masculine.

Exceptions:

côs, whetstone, *dōs*, dowry, f.; *os, ossis*, bone, *ōs, ōris*, mouth, n.
ēchō, echo, *carō*, flesh, f.
arbor, tree, f.; *aequor*, sea, *marmor*, marble, *cor*, heart, n.
vêr, spring, *cadāver*, corpse, *iter*, journey, *tūber*, hump, *ūber*, udder, *verber*, lash, n.; also some names of plants, as *papāver*, poppy.
compēs, fetter, *mercēs*, hire, *merges*, sheaf, *quiēs*, rest, *requiēs*, rest, *seges*, corn, *tēges*, mat, f.

52 Nouns which end in **-x, -ās, -ps, -dō, -gō, -iō,** and nouns in **-ūs** of more than one syllable are feminine.

Exceptions:

Nouns in **-ex, ēx** are masculine or common, but *lēx*, law, *nex*, death, *forfex*, shears, *supellex*, furniture, *īlex*, oak, f. *calix*, cup, *fornix*, arch, m.; *dux*, leader, c.
âs, coin; *fâs*, right, *nefâs*, wrong, *vās*, vessel, n. *manceps*, buyer, m.;
mūniceps, burgess, c.; *prīnceps*, chief, c. *cardō*, hinge; *ōrdō*, order, m.
ligō, hoe, m.; *margō*, brink, c.
Concrete nouns in **-iō** are masculine: *pūgiō*, dagger; *pāpiliō*, butterfly.
Abstract nouns in **-iō** are feminine: *ratiō*, reason; *regiō*, region.

53 Nouns ending in **-us, -ūs** (in words of one syllable), **-en, ēn, -l, -ar, -ur** are neuter.

Exceptions:

lepus, hare, m.; *pecus, pecudis*, single head of cattle, f.
mûs, mouse, m.; *grûs*, crane, *sûs*, pig, c.
pecten, comb, *rēn*, kidney, *splēn*, spleen, *tībīcen*, flute-player, m.
mūgil, mullet, *sāl*, salt, *sōl*, sun, m.
lâr, god of the hearth, m.
furfur, bran, *lemur*, goblin, *turtur*, turtle dove, *vultur*, vulture, m.
praes, bondsman, is masc; *laus*, praise, *fraus*, deceit, are fem.

54 **I- Stems**

Most parisyllabic nouns in **-is** and **-ēs** are feminine.

Exceptions:

the following nouns in **-is** are masculine: *acīnacēs*, scimitar, *amnis*, river, *axis*, axle, *canālis*, canal, *caulis*, cabbage, *clūnis*, buttock, *collis*, hill *crīnis*, hair, *ēnsis*, sword, *fascis*, bundle, *follis*, bag, *fūstis*, cudgel, *ignis*, fire, *mēnsis*, month *orbis*, circle, *pānis*, bread, *piscis*, fish, *postis*, post, *torris*, firebrand, *unguis*, nail,

vectis, lever, *vermis,* worm *verrēs,* boar.
Words which are usually masculine are: *callis,* path; *fīnis,* end; *fūnis,* rope; *sentis,* thorn; *torquis,* necklace.

Nouns in **-al, -ar,** and **-e** are neuter.
Nouns in **-x, -bs, -ls, -ns, -rs** are feminine.

Exceptions:
fōns, fountain, *mōns,* mountain, *dēns,* tooth, *bidēns,* fork, *rudēns,* rope, *torrēns,* torrent, *oriēns; east, occidēns,* west are masculine.
Infāns, infant, parēns, *parent,* common.

FOURTH DECLENSION

55   U- Stems (contracted)

The nominative of masculine and feminine nouns is formed by adding **s**; neuters have the plain stem with **ū**.

Stem	**gradu-**		**genū**
	step, m.		*knee,* n.
SINGULAR			
Nom.	**gradus**	*a step*	**genū**
Voc.	**gradus**	*o step*	**genū**
Acc.	**gradum**	*a step*	**genū**
Gen.	**gradūs**	*of a step*	**genūs**
Dat.	**graduī**	*to a step*	**genū**
Abl.	**gradū**	*from a step*	**genū**
PLURAL			
Nom.	**gradūs**	*steps*	**genua**
Voc.	**gradūs**	*o steps*	**genua**
Acc.	**gradūs**	*steps*	**genua**
Gen.	**graduum**	*of steps*	**genuum**
Dat.	**gradibus**	*to steps*	**genibus**
Abl.	**gradibus**	*from steps*	**genibus**

Decline like *gradus:* m. *frūctus,* fruit; *senātus,* senate; f. *manus,* hand. Decline like *genū: cornū,* horn; *verū,* spit (dat. abl. plur.,**-ibus** or **-ubus**).

Feminine nouns of this declension, besides *manus*, are: *acus*, needle; *porticus*, porch; *tribus*, tribe; *Īdūs*, Ides, and words feminine by meaning. Neuters are: *genū, cornū, verū*.

Note 1: The dat. sing. **-uī** is sometimes contracted into **-ū**. The dat. and abl. plur. **-ubus** is generally changed into **-ibus**; but *acus, tribus, arcus*, bow, *lacus*, lake, *partus*, birth, and *artūs* (plur.), limbs, have always **-ubus**; *portus*, harbor, has **-ibus** or **-ubus**.

Note 2: Some nouns have forms of both **u-** and **o-** stems, especially names of trees: *laurus*, bay; *myrtus*, myrtle. *Colus*, distaff, has gen. **-ī** and **ūs**, abl.**-ō** and **-ū**, acc. pl. **-ōs** and **ūs**. See § 56.

56 *Domus*, f., is declined thus:

	SINGULAR	PLURAL
N.V.	**domūs**	**domūs**
Acc.	**domum**	**domūs** or **domōs**
Gen.	**domūs** or **domī**	**domorum** or **domuum**
Dat.	**domuī** or **domō**	**domibus**
Abl.	**domō**	**domibus**

The locative **domī**, at home, is often used.

FIFTH DECLENSION

57 Ē- Stems

The nominative singular is formed by adding **s** to the stem.

Stem **rē**, *thing*

SINGULAR.			PLURAL.	
Nom.	**rēs**	*a thing*	**rēs**	things
Voc.	**rēs**	*o thing*	**rēs**	o things
Acc.	**rem**	*a thing*	**rēs**	things
Gen.	**reī**	*of a thing*	**rērum**	of things
Dat.	**reī**	*to a thing*	**rēbus**	to things
Abl.	**rē**	*from a thing*	**rēbus**	from things

Decline like **rēs:** *diēs,* day (gen. dat., *diēī*); *aciēs,* line of battle; *faciēs,* face; *seriēs,* series; *speciēs,* form; *spēs,* hope; *fidēs,* faith; *glaciēs,* ice; *meridiēs,* noon.

Rēs and *diēs* are the only nouns which occur in the gen., dat., and abl. plural. *Fidēs, meridiēs,* are singular only.

All nouns of this declension are feminine except *diēs* and *meridiēs. Diēs* also is feminine when it means 'an appointed day' or 'a period of time.'

Note 1: The greater number of nouns of this declension were originally **ia-** stems, and have forms both of **e-** and **a-** stems. They are declined like *māteriēs,* matter, singular only:

	māteriā-	māteriē -
Stem		
N.V.	māteriā	māteriēs
Acc.	māteriam	māteriem
Gen., Dat.	māteriae	māteriēī
Abl.	māteriā	māteriē

Note 2: The contracted gen. and dat. sing. in **-ē,** as *fidē* for *fideī,* is found in Virgil and Horace. An old gen. in **-ī** occurs in *tribūnus plēbī,* tribune of the people. The locative ends in **-ē.**

58 **Note 3:** **Rēspūblica,** the public interest, the republic, the state, is declined in both its parts:

	SINGULAR	PLURAL
N.V.	rēspūblica	rēspūblicae
Acc.	rēspūblicam	rēspūblicās
Gen.	rēspūblicae	rēspūblicārum
Dat.	rēspūblicae	rēspūblicīs
Abl.	rēspūblicā	rēspūblicīs

DEFECTIVE AND VARIABLE SUBSTANTIVES

59 Many nouns are found only in the singular; these are chiefly proper names and words of general meaning:

humus, ground.   *aevum,* an age   *iūstitia,* justice *aurum,* gold
laetitia, joy   *argentum,* silver *vēr,* spring   *caelum,* heaven
vesper, evening   *lētum,* death

Note: In poetry some words take plural form with singular meaning: *mella,* honey, *nivēs,* snow, *silentia,* silence, *rūra,* country.

60 Many nouns are used only in the plural

arma, arms	*artūs*, limbs	*cūnae*, cradle
dīvitiae, riches	*fāstī*, annals	*fēriae*, holidays
indūtiae, truce	*īnsidiae*, ambush	*līberī*, children
mānēs, departed spirits	*moenia*, town walls	*nūgae*, trifles
penātēs, household gods	*tenebrae*, darkness	

And names of towns, days, festivals: *Athēnae, Delphī, Kalendae,* Calends; *Bacchanālia,* festival of Bacchus.

61 Some words have a different meaning in singular and plural

SINGULAR	PLURAL
aedēs, temple	*aedēs*, house
auxilium, help	*auxilia*, allied forces
castrum, fort	*castra*, camp
cēra, wax	*cērae*, waxen tablet
cōpla, plenty	*cōpiae*, forces
fīnis, end	*fīnēs*, boundaries
grātia, favour	*grātiae*, thanks
impedīmentum, hindrance	*impedīmenta*, baggage
littera, letter of the alphabet	*litterae*, epistle, literature
lūdus, play	*lūdī*, public games
opem (acc), help	*opēs*, wealth
opera, labor	*operae*, work-people
sāl, salt	*salēs*, wit

62 Some nouns have two or more forms of declension

NOM.	GEN.		NOM.	GEN.	
tergum,	-ī n.	}back	*pecus*, n.	-oris	}cattle,
tergus,	-oris, n.		*pecus*, f.	-udis	head of cattle
ēventum,	-ī, n.	}event	*plēbs*,	-is, f.	}the common people
ēventus,	-ūs, m.		*plēbēs*,	-eī, f.	

			NOM.	GEN.	ABL.	
iūgerum,	-ī, n.	}acre	*vespera*,	-ae	-ā, f.	
[*iūger*],	-is, n.		*vesper*,	-ī,	-ō m.	}evening
			vesper,	—	-e m.	

Quiēs, f., rest, *-ētis*, is a **t-** stem only; but its compound *requiēs* takes also the **e-** forms (5th declension): *requiem, requiē*.

63   Some o- stems vary between masc. and neut. in sing. or plur.

E.g.: *baculus,* m., *baculum,* n., a stick; *plleus,* m., *pileum,* n., a hat.

locus, m. place, pl. $\begin{cases} loci \\ loca \end{cases}$ *frēnum,* n. bit, pl. $\begin{cases} frēnī \\ frēna \end{cases}$

iocus, m. jest pl. $\begin{cases} ioci \\ ioca \end{cases}$ *rāstrum,* n. harrow, pl. $\begin{cases} rāstrī \\ rāstra \end{cases}$

64   In many nouns some of the cases are wanting; thus:

	feast, f.,	fruit, f.,	help, f.,	prayer, f.,	change, f.
N.V.	—	—	—	—	—
Acc.	**dapem**	**frūgem**	**opem**	**precem**	**vicem**
Gen.	**dapis**	**frūgis**	**opis**	—	**vicis**
Dat.	**dapī**	**frūgī**	—	**precī**	—
Abl.	**dape**	**frūge**	**ope**	**prece**	**vice**

These have full plural **-ēs, -um, -ibus,** except gen. **vicium.**

65   Many are used in the ablative singular only

coāctū,	by force	**nātū,**	by birth
concessū,	by permission	**noctū,**	by night
(diū) interdiū,	by day	**rogātū,**	by reques
iussū,	by command	**sponte,**	by choice
iniussū	without command		

66   Some nouns have only nominative and accusative singular

E.g.: *fās,* right, *nefās,* wrong, *īnstar,* likeness, size, *nihil,* nothing.

DECLENSION OF GREEK NOUNS

67   First declension, a- stems

At an early time many Greek nouns were used in Latin, in an almost or entirely Latin form. Masculine nouns ending in **-as, -es,** and feminine nouns in **-a, -e,** all alike took the ending **-a** in the nominative, and were declined throughout like *mēnsa.* Such words are *nauta,* sailor, *poēta,* poet.

Afterwards the Greek forms, especially of proper names, were brought in by the poets, and thus in many instances both Greek and Latin forms of the same words are found, while of some words, used chiefly in poetry, the Greek forms alone occur.

Note: Patronymics (family names) are usually in the Greek form, as *Atrīdēs* (son of Atreus), *Pēlīdēs* (son of Peleus); and though they sometimes have -*a* for *ēs* in the nom. they always retain the Greek acc. in -**en**.
Names of people ending in -**ātēs**, -**ītēs**, or -**ōtes**, as *Eleātēs* (inhabitant of Elea), generally have -**em** or -**am** in acc., being nearer to Latin words.
All these usually follow the Latin declension in the plural, even when they have the Greek form in the singular.

Masculine nouns in -ās, -ēs, and feminine nouns in -ē

SINGULAR

Nom.	Aenēās	Atrīdēs, -a	Cybelē, a
Voc.	Aenēā	Atrīdē, -a, -ā	Cybelē, -a,
Acc.	Aenēan	Atrīdēn	Cybelēn
Gen.	Aenēae	Atrīdae	Cybelēs, -ae
Dat.	Aenēae	Atrīdae	Cybelae
Abl.	Aenēā	Atrīdē, -ā	Cybelē, -ā,

Plural in all cases like that of *mēnsa*.

Decline also: *Boreās*, the north wind, *Persa* (-*ēs*), a Persian, *Êpiretēs* (-*ōta*), native of Epirus, *Helenē*, f.

68   **Second declension, o- stems**
Greek nouns of the second declension, especially names of persons and places, often keep their Greek forms in the nom. and acc., but the other cases generally take the Latin forms.

SINGULAR

Nom.	Dēlos, f.	Athos, m.	Pēlion, n.
Voc.	(Dēle)	(Athōs)	(Pēlion)
Acc.	Dēlon, -um	Athōn	Pēlion
Gen.	Dēlī	Athō	Pēliī
Dat.	Dēlō	Athō	Pēliō
Abl.	Dēlō	Athō	Pēliō

Note 1: The feminine words of this declension are chiefly names of towns, islands, plants, and precious stones.

Note 2: Nouns ending in -**ros** sometimes take the Latin ending -**er** in the nom., as *Euander* (or -*dros*).

Note 3: Decline also: *scorpios*, m., scorpion; *lōtos*, f., lotus; *Samos, Īlion*.

Note 4: The Greek plural forms are rare, but plural nom. in **-oe**, as *Canēphoroe*, and plur. gen. in **-ōn**, as *Būcolicōn*, are sometimes found.

69   Third declension

These nouns are very numerous, having many different endings in the nominative singular.

	SINGULAR	PLURAL	SINGULAR.	PLURAL.
N.,V.	**hērōs**, m., *hero*	**hērōes**	**lynx,** c., *lynx*	**lynces**
Acc.	**hērō-a, -em**	**hērōas**	**lync-em, -a**	**lync-as, -ēs**
Gen.	**hērōis**	**hērōum**	**lyncis**	**lyncum**
Dat.	**hērōī**	**hērōibus**	**lyncī**	**lyncibus**
Abl.	**hērōe**	**hērōibus**	**lynce**	**lyncibus**

Note 1: Decline also: f. *lampas*, gen. *lampadis*, torch; m. *gigās, gigantis*, giant; *āēr, āēris*, air; *aethēr, aetheris*, the upper air.

Note 2: Names of this class are found in different forms, from the tendency to latinise Greek words. Thus Perseus is called *Persēūs* by Livy, but by Cicero latinised to *Persēs* in the nom., with the other cases like Greek names of the first declension, as *Atrīdēs*.

Note 3: Greek nouns in **-ōn** often drop the **n** in the nom., as *Platō, Platōnis;* but sometimes it is kept, as in *Cīmōn*. Some nouns have a second form, as *elephās*, elephant, which is usually declined like *gigās*, but sometimes latinised to *elephantus, elephantī*.
Dīdō also has two forms of declension, (1) as an **-ōn** stem, gen. *Dīdōnis*, (2) as a **u-** stem, gen. *Dīdūs*.

Note 4: *Poēma, poēmatis*, n., poem, is regularly declined, but Cicero has dat, and abl. plur. *poēmatīs*. *Poēsis*, f., poetry, is an **i-** noun, acc. *poēsin* or *poēsim*, abl. *poēsī*.

Note 5: The accusative singular endings in **-em** and in **-a** are both frequent. Gen. sing. usually in **-is**, but the Greek ending **-os** is often found in poetry. The abl. sing. is always in **-e**, and dat, sing. in **-ī**, but the latter is often short (ĭ) as in Greek. The nom. plur. is always in **-es**, often short. In acc. plur. the Greek **-as** is usual. The Greek ending of the abl. plur. in **-si (-sin)** is occasionally used by the poets.

Note 6: Many names in **-es, -eus,** and in **-is** have cases from two forms. **i-** forms and consonant forms appear in

Nom.	Voc.	Acc.	Gen.	Dat.	Abl.	
Thalēs	-ēs	-em, ēn, ēta	-is, -ētis	-ī, ēti	-ē, ēte	m.

Paris		{ -idem, ida	-idis, -idos -idi	-ide	f. m.
Iris	-i	{ -in, -im			

Forms of both the second and third declension appear in:

	Nom.	Voc.	Acc.	Gen.	Dat.	Abl.	
Orphēus		-eu	-eum,ea	-eī, eos	-ī	-eō, ēō	
Achillēus		-eu	-ea	-eī, eos	-ī	-e	m.
Achillēs		-ē	-em, ēn	-īs, ī	-ī	-e	m.

Note 7 *Tigris*, tiger, is declined throughout as an **i-** noun, like **cīvis**; but also as a consonant stem in **d**, like *Paris;* forming plur. *tigrides, tigridas, tigridum,* without dat. and abl. Decline *Ulixēus* (*Ulixēs*) like *Achillēus* (*Achillēs*).

70

DECLENSION OF ADJECTIVES

Adjectives are declined by gender, number and case.

71   **A. Adjectives declined like 2nd and 1st declension nouns**

Adjectives of three endings in *-us, -a, -um* or *-er, -a, -um* are declined like nouns of the second and first declension, **o-** and **a-** stems.

Stem	bono-	bona	bono-
		good	
SING.	M.	F.	N.
Nom.	bonus	bona	bonum
Voc.	bone	bona.	bonum
Acc.	bonum	bonam	bonum
Gen.	bonī	bonae	bonī
Dat.	bonō	bonae	bonō
Abl.	bonō	bonā	bonō
PLURAL			
Nom.	bonī	bonae	bona
Voc.	bonī	bonae	bona
Acc.	bonōs	bonās	bona
Gen.	bonōrum	bonārum	bonōrum
Dat.	bonīs	bonīs	bonīs
Abl.	bonīs	bonīs	bonīs

Note: Decline also: *cārus,* dear; *dūrus,* hard; *malus,* bad; *magnus,* great; *parvus,* small; *dubius,* doubtful.

Stem	tenero-	tenera-	tenero
	tender		
SING.	M.	F.	N.
Nom.	tener	tenera	tenerum
Voc.	tener	tenera	tenerum
Acc.	tenerum	teneram	tenerum
Gen.	tenerī	tenerae	tenerī
Dat.	tenerō	tenerae	tenerō
Abl.	tenerō	tenerā	tenerō
PLURAL.			
N.V.	tenerī	tenerae	tenera
Acc.	tenerōs	tenerās	tenera
Gen.	tenerōrum	tenerārum	tenerōrum
D., Abl.	tenerīs	tenerīs	tenerīs

Note: Also declined thus are: *asper*, rough; *lacer*, torn; *līber*, free; *miser*, wretched; *prōsper*, prosperous; *frūgifer*, fruit-bearing, *plūmiger*, feathered, and other compounds of *fero* and *gero*; also *satur*, full, *satura*, *saturum*.

Stem	nigro-	nigra-	nigro
		black	
SING.	M.	F.	N.
N.V.	niger	nigra	nigrum
Acc.	nigrum	nigram	nigrum
Gen.	nigrī	nigrae	nigrī
Dat.	nigrō	nigrae	nigrō
Abl.	nigrō	nigrā	nigrō
PLURAL			
N.V.	nigrī	nigrae	nigra
Acc.	nigrōs	nigras	nigra
Gen.	nigrōrum	nigrārum	nigrōrum
D.,Abl.	nigrīs	nigrīs	nigrīs

Note 1: Decline also: *aeger*, sick; *āter*, jet-black; *pulcher*, beautiful; *ruber*, red; *sacer*, sacred.

Note 2: *Dexter*, on the right hand, may be declined like *tener* or like *niger*.

72 Adjectives of 2 endings and 1 ending in nom. sing

Adjectives of two endings and of one ending in the nominative singular are declined like substantives of the third declension.

73 (1) Adjectives with nom. sing. in **-is**, masc. and fem.; in **-e** neuter: i- stems

Stem   **trīsti-,** sad

| | SINGULAR | | PLURAL | |
	M. F.	N.	M. F.	N.
N.V.	trīstis	trīste	trīstēs	trīstia
Acc.	trīstem	trīste	trīstēs, -īs	trīstia
Gen.	trīstis	trīstis	trīstium	trīstium
D. Abl.	trīstī	trīstī	trīstibus	trīstibus

Note: Decline also: *brevis,* short; *omnis,* all; *aequālis,* equal; *hostīlis,* hostile; *facilis,* easy; *illūstris,* illustrious; *lūgubris,* mournful.

Some stems in **ri-** form the masc. nom. sing. in **-er:**

Stem   **ācri-,** keen

SING.	M.	F.	N.
N.V.	ācer	ācris	ācre
Acc.	ācrem	ācrem	ācre
Gen.	ācris	ācris	ācris
Dat.	ācrī	ācrī	ācrī
Abl.	ācrī	ācrī	ācrī

PLURAL			
N.V.	ācrēs	ācrēs	ācria
Acc.	ācrēs, -īs	ācrēs, -īs	ācria
Gen.	ācrium	ācrium	ācrium
D., Abl.	ācribus	ācribus	ācribus

Decline like ācer: *celeber,* famous; *salūber,* healthy; *alacer,* brisk; *volucer,* winged; *campester,* level; *equester,* equestrian; *pedester,* pedestrian; *palūster,* marshy; *puter,* crumbling; with *September, Octōber, November, December,* masculine only.

Note: In *celer, celeris, celere,* swift, the stem ends in **-eri-** and the **e** is kept throughout.

74   (2) Adjectives with nom. sing. the same for all genders

(a) i- Stems

Stem **felīci-**, happy

	SINGULAR		PLURAL	
	M. F.	N.	M. F.	N.
N.V.	**fēlīx**	**fēlīx**	**fēlīces**	**fēlīcia**
Acc.	**fēlīcem**	**fēlīx**	**fēlīces, -īs**	**fēlīcia**
Gen.	**fēlīcis**	**fēlīcis**	**fēlīcium**	**fēlīcium**
Dat.	**fēlīcī**	**fēlīcī**	**fēlīcibus**	**fēlīcibus**
Abl.	**fēlīcī**	**fēlīcī**	**fēlīcibus**	**fēlīcibus**

Stem **ingenti-**, huge.

	SINGULAR		PLURAL	
	M. F.	N.	M. F.	N.
N.V.	**ingēns**	**ingēns**	**ingentēs**	**ingentia**
Acc.	**ingentem**	**ingēns**	**ingentēs, -īs**	**ingentia**
Gen.	**ingentis**	**ingentis**	**ingentium**	**ingentium**
Dat.	**ingentis**	**ingentis**	**ingentibus**	**ingentibus**
Abl.	**ingentī**	**ingentī**	**ingentibus**	**ingentibus**

Decline also: *audāx, audāci-*, bold; *simplex, simplici-*, simple; *duplex, duplici-*, double; *vēlōx, vēlōci-*, swift; *amāns, amanti-*, loving; *sapiēns, sapienti-*, wise; *concors, concordi-*, agreeing; *pār, pari-*, like.

Note 1: Some adjectives with stems in **ti** have genitive plural in **-um** as well as **-ium**: *recēns, recentum* or *recentium, cōnsors, cōnsortum* or *cōnsortium*. In participles, however, the gen. plur. is almost always in **-ium.**

Note 2: It is to be remarked that when either in a noun or an adjective a long vowel comes before the stem character, the genitive plural generally ends in **-ium**; when a short vowel comes before the stem character, it ends in **-um**; but this cannot be laid down as an invariable rule.

Note 3: The abl. sing. generally ends in **-ī** when an adjective is used with a substantive: *ā mīlite vigilī*, by a watchful soldier; and in **-e** when an adjective stands for a substantive: *ā vigile*, by a watchman, but a few have abl. sing. always in **-ī**. The same rule applies to present participles; but in the ablative absolute construction the ablative always ends in **-e**: *viridantī quercū cīnctus*, wreathed with green oak; *viridante quercū*, when the oak is green.

75 **(b) Consonant stems**

Stem **dīvet-, dīvit-**, rich.

SING.			PLUR.	
Nom.	**dīves**	PLUR.	**dīvitēs**	
Voc.	**dīves**	PLUR.	**dīvitēs**	
Acc.	**dīvitem**		**dīvitēs**	
Gen.	**dīvitis**		**dīvitum**	
Dat.	**dīvitī**		**dīvitibus**	
Abl.	**dīvite**		**dīvitibus**	

Decline like dives: *pauper, pauper-,* poor; *dēgener, dēgener-,* degenerate; *sōspes, sōspit-,* safe; *superstes, superstit-,* surviving; *dēses, dēsid-,* slothful; *compos, compot-,*possessing; *caelebs, caelib-,* unmarried; *vetus, veter-,* old.

Note. *Dives* has a contracted form *dīs*, nom.; *dītem*, acc. &c.; with abl. sing. *dītī* and neut. plur. *dītia*; gen. plur. *dītium*. *Dives* and *vetus* are used as neut. acc. sing. *Vetus* has neut. plur. *vetera*. The rest have no neuter forms.

COMPARISON OF ADJECTIVES

76 Adjectives are compared in three degrees.

(1) Positive: **dūrus**, hard, **trīstis**, sad.

(2) Comparative: **dūrior**, harder; **trīstior**, sadder.

(3) Superlative: **dūrissimus**, hardest, very hard; **trīstissimus**, saddest, very sad.

The **positive** is the adjective itself expressing the quality; the **comparative** expresses a greater degree; the **superlative** expresses a very great, or the greatest, degree of the quality. The comparative is formed from the positive by adding the suffix **-ior** to the last consonant of the stem; the superlative generally by adding **-issimus** to the last consonant of the Stem.

Stem	Positive	Comparative	Superlative
dūr-o-	**dūrus**	**dūr-ior**	**dūr-issimus**
trīst-i-	**trīstis**	**trīst-ior**	**trīst-issimus**
audāc-i-	**audāx**	**audāc-ior**	**audāc-issimus**

77 The Comparative is declined as follows:

	SING.		PLUR.	
	M.F.	N.	M.F.	N.
Nom.	trīstior	trīstius	trīstiōres	trīstiōra
Voc.	trīstior	trīstius	trīstiōres	trīstiōra
Acc.	trīstiōrem	trīstius	trīstiōr-es	trīstiōra
Gen.	trīstiōris	trīstiōris	trīstiōrum	trīstiōrum
Dat.	trīstiōrī	trīstiōrī	trīstiōribus	trīstiōribus
Abl.	trīstiōr-e, -ī*	trīstiōr-e, -ī*	trīstiōribus	trīstiōribus

* The ablative in -ī of the comparative is rare, and only used by late writers.

78 The superlative is declined from **o-** and **a-** stems, like *bonus*.

Adjectives with stems in **ro-**, **ri-**, form the superlative by doubling the last consonant of the stem and adding **-imus**. Words like **niger** insert **e** before **r** in the Superlative.

Stem	Positive	Comparative	Superlative
tenero-	tener	tenerior	tenerrimus
nigro-	niger	nigrior	nigerrimus
celeri-	celer	celerior	celerrimus

Six adjectives with Stems in **ili-** also form the superlative by doubling the last consonant of the stem and adding **-imus**:

facilis, easy	**similis**, like	**gracilis**, slender
difficilis, difficult	**dissimilis**, unlike.	**humilis**, lowly

e.g. root *facili-*, positive *facilis*, comparative *facilior*, superlative *facillimus*

79 Many participles are compared like adjectives:

amāns, loving	amantior	amantissimus
parātus, ready	parātior	parātissimus

Irregular Comparison

80 (1) Some comparatives and superlatives are formed from stems distinct from that of the positive:

Positive	Comparative	Superlative
bonus, good	**melior,** better	**optimus,** best
malus, bad	**peior,** worse	**pessimus,** worst
parvus, small	**minor,** less	**minimus,** least
multus, much	**plūs,** more	**plūrimus,** most
magnus, great	**maior**	**maximus**
nēquam*, wicked	**nēquior**	**nēquissimus**
frūgī*, honest	**frūgālior**	**frūgālissimus**
senex, old	{ **senior** / **nātū maior**	**nātū maximus**
iuvenis, young	{ **iūnior** / **nātū minor**	**nātū minimus**

* Indeclinable.

Note 1 *Senior, iūnior* are not used as true comparatives of *senex, iūvenis,* but with the meaning old rather than young, and young rather than old.

Note 2 *Dīves* has both uncontracted and contracted forms:

dīves, (**dīs**) } rich	**dīvitior** **dītior**	**dīvitissimus** **dītissimus**
vetus, (**veter**) } old has	{ **vetustior** (**veterior**)	**veterrimus**

Following its meaning, *plūs* as an adjective is always *more* than one, that is, plural, although it exists in the singular as a neuter noun:

	SING. (noun)	PLURAL	
	Neuter	M. F.	N.
N. V. Acc.	**plūs**	**plūres**	**plūra**
Gen.	**plūris**	**plūrium**	**plūrium**
Dat.	**plūrī**	**plūribus**	**plūribus**
Abl.	**plūre**	**plūribus**	**plūribus**

81 (2) Adjectives compounded with **-dicus, -ficus, -volus** (from *dīcō, faciō, volō*), form the comparative and superlative as if from participles in *-ēns*.

Positive	Comparative	Superlative:
maledicus, scurrilous	**maledīcentior**	**maledīcentissimus**
beneficus, generous	**beneficentior**	**beneficentissimus**
benevolus, well-wishing	**benevolentior**	**benevolentissimus**
also:		
egēnus, needy	**egentior**	**egentissimus**
prōvidus, provident	**prōvidentior**	**prōvidentissimus**

82 (3) Adjectives in **-eus, -ius, -uus** are generally compared with the adverbs *magis, maximē;* as *dubius*, doubtful, *magis dubius*, more doubtful, *maximē dubius*, most doubtful.

Note: Adjectives in **-quus** are compared regularly, the first **u** being consonantal: *aequus*, level, *aequior, aequissimus;* so, *antīquus*, ancient. *Ēgregius*, excellent, has comparative *ēgregior; strēnuus*, vigorous, sometimes has *strēnuior.*

---

83 (4) Some adjectives have no comparative forms; some no superlative; of some the comparative and superlative are found without the positive: *ōcior*, swifter, *ōcissimus*, swiftest.

84 Some comparatives denoting relations of place have no positive, but correspond to adverbs from the same stem.

Adverb	Comparative Adj	Superlative Adj.
extrā,* outside	**exterior**	**extrēmus, extimus**
intrā, within	**interior**	**intimus**
suprā,* above	**superior**	**suprēmus, summus**
īnfrā,* below	**īnferior**	**īnfimus, īmus**
citrā, on this side	**citerior**	**citimus**
ultrā, beyond	**ulterior**	**ultimus**
prae, before	**prior**	**prīmus,** first
post,* after	**posterior**	**postrēmus,** last
prope, near	**propior**	**proximus**

---

*Note: The adjectives *exterus, superus, īnferus, posterus*, are, however, sometimes found. Also: *dexter* (adj.), on the right, *dexterior dexterrimus, dextimus; sinister* (adj.), on the left, *sinisterior; dēter*, down [obs. adj. from prep *dē*], *deterior*, worse, *deterrimus*, worst.

Comparison of Adverbs

85 Adverbs derived from adjectives and ending in **-ē, -ō, -ter**, and rarely **-e**, form comparative in **-ius**, superlative in **-issimē**.

Note: These forms are the neut. acc. sing. of the comparative adjective and an old neut. abl. sing. of the superlative adjective.

Adjective	Adverb	Comparative	Superlative
dignus, worthy	**dignē**, worthily	**dignius**	**dignissimē**
tūtus, safe	**tūtō**, safely.	**tūtius**	**tūtissimē**
fortis, brave	**fortiter**, bravely	**fortius**	**fortissimē**
cōnstāns, firm	**cōnstanter**, firmly	**cōnstantius**	**cōnstantissimē**
audāx, bold	**audācter**, boldly	**audācius**	**audācissimē**
facilis, easy	**facile**, easily	**facilius**	**facillimē**

86 Irregular comparison has corresponding forms in adverbs.

Adverb	Comparative	Superlative
bene, well	**melius**	**optimē**
male, badly	**peius**	**pessimē**
paulum, little	**minus**	**minimē**
multum, much	**plūs**	**plūrimum**
magnopere, greatly	**magis**	**maximē**
—	**ōcius**, more quickly	**ōcissimē**

Note: *Magis*, more (in degree); *plūs*, more (in quantity).

87 In like manner are compared:

diū, long	**diūtius**	**diūtissimē**
intus, within	**interius**	**intimē**
(**prae**, before)	**prius**	**prīmō, prīmum**
post, after	**posterius**	**postrēmō**
prope, near	**propius**	**proximē**
saepe, often	**saepius**	**saepissimē**
nūper, lately	—	**nūperrimē**

88 Numerals (see also § 311)

Numeral adjectives are of three kinds:

1. **Cardinals**, answering the question *How many?*
2. **Ordinals**, answering the question *Which in order of number?*
3. **Distributives,** answering the question, How many each?

88a Numeral adverbs answer the question, *How many times?*

89 **Ūnus,** from **o-** and **a-** stems, is declined as follows:

	SINGULAR			PLURAL		
Nom.	ūnus	ūna	ūnum	ūnī	ūnae	ūna
Acc.	ūnum	ūnam	ūnum	ūnōs	ūnās	ūna
Gen.	ūnīus	ūnīus	ūnīus	ūnōrum	ūnārum	ūnōrum
Dat.	ūnī	ūnī	ūnī	ūnīs	ūnīs	ūnīs
Abl.	ūnō	ūnā	ūnō	ūnīs	ūnīs	ūnīs

Duo is an o- stem, and tres an i- stem:

	M.	F.	N.	M. and F.	N.
Nom.	duo	duae	duo	trēs	tria
Acc.	duōs, duo	duās	duo	trēs	tria
Gen.	duōrum	duārum	duōrum	trium	trium
D., Abl.	duōbus	duābus	duōbus	tribus	tribus

Note 1: *Ambō,* both, as *duo,* except for *ō* in nom. and acc. sing. m. & n.

Note 2: *Duum* is sometimes used for *duōrum, duārum.*

The **cardinals** from *quattuor* to *centum* are indeclinable. Hundreds from two to nine hundred are **o-** and **a-** stems: *ducentī, ducentae, ducenta. Mīlle* (a thousand) is an indeclinable adjective; but *mīlia* (thousands) is a neuter noun declined like *animālia. Mīlle passus,* a mile.

In **compound numbers** above twenty, either the smaller number with **et** comes first (as was common in English until quite recently), or the larger without **et** (as in current English usage): *septem et trīgīnta,* seven and thirty; or *trīgīnta septem,* thirty-seven. *Ūnus* usually stands first: *ūnus et vīgintī,* twenty-one. In numbers above a hundred the larger comes first, with or without **et.**

Thousands are expressed by putting (1) the numeral adverbs **bis, ter,** &c., before *mīlle: bis mīlle;* or (2) cardinal numbers before *mīlia: duo milia. Mīlia* is followed by a genitive: *duo mīlia hominum,* two thousand men.

90   **LIST OF NUMBERS**

Arabic	Roman	Cardinals	Ordinals	Distrubutive	Adverbs
1	I	ūnus	prīmus (prior), first	singulī, one each	semel, once
2	II	duo	secūndus (alter), second	bīnī, two each, etc.	bis, twice
3	III	trēs	tertius, third, &c.	ternī, or trīnī,	ter, thrice, &c.
4	IIII or IV	quattuor	quārtus	quaternī	quater
5	V	quīnque	quīntus	quīnī	quīnquiēns
6	VI	sex	sextus	sēnī	sexiēns
7	VII	septem	septimus	septēnī	septiēns
8	VIII or IIX	octō	octāvus	octōnī	octiēns
9	VIIII or IX	novem	nōnus	novēnī	noviēns
10	X	decem	decimus	dēnī	deciēns
11	XI	ūndecim	ūndecimus	ūndēnī	ūndeciēns
12	XII	duodecim	duodecimus	duodēnī	duodeciēns
13	XIII	tredecim	tertius decimus	ternī dēnī	tredeciēns
14	XIIII or XIV	quattuordecim	quārtus decimus	quaternī dēnī	quattuor-deciēns
15	XV	quīndecim	quīntus decimus	quīnī dēnī	quīndeciēns
16	XVI	sēdecim	sextus decimus	sēnī dēnī	sēdeciēns
17	XVII	septendecim	septimus decimus	septēnī dēnī	septiesdecēns
18	XVIII or XIIX	duodēvīgintī or octōdecim	duodēvīcēnsimus	duodēvīcēnī	duodēvīciēns
19	XVIIII or XIX	ūndēvīgintī or novendecim	ūndēvīcēnsimus	ūndēvīcēnī	ūndēvīciēns
20	XX	vīgintī	vīcēnsimus	vīcēnī	vīciēns
21	XXI	ūnus at vīgintī	ūnus et vīcēnsimus	vīcēnī singulī	semel et vīciēns
22	XXII	duo et vīgintī	alter et vīcēnsimus	vīcēnī bīnī	bis et vīciēns
28	XXVIII or XXIIX	duodētrīgintā	duodētrīcēnsimus	duodētrīcēnī	duodētrīciēns
29	XXVIIII or XXIX	ūndētrīgintā	ūndētrīcēnsimus	ūndētrīcēnī	ūndētrīciēns
30	XXX	trīgintā	trīcēnsimus	trīcēnī	trīciēns
40	XXXX or XL	quadrāgintā	quadrāgēnsimus	quadrāgēnī	quadrāgiēns
50	L	quīnquāgintā	quīnquāgēnsimus	quīnquāgēnī	quīnquāgiēns
60	LX	sexāgintā	sexāgēnsimus	sexāgēnī	sexāgiēns
70	LXX	septuāgintā	septuāgēnsimus	septuāgēnī	septuāgiēns
80	LXXX or XXC	octōgintā	octōgēnsimus	octōgēnī	octōgiēns
90	LXXXX or XC	nonāgintā	nonāgēnsimus	nonāgēnī	nonāgiēns
98	XCIIX or IIC	octo et nonāgintā	duodēcentēnsimus	duo-dēcentēnī	duodēcentiēns
99	XCIX or IC	ūndēcentum	ūndēcentēnsimus	ūndēcentēnī	ūndēcentiēns
100	C	centum	centēnsimus	centēnī	centiēns
101	CI	centum et ūnus	centēnsimus prīmus	centēnī singulī	centiēns semel

Arabic	Roman	Cardinals	Ordinals	Distrubutive	Adverbs
126	CXXVI	centum vīgintī sex	centēnsimus vīcēnsimus sextus	centiēnī vīcēnī sēnī	centiēns vīciēns sexiēns
200	CC	ducenti, ae, a	ducentēnsimus	ducēnī	ducentiēns
300	CCC	trecentī	trecentēnsimus	trecēnī	trecentiēns
400	CCCC	quadringentī	quadringentēnsimus	quadringēnī	quadringentiēns
500	IↃ or D	quīngentī	quīngentēnsimus	quīngēnī	quīngentiēns
600	IↃC	sescentī	sescentēnsimus	sescēnī	sescentiēns
700	IↃCC	septingentī	septingentēnsimus	septingēnī	septingen tiēns
800	IↃCCC	octingentī	octingentēnsimus	octingēnī	octingentiēns
900	IↃCCCC	nōngentī,	nōngentēnsimus	nōngēnī	nōngentiēns
1,000	CIↃ or M	mīlle	mīllēnsimus	singula mīlia	mīliēns
2,000	CIↃCIↃ or MM	duo mīlia	bis-mīllēnsimus	bīna mīlia	bis mīliēns
5,000	IↃↃ	quīnque mīlia	quīnquiēns mīllēnsimus	quīna mīlia	quīnquiēns mīliēns
10,000	CCIↃↃ	decem mīlia	deciēns mīllēnsimus	dēna mīlia	deciēns mīliēns
50,000	IↃↃↃ	quīnquāgintā mīlia	quīnquāgiēns mīllēnsimus	quīnquāgēna mīlia	quīnquāgiēns mīliēns
100,000	CCCIↃↃↃ	centum mīlia	centiēns mīllēnsimus	centēna mīlia	centiēns mīliēns
500,000	IↃↃↃↃ	quīngenta mīlia	quīngentiēns mīllēnsimus	quīngēna mīlia	quīngentiēns mīliēns
1,000,000	CCCCIↃↃↃↃ	deciēns centum mīlia	deciēns centiēns mīllēnsimus	deciēns centēna mīlia	deciēns centiēns mīliēns

Note 1: Multiplicatives answering the question *how many fold?* are: *simplex, duplex, triplex, &c., centuplex,* a hundredfold (formed with stem **plic-**, fold).

Note 2: Proportionals, answering the question *how many times as great?* are: *simplus; duplus,* double; *triplus,* treble; *quadruplus,* quadruple.

PRONOUNS

91 Pronouns either stand in the place of nouns, or stand in the place of adjectives, to define or point out nouns.

There are three persons:

First: The person speaking: I or we.

Second: The person spoken to: you (singular), you (plural).

Third: The person or thing spoken of: he, she, it, they.

Personal pronouns stand only in place of nouns.

Possessive pronouns (more correctly possessive pronominal adjectives), as *meus*, my.

Most of the others can stand for nouns or adjectives.

92a Personal and Pronouns

SINGULAR

	1st Person		2nd Person	
Nom.	**ego**	I	**tū**	you (so also vocative)
Acc.	**mē**	me	**tē**	you
Gen.	**meī**	of me	**tuī**	of you
Dat.	**mihi**	to me	**tibi**	to you
Abl.	**mē**	from me	**tē**	from you

PLURAL

	1st Person		2nd Person	
Nom.	**nōs**	we	**vōs**	you (so also vocative)
Acc.	**nōs**	us	**vōs**	you
Gen.	**nostrī** / **nostrum**	of us	**vestrī** / **vestrum**	of you
Dat.	**nōbīs**	to us	**vōbīs**	to you
Abl.	**nōbīs**	from us	**vōbīs**	from you

Note 1: **Nostrī, vestrī,** are called **objective genitives**: *memor nostrī,* mindful of us (§ 264). **Nostrum, vestrum,** are called **partitive genitives,** because they are used after words which express a part: *ūnus nostrum,* one of us (§ 259).

Note 2: For the personal pronoun of the 3rd person, he, she, it, the demonstrative **is, ea, id,** is used (see § 94).

92b Reflexive Pronouns

SINGULAR and PLURAL

Nom.	—	
Acc.	**sē** or **sēsē**	himself, herself, itself, or themselves
Gen.	**suī**	of himself, etc.
Dat.	**sibi, sibī**	to himself, etc.
Abl.	**sē** or **sēsē**	from himself, etc.

93 Possessive Pronominal Adjectives

SINGULAR	M.	F.	N.	
1st person:	meus	mea	meum	my
2nd person:	tuus	tua	tuum	your

PLURAL				
1st person:	noster	nostra	nostrum	our
2nd person:	vester	vestra	vestrum	your

Note 1: Suus, sua, suum, his, her, its, their, is the possessive pronoun of the reflexive.

Note 2: Meus, tuus, suus are declined lilte *bonus: noster, vester,* like *niger. Meus* has voc. sing. masc. *mī.* The other possessives, except *noster,* have no vocative.

94 Demonstrative Pronouns

Is, that, *or* he, she, it

	SINGULAR			PLURAL		
	M.	F.	N.	M.	F.	N.
Nom.	is	ea	id	eī, iī	eae	ea
Acc.	eum	eam	id	eō	eās	ea
Gen.	eius*	eius*	eius*	eōrum	eārum	eōrum
Dat.	eī	eī	eī	eīs, iīs	eīs, iīs	eīs, iīs
Abl.	eō	eā	eō	eīs, iīs	eīs, iīs	eīs, iīs

Hic, this (near me), or he, she, it.

	SINGULAR.			PLURAL.		
	M.	F.	N.	M.	F.	N.
Nom.	hic*	haec	hoc*	hī	hae	haec
Acc.	hunc	hanc	hoc*	hōs	hās	haec
Gen.	huius*	huius*	huius*	hōrum	hārum	hōrum
Dat.	huic	huic	huic	hīs	hīs	hīs
Abl.	hōc	hāc	hōc	hīs	hīs	hīs

* Although the first vowel of **eius, huius** is short, the **i** was pronounced as a double consonant, so the syllable is long. **Hic** and **hoc** are generally pronounced *hicc, hocc,* so the syllables are heavy.

Ille, that (over there), or he, she, it.

	SINGULAR.			PLURAL.		
	M.	F.	N.	M.	F.	N.
Nom.	ille	illa	illud	illī	illae	illa
Acc.	illum	illam	illud	illōs	illās	illa
Gen.	illīus	illīus	illīus	illōrum	illārum	illōrum
Dat.	illī	illī	illī	illīs	illīs	illīs
Abl.	iliō	illā	illō	illīs	illīs	illīs

Iste, that (near you)

	SINGULAR.			PLURAL.		
	M.	F.	N.	M.	F.	N.
Nom.	iste	ista	istud	istī	istae	ista
Acc.	istum	istam	istud	istōs	istās	illa
Gen.	istīus	istīus	istīus	istōrum	istārum	istōrum
Dat.	istī	istī	istī	istīs	istīs	istīs
Abl.	istō	istā	istō	istīs	istīs	istīs

95 Definitive Pronoun

Īdem, same

	SINGULAR		
	M.	F.	N.
Nom.	īdem	eadem	idem
Acc.	eundem	eandem	idem
Gen.	eiusdem	eiusdem	eiusdem
Dat.	eīdem	eīdem	eīdem
Abl.	eōdem	eādem	eōdem

	PLURAL		
Nom.	eīdem or īdem	eaedem	eadem
Acc.	eōsdem	eāsdem	eadem
Gen.	eōrundem	eārundem	eōrundem
Dat.	eīsdem or īsdem	eīsdem or īsdem	eīsdem or īsdem
Abl.	eīsdem or īsdem	eīsdem or īsdem	eīsdem or īsdem

96   Intensive Pronoun

Ipse, self

	SINGULAR			PLURAL		
	M.	F.	N.	M.	F.	N.
Nom.	ipse	ipsa	ipsum	ipsī	ipsae	ipsa
Acc.	ipsum	ipsam	ipsum	ipsōs	ipsās	ipsa
Gen.	ipsīus	ipsīus	ipsius	ipsōrum	ipsārum	ipsōrum
Dat.	ipsī	ipsī	ipsī	ipsīs	ipsīs	ipsīs
Abl.	ipsō	ipsā	ipsō	ipsīs	ipsīs	ipsīs

Note: The suffixes **-met, -te, -pte** or **-pse, -ce** are added to some cases of pronouns for emphasis: (a) **met** may be joined (1) to *ego* and its cases, except gen. plur.: *egomet*, I myself; (2) to the cases of *tū*, except nom. sing.: *vōsmet*, you yourselves; (3) to *sē* and its cases, except *suī: sibimet*; (4) to the cases of *suus: suamet facta;* (b) **tē** is joined to *tū: tūtē;* also *tūtēmet*, you youself; (c) **pte** is joined especially to the abl. sing. of the possessive pronouns: *meōpte cōnsiliō*, by my advice. (d) **ce** is joined to the demonstrative: *hunce, huiusce; istece, illece,* are written *istīc, illīc:*

SING.	M.	F.	N.
Nom.	istīc	istaec	istuc
Acc.	istunc	istanc	istuc
Gen.	istīusce	istīusce	istīusce
Abl.	istōc	istāc	istōc

Īdem (for *is-dem*), and **ipse** (for *is-pse*) are emphatic forms of *is*.

---

97   Relative Pronoun

Quī, who, which

SINGULAR.				PLURAL.		
	M.	F.	N.	M.	F.	N.
Nom.	quī	quae	quod	quī	quae	quae
Acc.	quem	quam	quod	quōs	quās	quae
Gen.	cuius	cuius	cuius	quōrum	quārum	quōrum
Dat.	cui	cui	cui	quibus or quīs		
Abl.	quō	quā	quō	quibus or quīs		

98   Interrogative Pronoun

Quis, who? what?

Nominative			Accusative		
M.	F.	N.	M.	F	N.
quis	(quis)	quid	quem	quam	quid
quī	quae	quod	quem	quam	quod

Note: In all other cases singular and plural *qui* interrogative is like the relative pronoun.

99   Indefinite Pronoun

Quis, anyone or anything

Nominative			Accusative		
M.	F.	N.	M.	F.	N.
quis	qua	quid	quem	quam	quid
quī	quae	quod	quem	quam	quod

Note: In the other cases singular and plural the indefinite is like the relative, except that *qua* or *quae* may be used in neut. nom. and acc. plural.

    Quis, both interrogative and indefinite, and its compounds, are used chiefly as nouns; **quī** and its compounds chiefly as adjectives.

    Quid and its compounds are used only as nouns; **quod** and its compounds only as adjectives.

EXAMPLES:

Homō quī venit. The man who comes. (*quī* relative)

Quis venit? Who comes? (*quis* interrogative)

Quī homō venit? What man comes? (*quī* interrogative)

Aliquid amārī. Some bitterness.

Aliquod verbum. Some word.

100　Compound Pronouns

MASC.	FEM.	NEUT.	
quīcumque	quaecumque	quodcumque	whosoever *or*
quisquis	quisquls	quidquld or quicquid	whatsoever
quīdam	quaedam	quiddam (quoddam)	a certain person *or* thing
aliquis	aliqua	aliquid	someone *or*
aliquī	aliqua	aliquod	something
quispiam	quaepiam	quippiam (quodpiam)	someone
quīvīs	quaevīs	quidvīs (quodvīs)	anyone
quīlibet	quaelibet	quidlibet (quodlibet)	you like
quisquam	—	quidquam or quicquam	anyone at all
quisque	quaeque	quidque (quodque)	each one severally
uterque	utraque	utrumque	each of two
ūnusquisque	ūnaquaeque	ūnumquidque (ūnumquodque)	each single one
ecquis	ecqua	ecquid (ecquod)	Is there any who?
quisnam	quaenam	quidnam (quodnam)	Who, pray?

Note 1: **Quisquis** is found only in nom. acc. and abl.

Note 2: **Quisquam** is used as a noun, sing. only, chiefly in negative sentences and the adjective which corresponds to it is *ūllus: haud quisquam,* not anyone.

Note 3: In the **compound pronouns** *quī, quis,* and *uter* follow their own declension in the oblique cases; the prefix or suffix is unaltered: *alicuius, cuiusque, cuivīs, utrōque, quamlibet.* But in *ūnusquisque* both *ūnus* and *quisque* are declined.

101　The following pronominal adjectives form the genitive singular in **-ius** or **īus** and the dative singular in **-ī** like *ille*: **alius**, other, another; **ūllus**, any; **nūllus**, none; **sōlus**, sole; **tōtus**, whole; **ūter**, which of two?; **alter**, one of two, the other; **neuter**, neither.

	SINGULAR			PLURAL		
	M.	F.	N.	M.	F.	N.
Nom.	alius	alia	aliud	aliī	aliae	alia
Acc.	alium	aliam	aliud	aliōs	aliās	alia
Gen.	alīus	alīus	alīus	aliōrum	aliārum	aliōrum
Dat.	aliī	aliī	aliī	aliīs	aliīs	aliīs
Abl.	aliō	aliā	aliō	aliīs	aliīs	aliīs

Note: Like **alius**, but with neuter singular in **-um**, are declined **ūllus, nūllus, sōlus, tōtus.**

SINGULAR

	M.	F.	N.
Nom.	alter	altera	alterum
Acc.	alterum	alteram	alterum
Gen.	alterīus	alterīus	alterīus
Dat.	alterī	alterī	alterī
Abl.	alterō	alterā	alterō

PLURAL

	M.	F.	N.
Nom.	alterī	alterae	altera
Acc.	alterōs	alterās	altera
Gen.	alterōrum	alterārum	alterōrum
Dat.	alterīs	alterīs	alterīs
Abl.	alterīs	alterīs	alterīs

Note1: Like **alter**, but casting out **e** before **r** in all cases except the nom. sing. masculine, are declined: *uter, utra, utrum*, which (of two); *neuter, neutra, neutrum*, neither. These are seldom used in the plural.

Note 2: **Uter** forms compounds by taking nearly all the same suffixes as *quis* and *quī: utercumque*, whichever of two; *utervīs, uterlibet. Alteruter*, one or the other, is usually declined only as *uter*, but sometimes both parts are declined.

Note 3: The genitive and ablative singular of *nūllus* are used for the genitive and ablative of the substantive *nēmō*, nobody, which are very rarely found.

102 Table of Correlative Pronouns, Adjectives and Adverbs

INTERROGATIVE	DEMONSTRATIVE	RELATIVE	INDEFINITE (1)	INDEFINITE (2)	DISTRIBUTIVE	UNIVERSAL RELATIVE
quis, quī, who, which?	**is** that	**quī** who, which	**(sī) quis** (if) anyone	**aliquis** some one	**quisque** each	**quīcumque** whoever, whatever
uter which of two?	**alter** one of two, other of two			**alteruter** one or other of two	**uterque** each of two	**utercumque** whichever of two
quālis of what kind?	**tālis** of such kind	**quālis** as				**quāliscumque** of whatever kind
quantus how great?	**tantus** so great	**quantus** as (great)		**aliquantus** some (in quantity)		**quantuscumque** however great
quot how many?	**tot** so many	**quot** as (many)		**aliquot** some (in number)		**quotcumque** however many
ubi where?	**ibi** there	**ubi** where	**sīcubi** if anywhere	**alicubi** anywhere	**ubique** everywhere	**ubicumque** wheresoever
unde from where?	**inde** from there	**unde** from where	**sīcunde** if from anywhere	**alicunde** from somewhere	**undique** from every side	**undecumque** from wherever
quō to where?	**eō** to there	**quō** to where	**(sī) quō** (if) to anywhere	**aliquō** to somewhere		**quōcumque** to anywhere at all
quā by what way?	**eā** by that way	**quā** by what way	**sī quā** if by any way	**aliquā** by some way		**quācumque** by whatsoever way
quam how?	**tam** so	**quam** as				
quandō when?	**tum** then	**quandō** when **ubi** when **cum** when	**(sī) quandō** (if) ever	**aliquandō** at some time		**quandōcumque** whensoever
quotiēns how often?	**totiēns** so often	**quotiēns** as (often)		**aliquotiēns** at some (various) times		**quotiēnscumque** however often

VERBS

103 The verb has:

3 persons: first, second, third

2 numbers: singular and plural

6 tenses: (1) present, (2) future simple,
(3) past imperfect, (4) perfect,
(5) future perfect, (6) pluperfect

3 moods: (1) indicative, (2) imperative,
(3) subjunctive

} The verb finite

The **infinitives** (verbal substantives)

3 participles (verbal adjectives)

The **gerund** and **gerundive** (verbal
substantive and adjective).

2 supines (verbal substantives)

2 voices: (1) active, (2) passive

} The verb infinite

The **verb finite** is so called because it is limited by **mood** and
persons, while the **verb infinite** is not so limited.

104 Person and number

In modern English, **pronouns** are used with **verbs** to express
the three persons singular and plural: **I** come, **we** come, with
only a vestige of inflection as in **he** come-**s**. But in Latin person
and number are expressed by the inflections alone:

su-**m**, I come	su-**mus**, we are
e-**s**, you (sing.) are	es-**tis**, you (pl.) are
es-**t**, he (she, it) is	su-**nt**, they are

am-**ō**, I love	amā-**mus**, we love
amā-**s**, you (sing.) love	amā-**tis**, you (pl.) love
ama-**t**, he (she, it) loves	ama-**nt,** they love

Table of Personal Endings in the Indicative and Subjunctive Moods

	ACTIVE VOICE	PASSIVE VOICE
Singular		
1	**-m** or **-ō**	**-r**
2	**-s**	**-ris** or **-re**
3	**-t**	**-tur**
Plural		
1	**-mus**	**-mur**
2	**-tis**	**-minī**
3	**-nt**	**-ntur**

The **imperative mood** has only the second and third person singular and plural, not the first.

105 Tenses

Tenses express the time of the action or state denoted by the verb, as being: (1) present, past, or future; (2) complete or incomplete; (3) momentary or continuous.

In English, by means of auxiliary verbs, differences of time can be more accurately expressed than in Latin; so that one tense in Latin may correspond to two tenses in English, of which one is momentary, the other continuous. Thus, *rogō*, I ask, has the following tenses:

Present	**Present**	incomplete	rogō	{ I ask { I am asking
	Perfect	complete	rogāvī	I have asked
Future	**Fut. Simple**	incomplete	rogābō	{ I shall ask { I shall be asking
	Fut. Perf.	complete	rogāverō	I shall have asked
Past	**Perfect** } **Imperfect** }	incomplete	rogāvī rogābam	{ I asked { I was asking
	Pluperfect	complete	rogāveram	I had asked

Note: Latin has no separate tenses corresponding to the Greek aorist and perfect; therefore the perfect has to fill the place of two tenses: the aorist, I loved, and the perfect, I have loved.

The present, the future simple, and the future perfect are called **primary tenses**.

The imperfect and the pluperfect are called **historic tenses**. The perfect in the sense of *I have loved* is **primary**; in the sense of *I loved* it is **historic**.

106 Mood

Moods are the forms in which the idea contained in the verb is presented.

The **indicative** is the mood which states a fact: *amō,* I love.

The **imperative** is the mood of command: *amā,* love!

Note: The forms of the Imperative in **-tō, -tōte,** are emphatic, and were used anciently in laws.

The **subjunctive** is the mood which represents something as thought of or as dependent: *ut amem,* that I may love; *si amārem,* if I were to love.

Note: In the paradigms the tenses of the subjunctive are given without any English translation, because their meaning varies so much according to the context that it is impossible to convey it by any one rendering.

---

107 The Verb Infinitive

The **infinitive** is a **verb noun** expressing action or state in general, without limit of person or number: *amāre,* to love.

The **gerund** is a **verbal noun** declined like neuters of the second declension. It supplies cases to the infinitive: as *amandī,* of loving.

The **gerundive** is a **participle,** or **verbal adjective**: *amandus, -a, -um,* fit to be loved.

The **supines** are cases of a **verbal substantive**: *amātum,* in order to love; *amātū,* for loving or in loving.

The **participles** are so called because they have partly the properties of verbs and partly those of adjectives; there are three besides the gerundive: (a) **active present participle** *amāns,* loving (declined like *ingēns*); (b) **active future participle** *amātūrus,* about to love (declined like *bonus*);(c) **passive perfect participle** *amātus,* loved (declined like *bonus*).

Note: The three participles wanting are: (a) **active perfect**; (b) **passive present**; (c) **passive future**.

---

108 Voice

The **active voice** expresses what the subject of a verb is or does: *sum,* I am; *valeo,* I am well; *amō,* I love; *regō,* I rule.

The **passive voice** expresses what is done to the subject of the verb: amor, I am loved; *regor,* I am ruled.

109 **Deponent verbs** are verbs which have chiefly the forms of the passive voice with the meaning of the active voice: *loquor,* I speak.

110 Verbs in the active voice and deponent verbs are: (a) **transitive** (*transīre,* to pass over), acting on an object: *amō eum,* I love him, *hortor vōs,* I exhort you; (b) **intransitive**, not acting on an object: *stō,* I stand, *loquor,* I speak. .

Only transitive verbs have the full passive voice.

111   THE CONJUGATIONS

Verbs are generally arranged according to the character of the present stem in four conjugations.

The **stem character** is most clearly seen before the suffix **-re** (or **-ere**) of the present active infinitive.

Conjugation	Stem	Pres. Act. Inf.
1st	**-ā-**	-āre
2nd	**-ē-**	-ēre
3rd	**consonant or -u-**	-ere
4th	**-ī-**	-īre

Deponent verbs are also divided into four conjugations with the same stem endings.

112 The following forms (the '**principle parts**') must be known in order to give the full conjugation (see § 147).

stems:	a-	e-	cons. & u-	i-
ACTIVE VOICE				
1 Pers. Pres. Indic.	amō	moneō	regō	audiō
Infin. Pres.	amāre	monēre	regere	audīre
Perfect.	amāvī	monuī	rēxī	audīvī
Supine in -um	amātum	monitum	rēctum	audītum
PASSIVE VOICE				
1 Pers. Pres. Indic.	amor	moneor	regor	audior
Infin. Pres.	amārī	monērī	regī	audīrī
Partie. Perf.	amātus	monitus	rēctus	audītus
Gerundive	amandus	monendus	regendus	audiendus

113 In the perfects **-āvi, -ēvi, -ōvi, v** sometimes drops out before **-is** or **-er**, and contraction follows: *amāvistī* becomes *amāstī, amāverunt* → *amārunt, amāvissem* → *amāssem*. In **i-** stems there is no contraction: **audīvī** becomes **audiī, audīvērunt audiērunt** (see § 14.).

For **-ērunt** (3rd pers. pl. perfect active), **-ēre** is often written: *amāvēre, implēvēre, audīvēre;* but these forms are not contracted.

The 2nd pers. sing. in the passive ends in **-ris** or **-re**: *amābāris, amābāre;* but in pres. indic. the ending in **-re** is rare.

> **Note:** An old form in **-ier** of the pres. infin. passive is some· times found in poetry: *amārier* for *amārī.*
> Poets sometimes use old forms in the future of **i-** stems; as *audibo, audibor,* for *audiam, audiar.*
> The gerundive sometimes ends in **-undus** in consonant and **i-** stems.

114 Periphrastic Conjugation

The **active future participle** and the **gerundive** may be used with all the tenses of the verb *sum: amātūrus, -a sum,* I am about to loved; *amandus, -a, sum,* I am fit to be loved. etc.

In the same way the participle *futūrus* may be used with the tenses of *sum: futurus sum,* I am about to be.

The active future participle with *fuisse* forms an imperfect future infinitive, which is only used conditionally: *amātūrus fuisse,* to have been about to love.

115 The verb sum, I am (sum, fuī, esse, futūrus)

Before the regular verbs it is necessary to conjugate the irregular verb *sum*, I am, *esse*, to be, because it is used as an auxiliary in the conjugation of other verbs. This verb is formed from two roots, (**es**, to be, and **fu**, to be or become). The **present stem**

TENSE	INDICATIVE	
Present	**sum**	I am
	es	you (sing.) are
	est	he is
	sumus	we are
	estis	you (pl.) are
	sunt	they are
Future Simple	**erō**	I shall be
	eris	you (sing.) will be
	erit	he will be
	erimus	we shall be
	eritis	you (pl.) be
	erunt	they will be
Imperfect	**eram**	I was
	erās	you (sing.) were
	erat	he was
	erāmus	we were
	erātis	you (pl.) were
	erant	they were
Perfect	**fuī**	I have been *or* I was
	fuistī	you (sing.) have been *or* were
	fuit	he has been *or* he was
	fuimus	we have been *or* we were
	fuistis	you (pl.) have been *or* were
	fuērunt	they have been *or* they were
Future Perfect	**fuerō**	I shall have been
	fueris	you (sing.) will have been
	fuerit	he will have been
	fuerimus	we shall have been
	fueritis	you (pl.) will have been
	fuerint	they will have been
Pluperfect	**fueram**	I had been
	fuerās	you (sing.) had been
	fuerat	he had been
	fuerāmus	we had been
	fuerātis	you (pl.) had been
	fuerant	they had been

is formed from the root **es-**, the perfect and participial stems from the root **fu**. In the tense forms **es-** sometimes drops **e**: *sum, sumus;* sometimes **s** changes to **r**: *eram.*

SUBJUNCTIVE	IMPERATIVE
sim *or* **siem** **sis** *or* **siès** **sit** *or* **siet** **sīmus** **sītis** **sint**	**es, estō,** be (sing.) **estō,** let him be **este, estōte** be (pl.) **suntō** let them be

THE VERB INFINITE

Infinitives

Present } **esse** to be
Imperf. }

Perfect } **fuisse,** to have been
Pluperf. }

Future { **futūrus esse** } to be about to be
{ **fore** }

Participles

Present   (*none*)
Future   **futūrus,** about to be

Gerunds and Supines
(*none*)

essem *or* **forem**
esses *or* **forès**
esset *or* **foret**
essēmus
essētis
essent *or* **forent**
fuerim
fueris
fuerit
fuerīmus
fuerītls
fuerint

Note: There is no present participle of *sum*. It is only seen in a few compounds: *abēns, praesēns.*

fuissem
fuissēs
fuisset
fuissēmus
fuissētis
fuissent

Like *sum* are conjugated its compounds: *absum,* I am absent; *adsum,* I am present; *dēsum,* I am wanting; *īnsum,* I am in or among; *intersum,* I am among; *obsum,* I hinder; *praesum,* I am set over; *prōsum,* I am of use; *subsum,* I am under; *supersum,* I survive. In *prōsum,* the final **d** of the old preposition is kept before **e**: *prōdes.*

116   First Conjugation, a- Stems, Active Voice

TENSE	INDICATIVE	
Present	amō	I love
	amās	you (sing.) love
	amat	he loves
	amāmus	we love
	amātis	you (pl.) love
	amant	they love
Future Simple	amābō	I shall love
	amābis	you (sing.) will love
	amābit	he (she, it) will love
	amābimus	we shall love
	amābitis	you (pl.) will love
	amābunt	they will love
Imperfect	amābam	I was loving, I loved
	amābās	you (sing.) were loving, you loved
	amābat	he (she, it) was loving, he loved
	amābāmus	we were loving, we loved
	amābātis	you (pl.) were loving, you loved
	amābant	they were loving, they loved
Perfect	amāvī	I have loved *or* I loved
	amāvistī	you (sing.) have loved *or* you loved
	amāvit	he (she, it) has loved *or* he loved
	amāvimus	we have loved *or* we loved
	amāvistis	you (pl.) have loved *or* you loved
	amāvērunt	they have loved *or* they loved
Future Perfect	amāverō	I shall have loved
	amāveris	you (sing.) will have loved
	amāverit	he (she, it) will have loved
	amāverimus	we shall have loved
	amāveritis	you (pl.) will have loved
	amāverint	they will have loved
Pluperfect	amāveram	I had loved
	amāverās	you (sing.) had loved
	amāverat	he (she, it) had loved
	amāverāmus	we had loved
	amāverātis	you (pl.) had loved
	amāverant	they had loved

SUBJUNCTIVE	IMPERATIVE
amem amēs amet amēmus amētis ament	amā, amātō, love (sing.) amātō, let him love amāte, amātōte love (pl.) amantō let them love

THE VERB INFINITE

amārem amārēs amāret amārēmus amārētis	Infinitives
	Present } Imperf. } amāre, to love
	Perfect } Pluperf. } amāvisse, to have loved

amārent   Future   amātūrus esse, to be about to love

amāverim
amāverīs
amāverit
amāverīmus
amāverītis
amāverint

Gerund
Nom. Acc.   amandum, the loving
Gen.   amandī, of loving
Dat. Abl.   amandō, for or by loving

Supines
amātum, in order to love
amātū, in or for loving

Participles
Pres. amāns, loving
Fut. amātūrus, about to love

amāvissem
amāvissēs
amāvisset
amāvissēmus
amāvissētis
amāvissent

117　Second Conjugation, e- Stems, Active Voice

TENSE	INDICATIVE	
Present	moneō	I advise or I am advising
	monēs	you (s.) advise or you are advising
	monet	he advises or he is advising
	monēmus	we advise or we are advising
	monētis	you (pl.) advise or you are advising
	monent	they advise or they are advising
Future Simple	monēbō	I shall advise
	monēbis	you (sing.) will advise
	monēbit	he (she, it) will advise
	monēbimus	we shall advise
	monēbitis	you (pl.) will advise
	monēbunt	they will advise
Imperfect	monēbam	I was advising, I advised
	monēbās	you (sing.) were advising, you advised
	monēbat	he (she, it) was advising, he advised
	monēbāmus	we were advising, we advised
	monēbātis	you (pl.) were advising, you advised
	monēbant	they were advising, they advised
Perfect	monuī	I have advised or I advised
	monuistī	you (s.) have advised or you advised
	monuit	he (she, it) has advised or he advised
	monuimus	we have advised or we advised
	monuistis	you (pl.) have advised or you advised
	monuērunt	they have advised or they advised
Future Perfect	monuerō	I shall have advised
	monueris	you (sing.) will have advised
	monuerit	he (she, it) will have advised
	monuerimus	we shall have advised
	monueritis	you (pl.) will have advised
	monuerint	they will have advised
Pluperfect	monueram	I had advised
	monuerās	you (sing.) had advised
	monuerat	he (she, it) had advised
	monuerāmus	we had advised
	monuerātis	you (pl.) had advised
	monuerant	they had advised

SUBJUNCTIVE	IMPERATIVE
moneam moneās moneat moneāmus moneātis moneant	monē, monētō, advise (sing.) monētō, let him advise monēte, monētōte advise (pl.) monentō let them advise

THE VERB INFINITE

monērem monērēs monēret monērēmus monērētis monērent monuerim monuerīs monuerit monuerīmus monuerītis monuerint	Infinitives Present } monēre, to advise Imperf. } Perfect } monuisse, to have advised Pluperf. } Future monitūrus esse, to be about to advise Gerund Nom. Acc. monendum, the advising Gen. monendī, of advising Dat. Abl. monendō, for or by advising
	Supines monitum, in order to advise monitū, in or for advising
monuissem monuissēs monuisset monuissēmus monuissētis monuissent	Participles Pres. monēns, advising Fut. monitūrus, about to advise

118 Third Conjugation, Consonant Stems, Active Voice

TENSE	INDICATIVE	
	regō	I rule *or* I am ruling
	regis	you (s.) rule *or* you are ruling
Present	regit	he rules *or* he is ruling
	regimus	we rule *or* we are ruling
	regitis	you (pl.) rule *or* you are ruling
	regunt	they rule *or* they are ruling
	regam	I shall rule
	regēs	you (sing.) will rule
Future Simple	reget	he (she, it) will rule
	regēmus	we shall rule
	regētis	you (pl.) will rule
	regent	they will rule
	regēbam	I was ruling, I ruled
	regēbās	you (sing.) were ruling, you ruled
Imperfect	regēbat	he (she, it) was ruling, he ruled
	regēbāmus	we were ruling, we ruled
	regēbātis	you (pl.) were ruling, you ruled
	regēbant	they were ruling, they ruled
	rēxī	I have ruled *or* I ruled
	rēxistī	you (s.) have ruled *or* you ruled
Perfect	rēxit	he (she, it) has ruled *or* he ruled
	rēximus	we have ruled *or* we ruled
	rēxistis	you (pl.) have ruled *or* you ruled
	rēxērunt	they have ruled *or* they ruled
	rēxerō	I shall have ruled
	rēxeris	you (sing.) will have ruled
Future Perfect	rēxerit	he (she, it) will have ruled
	rēxerimus	we shall have ruled
	rēxeritis	you (pl.) will have ruled
	rēxerint	they will have ruled
	rēxeram	I had ruled
	rēxerās	you (sing.) had ruled
Pluperfect	rēxerat	he (she, it) had ruled
	rēxerāmus	we had ruled
	rēxerātis	you (pl.) had ruled
	rēxerant	they had ruled

SUBJUNCTIVE	IMPERATIVE
regam **regās** **regat** **regāmus** **regātis** **regant**	**rege, regitō,** rule (sing.) **regtō,** let him rule **regite, regitōte** rule (pl.) **reguntō** let them rule
	THE VERB INFINITE Infinitives Present } **regere,** to rule Imperf. }
regerem **regerēs** **regeret** **regerēmus** **regerētis** **regerent**	Perfect } **rēxisse,** to have ruled Pluperf. } Future **rēctūrus esse,** to be about to rule Gerund
rēxerim **rēxerīs** **rēxerit** **rēxerīmus** **rēxerītls** **rēxerint**	Nom. Acc. **regendum**, the ruling Gen. **regendī**, of ruling Dat. Abl. **regendō,** for *or* by ruling Supines **rēctum,** in order to rule **rēctū,** in *or* for ruling
	Participles Pres. **regēns,** ruling Fut. **rēctūrus,** about to rule
rēxissem **rēxissēs** **rēxisset** **rēxissēmus** **rēxissētis** **rēxissent**	**Note:** *Faciō, dīcō, dūcō,* and the compounds of *dūcō* in the 2nd person of the present imperative make *fac, dīc, dūc, etc.*

119 Fourth Conjugation, i- Stems, Active Voice

TENSE	INDICATIVE	
Present	audiō	I hear *or* I am hearing
	audīs	you (s.) hear *or* you are hearing
	audit	he hears *or* he is hearing
	audīmus	we hear *or* we are hearing
	raudītis	you (pl.) hear or you are hearing
	audiunt	they hear or they are hearing
Future Simple	audiam	I shall hear
	audiēs	you (sing.) will hear
	audiet	he (she, it) will hear
	audiēmus	we shall hear
	audiētis	you (pl.) will hear
	audient	they will hear
Imperfect	audiēbam	I was hearing, I heard
	audiēbās	you (sing.) were hearing, you heard
	audiēbat	he (she, it) was hearing, he heard
	audiēbāmus	we were hearing, we heard
	audiēbātis	you (pl.) were hearing, you heard
	audiēbant	they were hearing, they heard
Perfect	audīvī	I have heard *or* I heard
	audīvistī	you (s.) have heard *or* you heard
	audīvit	he (she, it) has heard *or* he heard
	audīvimus	we have heard *or* we heard
	audīvistis	you (pl.) have heard *or* you heard
	audīvērunt	they have heard *or* they heard
Future Perfect	audīverō	I shall have heard
	audīveris	you (sing.) will have heard
	audīverit	he (she, it) will have heard
	audīverimus	we shall have heard
	audīveritis	you (pl.) will have heard
	audīverint	they will have heard
Pluperfect	audīveram	I had heard
	audīverās	you (sing.) had heard
	audīverat	he (she, it) had heard
	audīverāmus	we had heard
	audīverātis	you (pl.) had heard
	audīverant	they had heard

SUBJUNCTIVE	IMPERATIVE
audiam	
audiās	**audī, audītō,** hear (sing.)
audiat	**audītō,** let him hear
audiāmus	
audiātis	**audīte, audītōte** hear (pl.)
audiant	**audiuntō** let them hear

THE VERB INFINITE

audīrem

Infinitives

Present ⎱
Imperf. ⎰ **audīre,** to hear

Perfect ⎱
Pluperf. ⎰ **audīvisse,** to have heard

Future **audītūrus esse,** to be about to hear

audīrēs
audīret
audīrēmus
audīrētis
audīrent
audīverim
audīveris
audīverit
audīverīmus
audīverītis
audīverint

Gerund

Nom. Acc. **audiendum,** the hearing
Gen.   **audiendī,** of hearing
Dat. Abl. **audiendō,** for *or* by hearing

Supines
audītum, in order to hear
audītū, in *or* for hearing

Participles
Pres. **audiēns,** hearing
Fut. **audītūrus,** about to hear

audīvissem
audīvissēs
audīvisset
audīvissēmus
audīvissētis
audīvissent

120 First Conjugation, a- Stems, Passive Voice

TENSE	INDICATIVE	
Present	amor	I am loved *or* I am being loved
	amāris	you (s.) are loved *or* are being loved
	amātur	he is loved *or* he is being loved
	amāmur	we are loved *or* we are being loved
	amāminī	you (pl.) are loved *or* are being loved
	amantur	they are loved *or* are being loved
Future Simple	amābor	I shall be loved
	amāberis	you (sing.) will be loved
	amābitur	he (she, it) will be loved
	amābimur	we shall be loved
	amābiminī	you (pl.) will be loved
	amābuntur	they will be loved
Imperfect	amābar	I was being loved
	amābāris	you (sing.) were being loved
	amābātur	he (she, it) was being loved
	amābāmur	we were being loved
	amābāminī	you (pl.) were being loved
	amābantur	they were being loved
Perfect	amātus sum	I have been *or* was loved
	amātus es	you (s.) have been *or* were loved
	amātus est	he (she, it) has been *or* was loved
	amātī sumus	we have been *or* were loved
	amātī estis	you (pl.) have been *or* were loved
	amātī sunt	they have been *or* were loved
Future Perfect	amātus erō	I shall have been loved
	amātus eris	you (sing.) will have been loved
	amātus erit	he (she, it) will have been loved
	amātī erimus	we shall have been loved
	amātī eritis	you (pl.) will have been loved
	amātī erunt	they will have been loved
Pluperfect	amātus eram	I had been loved
	amātus erās	you (sing.) had been loved
	amātus erat	he (she, it) had been loved
	amātī erāmus	we had been loved
	amātī erātis	you (pl.) had been loved
	amātī erant	they had been loved

SUBJUNCTIVE	IMPERATIVE
amer	
amēris	**amāre, amātor,** be loved (sing.)
amētur	**amātor,** let him be loved
amēmur	
amēminī	**amāminī,** be loved (pl.)
amentur	**amantor,** let them be loved

amārer	
amārēris	THE VERB INFINITE
amārētur	
amārēmur	Infinitives
amārēminī	Present ⎫
amārentur	Imperf. ⎭ **amārī,** to be loved
amātus sim	Perfect ⎫
amātus sīs	Pluperf. ⎭ **amātus esse,** to have been loved
amātus sit	
amātī sīmus	Future **amātum īrī,** (see § 387)
amātī sītis	
amātī sint	
	Participle
	Pres. **amātus,** loved *or* having been loved
	Gerundive
	amandus, fit to be loved
amātus essem	
amātus essēs	
amātus esset	
amātī essēmus	
amātī essētis	
amātī essent	

121 Second Conjugation, e- Stems, Passive Voice

TENSE	INDICATIVE	
Present	moneor	I am advised or being advised
	monēris	you (s.) are advised or being advised
	monētur	he is advised or being advised
	monēmur	we are advised or being advised
	monēminī	you (pl.) are advised or being advised
	monentur	they are advised or being advised
Future Simple	monēbor	I shall be advised
	monēberis	you (sing.) will be advised
	monēbitur	he (she, it) will be advised
	monēbimur	we shall be advised
	monēbiminī	you (pl.) will be advised
	monēbuntur	they will be advised
Imperfect	monēbar	I was being advised
	monēbāris	you (sing.) were being advised
	monēbātur	he (she, it) was being advised
	monēbāmur	we were being advised
	monēbāminī	you (pl.) were being advised
	monēbantur	they were being advised
Perfect	monitus sum	I have been or was advised
	monitus es	you (s.) have been or were advised
	monitus est	he (she, it) has been or was advised
	monitī sumus	we have been or were advised
	monitī estis	you (pl.) have been or were advised
	monitī sunt	they have been or were advised
Future Perfect	monitus erō	I shall have been advised
	monitus eris	you (sing.) will have been advised
	monitus erit	he (she, it) will have been advised
	monitī erimus	we shall have been advised
	monitī eritis	you (pl.) will have been advised
	monitī erunt	they will have been advised
Pluperfect	monitus eram	I had been advised
	monitus erās	you (sing.) had been advised
	monitus erat	he (she, it) had been advised
	monitī erāmus	we had been advised
	monitī erātis	you (pl.) had been advised
	monitī erant	they had been advised

SUBJUNCTIVE	IMPERATIVE
monear **moneāris** **moneātur** **moneāmur** **moneāminī** **moneantur**	**monēre, monētor,** be advised (sing.) **monētor,** let him be advised **monēminī,** be advised (pl.) **monentor,** let them be advised

monērer
monērēris
monērētur
monērēmur
monērēminī
monērentur
monitus sim
monitus sīs
monitus sit
moniti sīmus
moniti sītis
moniti sint

monitus essem
monitus essēs
monitus esset
moniti essēmus
moniti essētis
moniti essent

THE VERB INFINITE

Infinitives

Present ⎱
Imperf. ⎰ **monērī,** to be advised

Perfect ⎱
Pluperf. ⎰ **monitus esse,** to have been

Future   **monitum īrī,** (see § 387)

Participle
Pres. **monitus,** advised *or* having been advised

Gerundive
monendus, fit to be advised

122 Third Conjugation, Consonant & u- Stems, Passive Voice

TENSE	INDICATIVE	
	regor	I am ruled *or* being ruled
	regeris	you (s.) are ruled *or* being ruled
Present	**regitur**	he is ruled *or* being ruled
	regimur	we are ruled *or* being ruled
	regiminī	you (pl.) are ruled *or* being ruled
	reguntur	they are ruled *or* being ruled
	regar	I shall be ruled
	regēris	you (sing.) will be ruled
Future Simple	**regētur**	he (she, it) will be ruled
	regēmur	we shall be ruled
	regēminī	you (pl.) will be ruled
	regentur	they will be ruled
	regēbar	I was being ruled
	regēbāris	you (sing.) were being ruled
Imperfect	**regēbātur**	he (she, it) was being ruled
	regēbāmur	we were being ruled
	regēbāminī	you (pl.) were being ruled
	regēbantur	they were being ruled
	rēctus sum	I have been *or* was ruled
	rēctus es	you (s.) have been *or* were ruled
Perfect	**rēctus est**	he (she, it) has been *or* was ruled
	rēctī sumus	we have been *or* were ruled
	rēctī estis	you (pl.) have been *or* were ruled
	rēctī sunt	they have been *or* were ruled
	rēctus erō	I shall have been ruled
	rēctus eris	you (sing.) will have been ruled
Future Perfect	**rēctus erit**	he (she, it) will have been ruled
	rēctī erimus	we shall have been ruled
	rēctī eritis	you (pl.) will have been ruled
	rēctī erunt	they will have been ruled
	rēctus eram	I had been ruled
	rēctus erās	you (sing.) had been ruled
Pluperfect	**rēctus erat**	he (she, it) had been ruled
	rēctī erāmus	we had been ruled
	rēctī erātis	you (pl.) had been ruled
	rēctī erant	they had been ruled

SUBJUNCTIVE	IMPERATIVE
regar	
regāris	**regere, regitor,** be ruled (sing.)
regātur	**regitor,** let him be ruled
regāmur	
regāminī	**regiminī,** be ruled (pl.)
regantur	**reguntor,** let them be ruled

regerer	
regerēris	THE VERB INFINITE
regerētur	
regerēmur	
regerēminī	Infinitives
regerentur	Present } **regī,** to be ruled Imperf.
rēctus sim	Perfect } **rēctus esse,** to have been ruled
rēctus sīs	Pluperf.
rēctus sit	
rēctī sīmus	Future **rēctum īrī,** (see § 387)
rēctī sītis	
rēctī sint	
	Participle
	Pres. **rēctus,** ruled *or* having been ruled
	Gerundive
	regendus, fit to be ruled
rēctus essem	
rēctus essēs	
rēctus esset	
rēctī essēmus	
rēctī essētis	
rēctī essent	

123 Fourth Conjugation, i- Stems, Passive Voice

TENSE	INDICATIVE	
Present	audior	I am heard *or* being heard
	audīris	you (s.) are heard *or* being heard
	audītur	he is heard *or* being heard
	audīmur	we are heard *or* being heard
	audīminī	you (pl.) are heard *or* being heard
	audiuntur	they are heard *or* being heard
Future Simple	audar	I shall be heard
	audiēris	you (sing.) will be heard
	audiētur	he (she, it) will be heard
	audiēmur	we shall be heard
	audiēminī	you (pl.) will be heard
	audientur	they will be heard
Imperfect	audiēbar	I was being heard
	audiēbāris	you (sing.) were being heard
	audiēbātur	he (she, it) was being heard
	audiēbāmur	we were being heard
	audiēbāminī	you (pl.) were being heard
	audiēbantur	they were being heard
Perfect	audītus sum	I have been *or* was heard
	audītus es	you (s.) have been *or* were heard
	audītus est	he (she, it) has been *or* was heard
	audītī sumus	we have been *or* were heard
	audītī estis	you (pl.) have been *or* were heard
	audītī sunt	they have been *or* were heard
Future Perfect	audītus erō	I shall have been heard
	audītus eris	you (sing.) will have been heard
	audītus erit	he (she, it) will have been heard
	audītī erimus	we shall have been heard
	audītī eritis	you (pl.) will have been heard
	audītī erunt	they will have been heard
Pluperfect	audītus eram	I had been heard
	audītus erās	you (sing.) had been heard
	audītus erat	he (she, it) had been heard
	audītī erāmus	we had been heard
	audītī erātis	you (pl.) had been heard
	audītī erant	they had been heard

SUBJUNCTIVE	IMPERATIVE
audiar	
audiāris	audīre, audītor, be heard (sing.)
audiātur	audītor, let him be heard
audiāmur	
audāminī	audīminī, be heard (pl.)
audiantur	audiuntor, let them be heard

	THE VERB INFINITE
audīrer	
audīrēris	
audīrētur	
audīrēmur	Infinitives
audīrēminī	Present ⎫ audīrī, to be heard
audīrentur	Imperf. ⎭
audītus sim	Perfect ⎫ audītus esse, to have been heard
audītus sīs	Pluperf. ⎭
audītus sit	
audītī sīmus	Future audītum īrī, (see § 387)
audītī sītis	
audītī sint	

Participle
Pres. **audītus,** heard *or* having been heard

Gerundive
audiendus, fit to be heard

audītus essem
audītus essēs
audītus esset
audītī essēmus
audītī essētis
audītī essent

124　Deponent Verb, Ūtor, Ūtī, Ūsus (3rd Conjugation)

TENSE	INDICATIVE	
Present	ūtor	I use *or* I am using
	ūteris	you (s.) use *or* are using
	ūtitur	he uses *or* is using
	ūtimur	we use *or* are using
	ūtiminī	you (pl.) use *or* are using
	ūtuntur	they use *or* are using
Future Simple	ūtar	I shall use
	ūtēris	you (sing.) will use
	ūtētur	he (she, it) will use
	ūtēmur	we shall use
	ūtēminī	you (pl.) will use
	ūtentur	they will use
Imperfect	ūtēbar	I was using
	ūtēbāris	you (sing.) were using
	ūtēbātur	he (she, it) was using
	ūtēbāmur	we were using
	ūtēbāminī	you (pl.) were using
	ūtēbantur	they were using
Perfect	ūsus sum	I have used *or* I used
	ūsus es	you (s.) have used *or* you (sing.) used
	ūsus est	he (she, it) has used *or* he (she, it) used
	ūsī sumus	we have used *or* we used
	ūsī estis	you (pl.) have used *or* you used
	ūsī sunt	they have used *or* they used
Future Perfect	ūsus erō	I shall have used
	ūsus eris	you (sing.) will have used
	ūsus erit	he (she, it) will have used
	ūsī erimus	we shall have used
	ūsī eritis	you (pl.) will have used
	ūsī erunt	they will have used
Pluperfect	ūsus eram	I had used
	ūsus erās	you (sing.) had used
	ūsus erat	he (she, it) had used
	ūsī erāmus	we had used
	ūsī erātis	you (pl.) had used
	ūsī erant	they had used

SUBJUNCTIVE	IMPERATIVE
ūtar	
ūtāris	**ūtere, ūtitor,** use (sing.)
ūtātur	**ūtitor,** let him use
ūtāmur	
ūtāminī	**ūtiminī,** use (pl.)
ūtantur	**ūtuntor,** let them use

THE VERB INFINITE

	Infinitives
	Present **ūtī,** to use
ūterer	Perfect **ūsus esse,** to have used
ūterēris	Future **ūsūrus esse,** to be about to use
ūterētur	
ūterēmur	Gerund
ūterēminī	**ūtendum**
ūterentur	
ūsus sim	Supines
ūsus sīs	**ūsum** to use
	ūsū in or for using
ūsus sit	
ūsī sīmus	Participles
ūsī sītis	Pres. **ūtēns,** using
ūsī sint	Future **ūsūrus** about to use
	Perfect **ūsus** having used

Gerundive
ūtendus, fit to be used

ūsus essem	**Note:** Deponent verbs are passive in form
ūsus essēs	but active in meaning.
ūsus esset	
ūsī essēmus	
ūsī essētis	
ūsī essent	

125 Deponent Verbs of the Four Conjugations

	1	vēnor	vēnātus sum	vēnārī, hunt
	2	vereor	veritus sum	verērī, fear
	3	ūtor	ūsus sum	ūtī, use
	4	partior	partītus sum	partīrī, divide

INDICATIVE

TENSE	1st Conj.	2nd Conj.	3rd Conj.	4th Conj.
Pres.	vēnor	vereor	ūtor	partior
	vēnāris (re)	verēris (re)	ūteris (re)	partīris (īre) etc.
Fut. S.	vēnābor	verēbor	ūtar	partiar
Imperf.	vēnābar	verēbar	ūtēbar	partiēbar
Perf.	vēnātus sum	veritus sum	ūsus sum.	partītus sum
Fut.Perf.	vēnātus erō	veritus erō	ūsus erō	partītus erō
Pluperf.	vēnātus eram	veritus eram	ūsus eram	partītus eram

SUBJUNCTIVE

Pres.	vēner	verear	ūtar	partiar
Imperf.	vēnārer	verērer	ūterer	partīrer
Perf.	vēnātus sim	veritus sim	ūsus sim	partītus sim
Pluperf.	vēnātus essem	veritus essem	ūsus essem	partītus essem

IMPERATIVE

	vēnāre	verēre	ūtere	partīre
	vēnātor	verētor	ūtitor	partītor

THE VERB INFINITE

Infinitives

Pres.	vēnārī	verērī	ūtī	partīrī
Perf.	vēnātus esse	veritus esse	ūsus esse	partītus esse
Fut.	vēnātūrus esse	veritūrus esse	ūsūrus esse	partītūrus esse

Participles

Pres.	vēnāns	verēns	ūtēns	partiēns
Fut.	vēnātūrus	veritūrus	ūsūrus	partītūrus
Perf.	vēnātus	verltus	ūsus	partītus

Gerundive

	vēnandus	verendus	ūtendus	partiendus

Gerunds

	vēnandum	verendum	ūtendum	partiendum

Supines

in -um	vēnātum	veritum	ūsum	partītum
in -ū	vēnātū	veritū	ūsū	partītū

Note: Some deponents also have an active form: *pūnior* and *pūniō*, punish.

126 Many perfect participles of deponent verbs are used passively as well as actively: as *cōnfessus* from *cōnfiteor,* confess; *imitātus* from *imitor,* imitate; *meritus* from *mereor,* deserve; *pollicitus* from *polliceor,* promise.

127 Some verbs have a perfect of passive form with a present of active form; they are called **semi-deponents**:

audeō, dare	**ausus sum,** I have dared or I dared
gaudeō, rejoice	**gāvīsus sum,** I have rejoiced or I rejoiced
soleō, am accustomed	**solitus sum,** I have been accustomed
fidō, trust	**fīsus sum,** I have trusted or I trusted

128 Some verbs have an active form with passive meaning; they are called **quasi-passive** (see § 303):

exsulō, am banished	**liceō,** am put up for sale
vāpulō, am beaten	**vēneō,** am on sale
fīō, am made (see § 141)	

129 Some verbs have perfect participles with active meaning, like the deponent verbs:

iūrō, swear	**iūrāvī,** I swore	**iūrātus,** having sworn
cēnō, dine	**cēnāvī,** I dined	**cēnātus,** having dined
prandeō, dine	**prandī,** I dined	**prānsus,** having dined

130 Inceptive verbs, with present stem in **-seō** (third conjugation), express beginning of action, and are derived from verb stems or from nouns:

> **pallēscō,** turn pale, from **palleō**
> **nigrēscō,** turn black, from **niger**

131 Frequentative verbs (first conj.) express repeated or intenser action, and are formed from supine stems:

> **rogitō,** ask repeatedly (**rogō**); **cantō,** sing with energy (**canō**)

132 Desiderative verbs (fourth conj.) express desire of action, and are formed from the supine stem:

> **ēsuriō,** am hungry (**ēdō, ēsūrus**)

133 Mixed Conjugation

Forms from present stem, **cap-i-**, take

	ACTIVE VOICE		PASSIVE VOICE	
PRESENT	INDIC.	SUBJUNC.	INDIC.	SUBJUNC.
	capiō	capiam	capior	capiar
	capis	capiās	caperis	capiāris
	capit	capiat	capitur	capiātur
	capimus	capiāmus	capimur	capiāmur
	capitis	capiātis	capiminī	capiāminī
	capiunt	capiant	capiuntur	capiantur

FUTURE SIMPLE

	capiam	capiar
	capiēs	capiēris
	capiet	capiētur
	capiēmus	capiēmur
	capiētis	capiēminī
	capient	capientur

IMPERFECT

	capiēbam	caperem	capiēbar	caperer
	capiēbās	caperēs	capiēbāris	caperēris
	capiēbat	caperet	capiēbātur	caperētur
	capiēbāmus	caperēmus	capiēbāmur	caperēmur
	capiēbātis	caperētis	capiēbāminī	caperēminī
	capiēbant	caperent	capiēbantur	caperentur

IMPERATIVE

2 sing.	**cape, capitō**		2 sing.	**capere, capitor**	
3 sing.	**capitō**		3 sing.	**capitor**	
2 pl.	**capite, capitōte**		2 pl.	**capiminī**	
3 pl.	**capiuntō**		3 pl.	**capiuntor**	

INFINITE

Infin. Pres.	**capere,**		**capī**
Gerund	**capiendum**	Gerundive	**capiendus**
Pres. Partic.	**capiēns**		
Perfect	**cēpi**	Supine	**captum**

The verbs in **-iō** are:

capiō, cupiō, faciō	} and their compounds	take, desire, make
fodiō, fugiō, iaciō		dig, flee, throw
pariō, rapiō, sapiō, quatiō		bring forth, seize, know, shake
compounds of speciō & laciō	obsolete verbs	look at, entice
Deponents: **gradior, patior, morior**		step, suffer, die
Semi-deponents (see §161): **potior, orior**		get possession of, arise

134 Irregular Verbs

Verbs are called irregular: (1) because they are formed from more than one root, as *sum*; (2) because their tense-forms differ from those of regular verbs.

135 **Possum,** I can, **posse, potuī**: the present indicative, **possum**, is compounded of *sum*, I am, and the adjective *potis*, able.

INDIC.	SUBJUNC.	INDIC.	SUBJUNC.
PRESENT		**PERFECT**	
possum	possim	potuī	potuerim
potes	possīs	potuistī	potueris
potest	possit	potuit	potuerit
possumus	possīmus	potuimus	potuerīmus
potestis	possītis	potuistis	potuerītis
possunt	possint	potuērunt	potuerint
FUTURE SIMPLE		**FUTURE PERFECT**	
poterō		potuerō	
poteris		potueris	
poterit		potuerit	
poterimus		potuerimus	
poteritis		potueritis	
poterunt		potuerint	
IMPERFECT		**PLUPERFECT**	
poteram	possem	potueram	potuissem
poterās	possēs	potuerās	potuissēs
poterat	posset	potuerat	potuisset
poterāmus	possēmus	potuerāmus	potuissēmus
poterātis	possētis	potuerātis	potuissētis
poterant	possent	potuerant	potuissent

Infinitive pres. and imperf. **posse** (*pot-esse*), perf. and pluperf. **potuisse. Potēns** is used as an adjective, powerful, able, never as a participle.

136   Fero, bear, ferre, tulī, lātum

ACTIVE VOICE		PASSIVE VOICE	
PRESENT INDIC.	SUBJUNC.	INDIC.	SUBJUNC.
ferō	feram	feror	ferar
fers	ferās	ferris	ferāris
fert	ferat	fertur	ferātur
ferimus	ferāmus	ferimur	ferāmur
fertis	ferātis	feriminī	ferāminī
ferunt	ferant	feruntur	ferantur

FUTURE SIMPLE

feram	ferar
ferēs	ferēris
feret	ferētur
ferēmus	ferēmur
ferētis	ferēminī
ferent	ferentur

IMPERFECT

ferēbam	ferrrem	ferēbar	ferrrer
ferēbās	ferrrēs	ferēbāris	ferrrēris
ferēbat	ferrret	ferēbātur	ferrrētur
ferēbāmus	ferrrēmus	ferēbāmur	ferrrēmur
ferēbātis	ferrrētis	ferēbāminī	ferrrēminī
ferēbant	ferrrent	ferēbantur	ferrrentur

IMPERATIVE

2 sing.	fer, fertō	2 sing.	ferre, fertor
3 sing.	fertō	3 sing.	fertor
2 pl.	ferte, fertōte	2 pl.	feriminī
3 pl.	feruntō	3 pl.	feruntor

INFINITE

Infin. Pres.	ferre,		ferrī
Gerund	ferendum	Gerundive	ferendus
Pres. Partic.	ferēns		

Perfect stem forms are regular:

tul-ī, -erō, -eram, -erim, -issem   Infin. **tulisse**

The supine stem forms are also regular.

137 Eō (for **eiō**), go, **ire, iī** (or **īvī**), **itum**

INDICATIVE	SUBJUNCTIVE	IMPERATIVE
Present		
eō	eam	
īs	eās	ī, ītō
it	eat	ītō
īmus	eāmus	
ītis	eātis	īte, itōte
eunt	eant	euntō

Future Simple		
ībō		
ībis		THE VERB INFINITIVE
ībit		
ībimus		Infinitives
ībitis		
ībunt		Present ⎱ īre
Imperfect		Imperfect ⎰
ībam	īrem	
ībās	īrēs	Perfect ⎱ īsse, īvisse
ībat	īret	Pluperfect ⎰
ībāmus	īrēmus	
ībātis	īrētis	Gerund **eundem**
ībant	īrent	
		Supines **itum, itū**
Perfect		
iī or īvī	ierim	Participles
īstī, īvīstī	ierīs	Pres. **iēns** (acc. **euntem**)
iit	ierit	Future. **itūrus**
iimus, īvimus	ierīmus	
īstis, īvistis	ierītis	
iērunt, īvērunt	ierint	

Note: In the perfect tense of **eō** the forms **iī, īstī** &c. are more usual than **īvī** &c.; also in the compounds **rediī, rediistī, redistī**.

The impersonal passive, **ītur, itum est**, is often used.

---

138 Queō, can, **nequeō**, cannot, are conjugated like **eo** in the forms which are found, but many are wanting; they have no imperative and no gerunds. **Ambiō**, go round, canvass, is conjugated like *audiō*.

139 **Volō,** am willing, wish; **nōlō,** am unwilling, do not wish; **mālō,** prefer, wish rather. **Nōlō** is compounded of **ne** and **volō. Mālō** of **magis** and **volō.**

INDICATIVE			IMPERATIVE
Present			nōlī, nōlītō
volō	**nōlō**	**mālō**	nōlītō
vīs	**nōnvīs**	**māvis**	nōlīte
vult	**nōn vult**	**māvult**	nōlītōte, nōluntō
volumus	**nōlumus**	**mālumus**	**volō** and **mālō** have
vultis	**nōn vultis**	**māvultis**	no imperative.
volunt	**nōlunt**	**mālunt**	
Future Simple			
volam	**(nōlam)**	**(mālam)**	
volēs	**nōlēs**	**mālēs**	
volet	**nōlet**	**mālet**	
volēmus	**nōlēmus**	**mālēmus**	THE VERB INFINITE
volētis	**nōlētis**	**mālētis**	
volent	**nōlent**	**mālent**	Infinitives
Imperfect			Present ⎫ **velle**
volēbam	**nōlebam**	**mālebam**	Imperfect ⎬ **nōlle**
volēbās	**nōlebās**	**mālebās**	⎭ **mālle**
&c.	&c.	&c.	
SUBJUNCTIVE			Gerunds
Present			**volendum, -ī, -ō**
velim	**nōlim**	**mālim**	**nōlendum, -ī, -ō**
velīs	**nōlīs**	**mālīs**	**mālendum, -ī, -ō**
velit	**nōlit**	**mālit**	
velīmus	**nōlīmus**	**mālīmus**	Supines
velītis	**nōlītis**	**mālītis**	None
velint	**nolint**	**mālint**	
Imperfect			Participles
vellem	**nōllem**	**māllem**	Present ⎰ **volēns**
vellēs	**nōllēs**	**māllēs**	⎱ **nōlēns**
vellet	**nōllet**	**māllet**	
vellēmus	**nōllēmus**	**māllēmus**	
vellētis	**nōllētis**	**māllētis**	
vellent	**nōllent**	**māllent**	

The perfect-stem forms are regular:

volu-ī	**-erō**	**-eram**	**-erim**	**-issem**	⎧ voluisse
nōlu-ī	**-erō**	**-eram**	**-erim**	**-issem**	Infin.⎨ nōluisse
mālu-ī	**-erō**	**-eram**	**-erim**	**-issem**	⎩ māluisse

140 Edō, I eat, ēsse, ēdī, ēsum

Pres. ind. act.	edō, ēs, ēst, edimus, ēstis, edunt
Imperf. subj. act.	ēssem, ēssēs, ēsset, etc.
Imperat. pres. act.	ēste
Imperat. fut. act	ēstō, ēstōte
Inf. pres. act.	ēsse
3rd pers. s. pres. pass.	ēstur

The other forms of this verb are regular; except that **edim, edīs, edit,** are usually found in the present subjunctive.

141 Fīō, am made, become, fierī, factus sum

Fīō is defective, having only present, future and imperfect forms. The perfect is supplied by the perfect passive of **faciō**, make: *factus sum,* I have been made.

INDICATIVE	SUBJUNCTIVE	IMPERATIVE
Present		
fīō	fīam	fī
fīs	fīās	fīte
fit	fīat	
(fīmus)	fīāmus	
(fītis)	fīātis	
fīunt	fīant	THE VERB INFINITE
Future Simple		
fīam		Infinitives
fīēs		Present ⎫
fīet		Imperf. ⎭ **fierī**
fīēmus		Perfect ⎫
fīētis		Pluperf. ⎭ **factus esse**
fīent		Future **factum īrī**
Imperfect		
fīēbam	fierem	Gerundive
fīēbās	fierēs	**faciendus**
fīēbat	fieret	
fīēbāmus	fierēmus	
fīēbātis	fierētis	
fīēbant	fierent	
Perfect **factus sum &c.** Perf. subj. **factus sim, &c.**		

142 Defective Verbs

Defective verbs are those of which only some forms are used.

coepī, began ⎫   have only perfect-stem forms in the classical
meminī, remember ⎬   period; **meminī** and **ōdī** have present
ōdī, hate ⎭   meanings despite their forms.

INDICATIVE

Perfect.	**coepī,** I began	**meminī,** I remember	**ōdī,** I hate.
Fut. Perf.	**coeperō,** I shall have begun	**meminerō,** I shall remember	**ōderō,** I shall hate
Pluperf.	**coeperam,** I had begun	**memineram,** I rememered	**ōderam,** I hated

SUBJUNCTIVE

Perfect.	**coeperim**	**meminerim**	**ōderim**
Pluperf.	**coepissem**	**meminissem**	**ōdissem**

INFINITIVE, PARTICIPLES, IMPERATIVE

Infin.	**coepisse,** to have begun	**meminisse**	**ōdisse**
Perf. Part.	**coeptus**	—	**ōsus,** hating
Fut. Part.	**coeptūrus esse,** about to have begun	—	**ōsūrus esse** about to hate
Imperat.	—	**mementō,** **mementōte**	—

Nōvī (Perf. of *nōscō*) is used with present meaning, I know.

nōverō { **nōveram** / **nōram** } **nōverim** { **nōvissem** / **nōssem** } infin. { **nōvisse** / **nōsse** }

Aiō, I say or affirm

Ind. Pres.	**aiō, ais, ait, —,—, aiunt**
Impf.	**aiēbam, aiēbās, aiēbat, aiēbāmus, aiēbātis, aiēbant**
Subj. Pres.	**—,—, aiat, —,—, aiant**
Participle	**aiēns**

Inquam, I say

Ind. Pres.	**inquam, inquis, inquit, inquimus, inquitis, inquiunt**
Imperfect	**—,—, inquiēbat —,—, inquiēbant**
Future S.	**—, inquiēs, inquiet —, —, —**
Perf.	**—, inquīstī, inquit, —,—,—**
Imperative	**inque, inquitō**

Fārī, to speak

Indic. Pres.	**fāris, fātur**		
Indic. Fut.	**fābor, fābitur**		
Imperative	**fāre,** speak!		
Participles:	Pres. Acc. **fantem**	Perf. **fātus**	
Gerund.	**fandī, fandō**	Gerundive **fandus**	

Quaesō, entreat (an old form of *quaerō*), has first pers. plur. *quaesumus.*

The following imperatives are found:
 apage, be gone
 avē (havē), avēte, hail!   Infin. **avēre,** to have a desire
 cedo, cedite (cette), give!
 salvē, salvēte hail!   Infin. **salvēre,** to be well.

Note: **Age, igite,** come; **valē, valēte,** farewell, are used with special mean-ing; but the verbs **agō,** I do, **valeō,** I am well, are fully conjugated.

---

143 Impersonal Verbs

Impersonal verbs are used only in the forms of the third person singular of each tense, and do not refer to a subject in the nominative. They have also infinitive and gerund (see § 288–295).

144 The principal impersonal verbs are the following:

Present	Perfect	Infinitive
miseret, it moves to pity	**(miseruit)**	**(miserēre)**
piget, it vexes	**piguit**	**pigēre**
paenitet, it repents	**paenituit**	**paenitēre**
pudet, it shames	**puduit**	**pudēre**
taedet, it wearies	**taeduit**	**taedēre**
decet, it is becoming	**decuit**	**decēre**
dēdecet, it is unbecoming	**dēdecuit**	**dēdecēre**
libet, it pleases	**libuit**	**libēre**
licet, it is lawful	**licuit**	**licēre**
oportet, it behoves	**oportuit**	**oportēre**
rēfert, it matters, it concerns	**rētulit**	**rēferre**

Note 1: Decet, dēdecet have also 3rd. pers. plur., **decent, dēdecent.**

Note 2: A few passive forms are found: *misereor,* I pity, *miserētur; miseritum est, pigitum est, puditum est, pertaesum est.* Other forms are oocasionally found: *paenitendus, pudendus.*

145 Some impersonal verbs express change of weather and time:

fulgurat, it lightens	**tonat,** it thunders
ningit, it snows	**lūcēscit,** it dawns
pluit, it rains	**vesperāscit,** it grows late

146 Of some verbs which have all the personal forms, the third person singular is used impersonally with special meaning:

accēdit, it is added	**expedit,** it is expedient
accidit, it happens	**fallit, fugit,** it escapes one
appāret, it is evident	**interest,** it concerns
attinet, it belongs	**iuvat,** it delights
cōnstat, it is agreed	**pertinet,** it pertains
contingit, it befalls	**placet,** it seems good
convenit, it suits	**rēfert,** it matters
dēlectat, it charms	**restat,** it remains
ēvenit, it turns out	

Intransitive Verbs are used impersonally in the passive (see § 293).

147   DERIVATION FROM THE THREE TENSE STEMS

1. From the Present-Stem.

Pres. Indic. Act.	am-ō	mone-ō	reg-ō	audi-ō
Pres. Indic. Pass.	-or	e-or	-or	i-or
Pres. Subj. Act.	-em	e-am	-am	i-am
Pres. Indic. Pass.	-er	e-ar	-ar	i-ar
Imperf. Indic. Act.	ā-bam	ē-bam	-ēbam	i-ēbam
Imperf. Indic. Pass.	ā-bar	ē-bar	-ēbar	i-ēbar
Imperf. Subj. Act.	ā-rem	ē-rem	-ērem	ī-rem
Imperf. Subj. Pass.	ā-rer	ē-rer	-erer	ī-rer
Fut. Indic. Act.	ā-bō	ē-bō	-am	i-am
Fut. Indic. Pass.	ā-bor	ē-bor	-ar	i-ar
Imperative Act.	ā	ē	-e	ī
Imperative Pass.	ā-re	ē-re	-ere	ī-re
Infin. Pres. Act.	ā-re	ē-re	-ere	ī-re
Infin. Pres. Pass.	ā-rī	ē-rī	-ī	ī-rī
Partic. Pres. Act.	ā-ns	ē-ns	-ēns	i-ēns
Gerund	a-ndum	e-ndum	-endum	i-endum
Gerundive	a-ndus	e-ndus	-endus	i-endus

2. From the Perfect-Stem

Perfect Indic. Act.	amāv-ī	monu-ī	rēx-ī	audīv-ī
Perfect Subj. Act.	-erim	-erim	-erim	-erim
Future Perf. Ind. Act	-erō	-erō	-erō	-erō
Pluperfect Indic. Act.	-eram	-eram	-eram	-eram
Pluperfect Subj. Act.	-issem	-issem	-issem	-issem
Infin. Perf. Act.	-isse	-isse	-isse	-isse

3. From the Supine-Stem

Supine I	amāt-um	monit-um	rect-um	audit-um
Infin. Fut. Pass.	-um īrī	-um īrī	-um īrī	-um īrī
Supine II	-ū	-ū	-ū	-ū
Partic. Fut. Act.	-ūrus	-ūrus	-ūrus	-ūrus
Partic. Perf. Pass.	-us	-us	-us	-us
Perf. Indic. Pass.	-us sum	-us sum	-us sum	-us sum
Perf. Subj Pass.	-us sim	-us sim	-us sim	-us sim
Fut. Perf. Pass.	-us erō	-us erō	-us erō	-us erō
Plup. Ind. Pass	-us eram	-us eram	-us eram	-us eram
Plup. Subj. Pass.	-us essem	-us essem	-us essem	-us essem
Infin. Pass.	-us esse	-us esse	-us esse	-us esse

148   FORMATION OF THE THREE STEMS IN VERBS

The forms of the Latin verb vary in many respects from those of the parent and related languages. Both in the past and in the future tenses the Latin has developed new endings of its own, so that the original forms are only seen in the present.

The verbs in the older language were divided into two principal classes:

1. In which the personal endings were joined immediately to the root, the tenses being partly formed by changes in the root vowel.
2. In which the verb-stem was formed by a so-called **thematic vowel** (see § 149) added to the root.

Of the first class there are very few remains in Latin, most of the verbs which belonged to it having gone over into the second class.

The old ending -**m** (for -**mi**) for the first person singular is seen in *sum*, I am, and in other tenses, as *eram*. A few verbs retain part of their old forms side by side with later forms borrowed from the thematic verbs. These are:

Vowel-ending stems: **eō,** I go; **dō,** I give **stō,** I stand

Consonant-ending stems: **edō,** I eat; **volō,** I will; **nōlō,** will not; **mālo,** I prefer

Note: for the forms of these verbs see § 115 and 136 to 140.

PERSONAL ENDINGS IN ATHEMATIC AND THEMATIC VERBS

	ACTIVE VOICE		PASSIVE VOICE
	Athematic	Thematic	
Singular 1	-m	-ō	-r
2	-a	-s	-ris *or* -re
3	-t	-t	-tur
Plural 1	-mus	-mus	-mur
2	-tis	-tis	-minī
3	-int	-nt	-ntur

Note: The -**r** of the passive probably comes from an old form of a third voice, called the **middle voice**, which is not preserved in Latin.

149 Present-Stem Formation

The thematic verbs are divided into six groups according to the formation of their present stems.

1. The present stem is the same as the verb-stem, being formed by the addition of the thematic vowel to the stem-syllable either with or without lengthening of the stem-vowel: **petō, vehō, cēdō, fendō, dīcō, fīdō, dūcō, claudō, agō, rudō,** etc.

> **Note.** This class had originally two divisions: (a) with long root vowel, (b) with short root vowel, but in Latin the distinction between them is not clear.

2. Reduplicated presents. Of this class very few are preserved in Latin: **gignō** for **gi-g(e)nō** (c.f. **genus,** race); **si-stō; bi-bō.**

3. With suffix **-t** added to the stem-syllable (i.e. with a **t** inserted between the verb-root and the thematic vowel): **plec-t-ō, flec-t-ō, nec-t-ō.**

4. Nasalized stems:

   (a) with addition of the suffix **-n: cer-n-ō, ster-n-ō, sper-n-ō, tem-n-ō,** and two roots ending in **-i: si-n-ō, li-n-ō.** Verbs in **-llō, fallō, pellō, percellō,** etc., also belong to this class, **-llō** standing for older **-lnō.**

   (b) Verbs in which the **-n-** is inserted in the stem-syllable, as **plangō** (verb-stem **plag-), iungō, findō, scindō.** The **n** becomes **m** before labials, as in **rumpo.** In some of these verbs the nasal goes through all the tenses, as in **ungō, unxi, unctum.** In others it appears only in the present stem, as in **frangō, frēgī, frāctum.** A few have the nasal in the perfect, but not in the supine, as **pingō, pīnxī, pictum.**

5. With suffix **-scō.** This class also has two divisions:

   (a) With the suffix joined immediately to the root-syllable: **nōscō, crēscō, discō, pāscō.**

   (b) Derivative verbs in **-āscō, -ēscō, -īscō,** derived from other verbs or from nouns: **congelāsco,** from gelo; **calēscō,** from caleo; **gemīscō,** from **gemō; dūrēscō,** from **dūrus,** etc.

6. With suffix **-iō.** The verbs in **-iō** of the 3rd Conj. (consonant-stems) belong to this class. **Capio, facio,** etc. It included originally the large number of derivative verbs with vowel-stems, as **amō** (for **ama-iō**), **moneō (mone-iō)** (see § 14).

150 Formation of the Perfect

The perfect first person singular ends in **ī**. When the suffix **-ī** is joined to the stem, with or without change in the stem-syllable, it is called a **strong formation**. When the perfect is formed by adding to the stem one of the suffixes **-sī, -vī, -uī,** the formation is called **weak.**

In some vowel-stems, especially in many **e-** stems, the final or character vowel of the verb-stem is dropped before the perfect suffix, and the stem is then called the **clipped stem.** This is seen in **mon-uī** (Stem **mone-**), **mān-sī, cāv-ī, pepend-ī,** and also in some **a-** and **i-** stems, as **dom-uī, sal-uī.**

Strong Formation of the Perfect

1. With **reduplication.** This is the oldest way of forming the perfect, and arose from a doubling of the stem-syllable. In Latin it is formed by a vowel (originally **e**) prefixed to the stem. When the stem begins with a single consonant, this vowel is preceded by the same consonant: **pendō, pependī.** When the stem begins with **s,** followed by another consonant (**sc, sp, st**), the reduplicating syllable begins with the double consonant, but the stem-syllable drops the **s: spondeō, spopondī; stō, stetī.** The **e** of the reduplicating syllable is often assimilated to the stem-vowel, **mo-mordī, pupugī, didicī** (§ 13). In compounds it is sometimes partly lost, as in **rettulī** (§ 15). In many reduplicated perfects, the vowel of the stem-syllable is weakened through loss of the accent: **cadō, cecidī.**

2. With **lengthened stem-vowel.** This formation is seen in two a-stems: **iūvī, lāvī** in a few e- Stems: **sēdī, vīdī, cāvī, fōvī,** etc.; in consonant-stems: **vīcī, fūgī, lēgī, fūdī,** etc.; and in one i- stem: **vēnī.**

A few consonant-stems, **agō, capiō, iaciō, frangō,** and the compounds of **pangō** (**compingō, impingō**) form their perfect with vowel change as well as lengthening. In many of these verbs the perfect was originally reduplicated and the vowel was lengthened after loss of reduplication. The perfects **ēgī, ēdī, ēmī,** of **agō, edō, emō,** are contractions of an old reduplication (**e-ag-, e-ed-, e-em-**).

Note: A few of the above have long vowel in present as well as perfect : **īcō, cūdō, sīdō, vīsō.**

---

3. With **unchanged stem-syllable.** This class includes the u- stems **acuī, arguī,** etc., and a number of consonant-stems, as **verrī, vertī, scandī,** the compounds of **-cendō, -fendō,** etc., and two **e-** verbs, **prandī** and **strīdī.**

Weak Formation of the Perfect

1. The perfect suffix in **-sī** is joined to the clipped stem of many **e-** and some **i-** verbs; also to a large number of consonant-stems with which it combines according to the laws of consonant change. Thus **gs, cs, hs,** become **x,** as in **rēxī, pīnxī, dūxī, vēxī.** Also **qs** in **coxī.** The guttural drops after **l, r** in **fulsī, mersī,** also in **vīxī** from stem **gvigv-** (compare Old English *cwicu,* alive). In **struxī, fluxī,** the perfect preserves the guttural sound which is lost in the present. Dental sounds are dropped, **plausī, flexī;** with lengthening of short vowels, as in **mīsī.** The labial **p** remains unchanged, as in **sculpsī,** but **b** becomes **p, scrīpsī, nūpsī.** After **m, p** is inserted, in **sumpsī, tempsī; s** remains, as in **gessī, ūsī,** where in the present it changes to **r.** It becomes single after a long vowel or diphthong, as **haesī, hausī.**

2. The weak perfect forms in **-vī** and **-uī** are peculiar to the Latin language. They were probably formed by analogy from the **v-** and **u-** stems like **favī, acuī,** and extended to a very large number of verbs. All the **a-** and **i-** Stems which keep their character vowel throughout the tenses as **amāvī, audīvī,** form their Perfect tense in **-vī** as well as many consonant-stems. The perfect in **-uī** is joined to the clippped **e-** stems, as **mon-uī,** also to a few clipped stems in **a-** and to a large number of consonant verbs. This form had a tendency to spread in later Latin, and many verbs formed new perfects in **-ui** after the classical period.

151 The Past Participle Future Participle and Supine

The supine or participial stem ends in **-to.** This suffix is joined to the verb stem or to the clipped stem, either immediately or by the vowel **i.** When it is joined immediately to the vowel stem, as in most of the **a-, i-** and **u-** stems, the character vowel is lengthened. When it is joined to a consonant stem, the laws of consonant change again come into force. **g** before **t** becomes **c;** the guttural is dropped after **l** or **r:** *fultum, tortum;* **p** is inserted between **m** and **t:** *emptum.* In a few verbs the stem vowel is changed, as in *lavō,* which has besides *lavātum,* a contracted supine form *lautum.* afterwards becoming *lōtum,* in *satum* (from *serō), cultum* (from *colō).*

The supine in **-sum** was formed in dental stems by a regular change of medial **-dt-, -tt-** to ss; thus *ced-to-, mit-to-,* would become *cesso-, misso-,* and the double **s** would become single after a long vowel or diphthong (§ 20). From the dental stems the supine in **-sum** spread to many other verbs by analogy. It combines with consonant stems according to the same laws of letter change as the perfect **sī**.

PRINCIPAL PARTS OF VERBS

152 ## 1st Conjugation, a- stems

PRESENT	INFINITIVE	PERFECT	SUPINE	
		Usual Form		
-ō	-āre	-āvī	-ātum	
amō	amāre	amāvī	amātum	

Exceptions

Perfect in -uī, Supine in -itum

crepō	-āre	crepuī	crepitum	creak
cubō	-āre	cubuī	cubitum	lie down
dōmō	-āre	domuī	domitum	tame
plicō	-āre	-plicāvī / -plicuī	-plicātum / -plicitum	fold
sonō	-āre	sonuī	sonitum	sound
tonō	-āre	tonuī	tonitum	thunder
vetō	-āre	vetuī / vetavī	vetitum	forbid

Perfect in -uī, Supine in -ātum

micō	-āre	micuī / micāvī	-micatum	glitter

Perfect in -uī, Supine in -tum

ēnecō	-āre	ēnecuī	ēnectum	kill
fricō	-āre	-fricuī	frictum / fricatum	rub
secō	-āre	secuī	sectum	cut

Perfect in -ī, Supine in-tum

(a) Reduplicated

dō	-āre	dedī	datum	give
stō	-āre	stetī, -stiti	statum	stand

(b) Lengthened Vowel

iuvō	-āre	iūvī	iūtum / iuvātum	help
lavō	-āre	lāvī	lautum / lōtum	wash

Note: For very many supines no authority exists; but the form is inferred from the perfect participle or future participle. Forms printed with a hyphen, as **-plicāvī, -plicătum** are only found in compounds.

153   2nd Conjugation, E- Stems

PRESENT	INFINITIVE	PERFECT	SUPINE	
		Usual Form		
moneō	monēre	monuī	monitum	
		Exceptions		
		Perfect in -uī, Supine in -tum		
doceō	-ēre	docuī	doctum	teach
misceō	-ēre	miscuī	mistum ⎫ mixtum ⎭	mix
teneō	-ēre	tenuī	tentum	hold
torreō	·ere	torruī	tostum	scorch
		Perfect in -uī, Supine in -sum		
cēnseō	-ēre	cēnsuī	cēnsum	deem, vote
		Perfect in -vī, Supine in -tum		
aboleō	-ēre	abolēvī	abolitum	destroy
cieō	-ēre	cīvī	cītum	stir up
dēleō	-ēre	dēlēvī	dēlētum	blot out
fleō	-ēre	flēvī	flētum	weep
neō	-ēre	nēvī	—	spin
-pleō	-ēre	-plēvī	-plētum	fill
		Perfect in -sī, Supine in -tum		
augeō	-ēre	auxī	auctum	increase (tr.)
cōnīveō	-ēre	conīxī	—	wink
frīgeō	-ēre	frīxī	—	freeze
lūgeō	-ēre	lūxī	—	mourn
pollūceō	-ēre	—	pollūctum	make a feast
fulgeō	-ēre	fulsī	—	shine
indulgeō	-ēre	indulsī	—	indulge
mulgeō	-ēre	mulsī	—	milk
torqueō	-ēre	torsī	tortum	twist
		Perfect in -sī, Supine in -sum		
ārdeō	-ēre	ārsī	ārsum	burn (intr.)
iubeō	-ēre	iussī	iussum	command
lūceō	-ēre	lūxī	—	shine
maneō	-ēre	mānsī	mānsum	remain
mulceō	-ēre	mulsī	mulsum	soothe
rīdeō	-ere	rīsī	rīsum	laugh
suādeō	-ere	suāsī	suāsum	advise
tergeō	-ere	tersī	tersum	wipe

turgeō	-ere	tursī	—	swell
urgeō	-ere	ursī	—	press

Note: **Ārdeō, haereō** have Fut. Part. *ārsūrus, haesūrus.*

Perfect in -ī, Supine in -sum or -tum

(a) Lengthened Perfect Stem, Supine in -tum

caveō	-ēre	cāvī	cautum	beware
faveō	-ēre	fāvī	fautum	favour
foveō	-ēre	fōvī	fōtum	cherish
moveō	-ēre	mōvī	mōtum	move (tr.)
paveō	-ēre	pāvī	—	quake
voveō	-ēre	vōvī	vōtum	vow

(b) Reduplicated Perfect Stem, Supine in -sum

pendeō	-ēre	pependī	pensum	hang (intr.)
mordeō	-ēre	momordī	morsum	bite
spondeō	-ēre	spopondī	sponsum	pledge
tondeō	-ēre	totondī	tons urn	shear

(c) Lengthened Perfect Stem, Supine in -sum

sedeō	-ēre	sēdī	sessum	sit
videō	-ēre	vīdī	visum	see

(d) Unchanged Perfect Stem

langueō	-ēre	languī	—	
prandeō	-ēre	prandī	prānsum	lunch, dine
strīdeō	-ēre	strīdī	—	creak

154   3rd Conjugation, Consonant and U- Stems

Consonant Stems

rego	regere	rēxi	rēctum	

Perfect in sī, Supine in -tum

adflīgō	-ere	-flīxī	-flīctum	smite down
angō	-ere	—	—	distress
carpō	-ere	carpsī	carptum	pluck
cingō	-ere	cīnxī	cīnctum	surround
clangō	-ere	—	—	clash
coquō	-ere	coxī	coctum	cook
cōmō	-ere	cōmpsi	cōmptum	adorn
dēmō	-ere	dēmpsi	dēmptum	take away
dīcō	-ere	dīxī	dictum	say
dīligō	-ere	dīlēxī	dīlēctum	love
dūcō	-ere	dūxī	ductum	lead

exstinguō	-ere	exstinxī	exstinctum	quench
fingō	-ere	fīnxī	fictum	feign
fluō	-ere	fluxī	fluctum	flow
frīgō	-ere	frīxī	frīctum	roast
gerō	-ere	gessī	gestum	carry on
intellegō	-ere	intellēxī	intellēctum	understand
iungō	-ere	iūnxī	iūnctum	join
neglegō	-ere	neglēxī	neglēctum	neglect
ninguit, ningit	-ere	ninxit	—	it snows
nūbō	-ere	nūpsi	nūptum	marry
pangō	-ere	pegī, pepigī	pāctum	fasten
pergō	-ere	perrēxī	perrēctum	proceed
pingō	-ere	pīnxī	pictum	paint
prōmō	-ere	prōmpsī	prōmptum	bring out
rēpō	-ere	rēpsī	rēptum	creep
scalpō	-ere	scalpsī	scalptum	scratch
scrībō	-ere	scrīpsī	scriptum	write
sculpō	-ere	sculpsī	sculptum	carve
stringō	-ere	strīnxī	strictum	bind
struō	-ere	struxī	structum	build
sūgō	-ere	sūxī	sūctum	suck
sūmō	-ere	sūmpsī	sūmptum	take
surgō	-ere	surrēxī	surrēctum	arise
tegō	-ere	tēxī	tēctum	cover
temnō	-ere	-tempsī	-temptum	despise
tingō	-ere	tīnxī	tīnctum	dye
trāhō	-ere	trāxī	tractum	draw
unguō (ungo)	-ere	ūnxi	ūnctum	anoint
ūrō	-ere	ūssī	ūstum	burn (tr.)
vehō	-ere	vēxī	vēctum	carry
vīvō	-ere	vīxī	vīctum	live

Perfect in -sī, Supine in -sum

fīgō	-ere	fīxī	fixum	fix
mergō	-ere	mersī	mersum	drown
spargō	-ere	sparsī	sparsum	sprinkle
cedō	-ere	cessī	cessum	yield
claudō	-ere	clausī	clausum	shut
dīvidō	-ere	dīvīsī	dīvīsum	divide
laedō	-ere	laesi	laesum	hurt
lūdō	-ere	lūsī	lūsum	play
mittō	-ere	mīsī	missum	send
plaudō	-ere	plausī	plausum	applaud
rādō	-ere	rāsī	rāsum	scrape
rōdō	-ere	rōsī	rōsum	gnaw
trūdō	-ere	trūsī	trūsum	thrust

vādō	-ere	(in)vāsī	(in)vāsum	go (attack)
premō	-ere	pressī	pressum	press
flectō	-ere	flexī	flexum	bend
nectō	-ere	nexī, nexuī	nexum	bind
pectō	-ere	pexī	pexum	comb

* **Nexuī**, the more usual Perf. of **nectō**, is from an obsolete verb, **nexō**.

Perfect in -vī, Supine in -tum

aboléscō*	-ere	abolēvī	—	decay
adolēscō	-ere	adolēvī	—	grow up
cernō	-ere	crēvī	crētum	sift, discern
cognōscō	-ere	cognōvī	cognitum	get to know
crēscō	-ere	crēvī	crētum	grow -
linō	-ere	lēvī, līvī	litum	smear
nōscō	-ere	nōvī	nōtum	get to know
obsolēscē	-ere	obsolēvī	obsolētum	grow out of use
pāscō	-ere	pāvī	pāstum	feed (tr.)
quiēscō	-ere	quiēvī	quiētum	rest
serō	-ere	sēvī	situm	sow
sinō	-ere	sīvī	situm	allow
spernō	-ere	sprēvī	sprētum	despise
sternō	-ere	strāvī	strātum	strew
suēscō	-ere	suēvi	suētum	grow accustomed

* **Adolēscō** has adjective **adultus**.

Perfect in -īvī, Supine in -ītum

arcessō	-ere	arcessīvī	arcessītum	send for
capessō	-ere	capessīvī	capessītum	take in hand
incessō	-ere	incessīvī	—	attack
lacessō	-ere	lacessīvī	lacessītum	provoke
quaerō	-ere	quaesīvī	quaesītum	seek
terō	-ere	trīvī	trītum	rub

Perfect in -uī, Supine in -tum

alō	-ere	aluī	altum	nourish
colō	-ere	coluī	cultum	till, worship
cōnsulō	-ere	cōnsuluī	cōnsultum	consult
occulō	-ere	occuluī	occultum	hide
pīnsō	-ere	pīnsuī, pīnsī	pistum	beat, pound
serō	-ere	seruī	sertum	join
texō	-ere	texuī	textum	weave
rapiō	-ere	rapuī	raptum	seize

Perfect in -uī, Supine in -itum

| fremō | -ere | fremuī | fremitum | bellow |
| gemō | -ere | gemuī | gemitum | groan |

molō	-ere	moluī	molitum	grind
strepō	-ere	strepuī	strepitum	roar
tremō	-ere	tremuī	compescuī —	tremble
vomō	-ere	vomuī	vomitum	vomit
gignō	-ere	genuī	genitum	produce
pōnō	-ere	posuī	positum	place
compēscō	-ere	compēscuī	—	restrain

Perfect in -uī, Supine in -sum

metō	-ere	messuī	messum	reap
excellō	-ere	excelluī	—	excel

Reduplicated Perfect Stem, Supine in -tum

canō	-ere	cecinī	cantum	sing
pungō	-ere	pupugī	pūnctum	prick
tangō	-ere	tetigī	tāctum	touch
tendō	-ere,	tetendi	tendum } tēnsum }	stretch,
discō	-ere	didicī	—	learn
poscō	-ere	poposcī	—	demand

Reduplicated Perfect Stem, Supine in -sum

cadō	-ere	cecidī	cāsum	fall
caedō	-ere	cecīdi	caesum	beat, kill
currō	-ere	cucurrī	cursum	run
fallō	-ere	fefellī	falsum	deceive
parcō	-ere	pepercī	parsum	spare
pellō	-ere	pepulī	pulsum	drive
pendō	-ere	pependī	pēnsum	hang
tundō	-ere	tutudī	tūsum, tūnsum	bruise

Compounds of dō

abdō	-ere	abdidī	abditum	hide
addō	-ere	addidī	additum	add
condō	-ere	condidī	conditum	found, hide
crēdō	-ere	crēdidī	crēditum	believe
dēdō	·ere	dēdidī	dēditum	give up
ēdō	-ere	ēdidi	ēditum	give out
perdō	-ere	perdidī	perditum	lose
prōdō	-ere	prōdidī	prōditum	betray
reddō	-ere	reddidī	redditum	restore
subdō	-ere	subdidī	subditum	substitute
trādō	-ere	trādidī	trāditum	deliver
vēndō	-ere	vendidī	venditum	sell

Note: **Pereō**, perish, **vēneō**, go for sale, are used as passives of **perdo** and **vēndo**.

Reduplicated from sto

sistō	-ere	stitī	statum	make to stand

(b) Lengthened Stem, -tum

emō	-ere	ēmī	ēmptum	buy
legō	-ere	lēgī	lēctum	choose, read
rumpō	-ere	rūpī	ruptum	break
vincō	-ere	vīcī	victum	conquer
linquō	-ere	līquī	-lictum	leave
agō	-ere	ēgī	actum	do
frangō	-ere	frēgī	fractum	break (tr.)
iaciī	-ere	iēcī	iactum	throw

Lengthened Stem, Perfect in -ī, Supine in -sum

fundō	-ere	fūdī	fūsum	pour
retundō	-ere	retudi	retūsum	beat back
fodiō	-ere	fōdī	fossum	dig
edō	-ere	ēdī	ēssum	eat

Perfect in -ī, no Reduplication, Supine in -tum, -sum

bibō	-ere	bibī	bibitum	drink
īcō	-ere	īcī	īctum	strike
cūdō	-ere	cūdī	cūsum	stamp
sīdō	-ere	sīdī	—	settle
vīsō	-ere	vīsī	vīsum	visit
psallō	-ere	psallī	—	play on strings
verrō	-ere	verrī	versum	sweep
vertō	-ere	vertī	versum	turn (tr.)
-cendō	-ere	-cendī	-cēnsum	kindle
-fendō	-ere	-fendī	-fēnsum	strike
findō	-ere	fidī	fissum	cleave
mandō	-ere	mandī	mānsum	chew
pandō	-ere	pandī	pansum } passum }	open, spread
prehendō	-ere	prehendī	prehēnsum	grasp
scandō	-ere	scendī	scēnsum	climb
scindo	-ere	scidī	scissum	tear
percello	-ere	perculī	perculsum	thrill
vellō	-ere	vellī (vulsī)	vulsum	rend

u- Stems, perfect in -ī, Supine in -tum

acuō	-ere	acuī	acūtum	sharpen
arguō	-ere	arguī	argūtum	prove
congruō	-ere	congruī	—	come together
exuō	-ere	exuī	exūtum	put off
induō	-ere	induī	indūtum	put on
imbuō	-ere	imbuī	imbūtum	tinge
luō	-ere	luī	-lūtum	wash, atone
metuō	-ere	metuī	—	fear
minuō	-ere	minuī	minūtum	lessen
adnuō	-ere	adnuī	—	nod
pluit	-ere	pluit	—	rain
ruō	-ere	ruī	rutum	rush, fall
spuō	-ere	spuī	spūtum	spit

statuō	-ere	statuī	statūtum	set up
sternuō	-ere	sternuī	—	sneeze
suō	-ere	suī	sūtum	sew
tribuō	-ere	tribuī	tribūtum	assign, render

155 Fourth Conjugation, i- Stems

PRESENT	INFIN.	PERFECT	SUPINE	

Usual Form

audiō	audīre	-īvī	audītum	

Exceptions

Perfect in -īvī, Supine in -ītum

sepeliō	-īre	sepelīvī	sepultum	bury

Perfect in -uī, Supine in -tum

saliō	-īre	saluī	—	dance
aperiō	-īre	aperuī	apertum	open
operiō	-īre	operuī	opertum	cover

Perfect in -sī, Supine in -tum

amiciō	-īre	amixī ⎫ amicuī ⎭	amictum	clothe
fulciō	-īre	fulsī	fultum	prop
hauriō	-īre	hausī	haustum	drain
saepiō	-īre	saepsī	saeptum	hedge in
sarciō	-īre	sarsī	sartum	patch
sanciō	-īre	sānxī	sānctum	hallow
vinciō	-īre	vīnxī	vīnctum	bind

Perfect in -sī, Supine in sum

| sentiō | -īre | sēnsī | sēnsum | feel |

Perfect in -ī, Supine in tum

veniō	-īre	vēnī	ventum	come
comperiō	-īre	comperī	compertum	find
reperiō	-īre	repperī	repertum	discover

155a Mixed Conjugation

capiō	-ere	cēpī	captum	take
cūpiō	-ere	cupīvī, cupiī	cupītum	desire
faciō	-ere	fēcī	factum	make
fugiō	-ere	fūgī	fugitum	flee
pariō	-ere	peperī	partum	bring forth
quatiō	-ere	quassī	quassum	shake (tr.)
salvō	-ere	solvī	solūtum	loosen, pay
sapiō	-ere	sapīvī, sapuī	—	be wise
volvō	-ere	volvī	volūtum	roll (tr.)

156   DEPONENT VERBS

1st Conjugation, a- Stems (Perfect -ātus sum)
About 160, all regular.

157 2nd Conjugation, e- Stems (Perfect usually -itus sum)

Present	Infin.	Perfect	
fateor	-ērī	fassus sum	confess
liceor	-ērī	licitus sum	bid in auction.
medeor	-ērī	—	heal
mereor	-ērī	meritus sum	deserve
misereor	-ērī	miseritus } sum mīsertus }	have pity on
tueor	-ērī	tuitus (tūtus) sum	protect
reor	-ērī	ratus sum	think

158 Semi-deponent Verbs

Present	Infin.	Perfect		
audeō	-ēre	ausus sum	—	dare
gaudeō	-ēre	gāvīsus sum	—	rejoice
soleō	-ēre	solitus sum	—	be wont

159 3rd and Mixed Conjugations, Consonant and u- Stems (Perfect -tus or -sus sum)

amplector	-ī	amplexus sum	embrace
adipīscor		adeptus sum	acquire
apīscor	-ī	aptus sum	acquire
expergīscor	-ī	experrēctus sum	waken
fatīscor	-ī	fessus sum	grow weary
fruor	-ī	frūctus sum	enjoy
fungor	-ī	fūnctus sum	perform
gradior	-ī	gressus sum	step
īrāscor	-ī	īrātus sum	be angry
lābor	-ī	lāpsus sum	glide
-mīnīscor	-ī	-mentus sum	have in mind
morior	-ī	mortuus sum	die
nancīscor	-ī	nactus } nānctus sum }	obtain
nāscor	-ī	nātus sum	be born
nītor	-ī	nīsus (nīxus) sum	strive
oblīvīscor	-ī	oblītus sum	forget
pacīscor	-ī	pactus sum	bargain

patior	-ī	passus sum	suffer
proficīscor	-ī	profectus sum	set out
queror	-ī	questus sum	complain
ulcīscor	-ī	ultus sum	avenge
vēscor	-ī	—	feed on
līquor	-ī	—	melt
loquor	-i	locūtus sum	speak
sequor	-ī	secūtus sum	follow

Note: The form **gressus** is very rarely found except in compounds. **Morior** has future participle **moritūrus**.

160 Semi-Deponent Verbs

fīdō	-ere	fīsus sum	trust

161 4th Conjugation, I- Stems (Perfect -ītus, -tus, or -sus sum)

blandior	-īrī	blandītus sum	coax, carress, flatter
experior	-īrī	expertus sum	try
largior	-īrī	largītus sum	bestow
mōlior	-īrī	mōlītus sum	contrive, work
opperior	-īrī	oppertus sum	wait, wait for
orior	-īrī	ortus sum	arise
potior	-īrī	potītus sum	acquire
pūnior	-īrī	pūnītus sum	punish
sortior	-īrī	sortītus sum	take by lot
adsentior assentior	-īrī	adsēnsus sum assēnsus sum	agree
mētior	-īrī	mēnsus sum	measure
ōrdior	-īrī	ōrsus sum.	begin

Note: **Orior** has some forms like capior (§ 133): *oreris, oritur, ortus*. **Potior** has *potītur* or *potitur, potīmur* or *potimur, potīrer* or *poterer*.

162   PARTICLES

The term **particles** is used as a catch-all expression, grouping together the uninflected parts of speech: adverbs, prepositions, conjunctions and interjections. They are for the most part old cases of nouns or adjectives, which have become limited to special uses. The oldest of these is the adverbial use, which was originally to limit or qualify the action expressed by the verb, but was afterwards extended to qualify adjectives, and sometimes other adverbs.

Latin prepositions are adverbs which have acquired the special use of standing before nouns to express relations of place and time.

Many conjunctions are also adverbs which have come to be used merely as links between words or sentences.

163 Adverbs

Adverbs are formed either from cases of substantives, adjectives or participles, or from pronoun roots. Those which are formed from adjectives or participles generally have comparison (§ 85). Those which are derived from pronoun roots have no comparison.

In regard to meaning, they are divided. chiefly into ad verbs of (1) manner; (2) degree; (3) cause; (4) place; (5) time; (6) order. The following are a few of each class :

164 Adverbs of Manner

lentē, slowly	**celeriter**, quickly
facile, easily	**sapienter**, wisely
falsō, falsely	**vehementer**, strongly
ultrō, spontaneously	**adeō**, so far
aequē, ⎫	**aliter,** ⎫ otherwise,
perinde, ⎪ in like	**secus,** ⎭ differently
proinde, ⎬ manner, in the	**ita,** ⎫
similiter, ⎪ same way	**sīc,** ⎬ so
itidem, ⎭	**tam,** ⎭
quam, how?	**ut**, as, how

165 Adverbs of Degree

multum, much	**paulum**, little
quantum, how much	**tantum**, so much
satis, enough.	**magis**, more
nimis, ⎫ too much	**potius**, rather
nimium, ⎭	**potissimum**, by preference
valdē, very	**parum**, too little
fermē, ⎫ almost	**magnopere**, greatly
ferē, ⎭	**vix,** ⎫ scarcely
	aegrē, ⎭

166 Adverbs of Cause

ideō, idcircō, proptereā, on that account

167 Adverbs of Place

Where	**ubi,** where?	**hīc,** here	
	ibi, ⎱ there	**ibidem,** in the same place	
	illic, ⎰	**alibi,** elsewhere	
	ūsquam, anywhere	**nūsquam,** nowhere	
To where	**quō,** to where	**hūc,** hither	
	eō, ⎱ to there	**eōdem,** to the same place	
	illūc, ⎰	**ūsque,** so far	
From where	**unde,** from where?	**hinc,** hence	
	inde, ⎱ from there	**indidem,** from the same place	
	illinc, ⎰	**hāc,** by this way	
	quā, by what way?	**eā, illāc,** by that way	

168 Adverbs of Time

When	**quandō, ubi,** when?	**tum, tunc,** then	
	nunc, modo, now	**iam,** now, already	
	simul, at the same time	**aliās,** at another time	
	umquam, ever	**nunquam,** never	
	semper, always	**interdum,** now and then	
	ōlim ⎱ at some time	**mox,** by and by	
	quondam ⎰	**nūper,** lately	
	ante, before	**post,** after	
	dēmum, at length	**nōndum,** net yet	
How long	**quam diū,** how long?	**tam diū,** so long	
	diū, long	**ūsque,** continuously	
	iam diū, long since		
How often	**quotiēns,** how often?	**totiēns,** so often	
	semel, once	**iterum,** a second time	
	saepe, often	**rārō,** seldom	
	crēbrō, frequently	**identidem,** repeatedly	

169 Adverbs of Order

prīmum, first   **prīmō,** in the beginning
deinde, in the next place   **praetereā,** ⎱ moreover
deinceps, afterwards   **īnsuper,** ⎰

                        dēnique, ⎱ lastly
tertiō, thirdly   **postrēmō,** ⎰

170 Sometimes an adverb qualifies a sentence or phrase, rather than any particular word.

Adverbs of Affirmation	**etiam,** also; **quidem, equidem,** indeed; **vērō,** but; **plānē,** quite; **sānē,** certainly; **profectō, omnīnō, certē,** surely, by all means
Limitation	**pariter,** alike; **simul,** together; **plērumque,** usually; **sōlum, tantum, modo,** only; **partim,** partly
Negation	**nōn, haud,** not; **haudquāquam, neutiquam,** by no means
Doubt	**fortasse, forsan, forsitan,** perhaps; **forte,** by chance
Question	**cūr, quārē, quamobrem?** why? **quōmodo, quemadmodum, quam, ut?** how?

171   PREPOSITIONS

Prepositions are placed before nouns to show their relation to other words in the sentence. They are also compounded with verbs to modify their meaning.

172 The following prepositions are used with the accusative:

ad, to, at	**iūxta,** next to, beside
adversus } towards, against	**ob,** over against, on account of
adversum } opposite to	**penes,** in the power of
ante, before	**per,** through
apud, at, near, among	**pōne,** behind
circum, around	**post,** after, behind
circā, circiter, about	**praeter,** beside, past
cis, citrā, on this side of	**prope,** near
clam, unknown to	**propter,** near, on account of
contrā, against	**secundum,** next, along, according to
ergā, towards	**suprā,** above
extrā, outside of, without	**trāns,** across
infrā below	**ultrā,** beyond
inter between amidst	**versus, versum,** towards
intrā within	

173 The following are used with the ablative:

ā, ab, abs, by, from	**palam,** in sight of
absque, without	**prae,** befo'te, in front of
cōram, in the presence of	**prō,** before, for
cum, with	**sine,** without
dē, from, concerning	**tenus,** as far as, reaching to
ex, ē, out of, from	

Note: **Clam** is also used with the ablative; **tenus** is placed after the noun; it is sometimes used with the genitive.

174 The following take the accusative when they denote motion towards and the ablative when they denote rest:

in, into, against, in, on **super** over, upon

sub, up to, under **subter,** under

175 Prepositions used only in verb compounds are:

ambi, amb-, am-, an-, around **ambiō,** go around

dī, dis-, apart **dissolvō,** separate; **dīrigō,** direct

red-, rē-, back, again **red-eō,** go back; **referō,** bring back

sed-, sē-, apart **sēcēdō,** step apart

176   CONJUNCTIONS

Conjunctions are: (1) co-ordinative (§ 400); (2) subordinative (§ 421–429).

177 1. Co-ordinative conjunctions are:

Connective: **et,** **-que,** **atque (adque), ac,** } and **neque, nec,** } no **etiam, quoque, item,** } also

Separitive: **aut, vel, -ve,** } or, either. **sīve, seu,** } whether, or

Adversative: **sed, at (ast),** } but **autem,** { but, now, however

atquī, but, yet

at enim, but it will be said **cēterum, vērum, vērō,** } but, moreover

tamen, { yet, however, nevertheless **attamen, vērumtamen,** { but, nevertheless

Causal: **nam, namque, enim, etenim** } for **enimvērō,** for indeed

Conclusive: **ergō, itaque, igitur,** } therefore **quārē, quamobrem, quāpropter, quōcircā,** } wherefore

Comparative: **ut, utī, velut, velutī, sicut, sicutī, ceu,** } as **quōmodo, quemadmodum,** } as, how **quam,** than, as utpote, as being

Interrogative: num,
-ne, } [see § 405]
nonne,

quasi,
tamquam, as it were.
utrum... an, whether... or

necne, or not?

178 2. Subordinative conjunctions are:

Consecutive: ut, so that
ut nōn, so that not

quin, that not, but that

Final: ut, in order that.

nēve, neu, { and that not, and lest

quō, { whereby / in order that

nē, lest

ut nē, that not, lest

quōminus, { whereby not, in order that not

Causal: quod, because
cum, since

quia, because
quoniam,
quandōquidem, } since

quippe, { for as much as, seeing that

siquidem, inasmuch as

Temporal: cum (quum), when
ut, when
dum,
dōnec, } while,
quoad, } so long as

quandō, when
ubi, when
dum,
dōnec, } until
quoad,

quātenus, how long

antequam,
priusquam, } before that

postquam, after that

simul ac, as soon as

quotiēns, as often as

Conditional: sī, if
sīve, } whether,
seu, } or if
sī modo, if only

sīn (sī ne), but if
nisi, nī, unless
sī nōn, if not.
modo,
tantum } only

modo, dummodo, provided that

Concessive: etsī, } even if,
etiamsī } although

tametsī although

quamquam,
utut, } although

quamvīs, } however, however much

cum, whereas, although
ut, licet, granting that, although

Comparative: quasi (quam sī),
ut sī, } as if
velut sī,

ceu,
tamquam } as though

179 The following pairs are often used as correlatives

et... et		**sīve... sīve**		
-que... -que } both... and		**seu... seu** } whether... or		
-que... et				
aut... aut } either... or		**sīc... ut**	so... as	
vel... vel		**ut... ita**	as... so	
neque... neque		**ita... ut**	so... that	
nec... nec } neither... nor		**adeō... ut**	so far... that	
nēve... nēve				

180 Interjections

An interjection is an exclamatory word, used either to draw attention or to express feeling. The most usual are:

ō, O! oh!	**prō or prōh,** forbid it!
ā or āh, alas!	**vae,** woe!
ēheu, heu, ei, alas!	**ēn, ecce,** lo! behold!

Syntax

THE SIMPLE SENTENCE

INTRODUCTORY OUTLINE

181   **Syntax** teaches how sentences are made.
Sentences are **simple** or **compound**.

182   A simple sentence has two parts:
1. The **subject**: the person or thing spoken about.
2. The **predicate**: that which is said about the subject.

183   The subject must be a noun, or some word or words taking the place of a noun:

A **noun**: *lex*, the law;
A **pronoun**: *ego*, I;*
An **adjective, participle,** or **adjectival pronoun**: *Rōmānus*, a Roman; *īrātus*, an angry man; ille, that (man);†
A **verb noun infinitive**: *nāvigāre*, to sail, or sailing;
A **phrase**: *satis temporis*, enough time.

---

* Latin nearly always omits pronouns used as subjects; they are *implied* by the verb inflections.

† The word 'man' is understood if a masculine adjective stands without a noun. The word 'woman' is understood if the adjective is feminine: *īrāta*, an angry woman. The word 'thing' is understood in the case of neuter adjectives.

---

184   The **predicate** must either be a verb or contain a verb, because it makes a statement or assertion about the subject; and it is usually a finite verb.

185   **Examples of the Simple Sentence**

SUBJECT	PREDICATE	SUBJECT	PREDICATE
Lēx	**iubet.**	**Nāvigāre**	**dēlectat.**
The law	commands.	Sailing	delights.
[Nōs]	**pārēmus.**	**Satis temporis**	**datur.**
We	obey.	Enough time	is given.

Note: A single verb may be a sentence. *Vēnī*, I came.

186 Some verbs cannot by themselves form complete predicates. The verb **sum** is a complete predicate only when it implies mere existence:

Seges	**est**	**ubī**	**Trōia**	**fuit.**	Ovid
Corn	is	where	Troy	was.	

It more often links the subject with the **complement**, which completes what is said about it.

187 Verbs which link a subject and **complement** are called **copulative verbs**. Others besides *sum* are:

appāreō, appear	**audiō,** am called	**maneō,** remain
videor, seem	**ēvādō, existō,** turn out	

The passives of verbs of making, saying, thinking (**factive verbs***) are also used as copulative verbs (§ 206):

fiō (*facio*), become *or* am made	**feror,** am reported
appellor, am called	**legor,** am chosen
creor, am created	**putor,** am thought
dēclāror, am declared	**vocor,** am called

---

* So-called from *facere*, to make, because they contain the idea of making.

---

188 Copulative verbs have the same case after them as before them.

189 The **complement** may be:
1. An adjective or adjectival word.
2. A substantive.

SUBJECT	PREDICATE	
	Copulative Verb	*Complement*
1. **Leō**	est	**validus.**
The lion	is	strong.
2. **Illī**	**appellantur**	**philosophī.**
They	are called	philosophers.

190 Many verbs usually require another verb in the infinitive to carry on their construction; such are: **soleō,** am wont; **possum,** am able; **queō,** can; **dēbeō,** ought; **volō,** wish; **cōnor,** endeavor.

Solet legere.	Possum īre.
He is wont to read.	I am able to go.

These verbs are called **indeterminate**, and the infinitive following them is called **prolative**, because it carries on (*prōfert*) their construction

191 A simple sentence may be enlarged in many ways.

The **subject** may be qualified by adjectives or pronouns in agreement, or may have words in apposition added to it.

The **verb** may be qualified by adverbs or adverbial phrases; it may have a preposition with a case, or some part of the verb infinite depending on it; if transitive, it has a direct object and may have also an indirect object; if intransitive, it may have an indirect object in the dative.

The **complement** may again be qualified by an adjective or an adverb, or by a case of a noun, or a preposition with a case.

AGREEMENT

Rules of the Four Concords

192 1. A verb agrees with its subject in number and person:

Tempus fugit.	Librī leguntur.
Time flies.	Books are read.

193 2. An adjective or participle agrees in gender, number and case with the substantive it qualifies:

Vir bonus bonam uxōrem habet.
The good man has a good wife.

Vērae amīcitiae sempiternae sunt.   Cicero
True friendships are everlasting.

194 3. When a nousubstantive is followed by another substantive, so that the second explains or describes the first, and has the same relation to the rest of the sentence, the second noun agrees in case with the first, and is said to be in apposition:

Nōs līberī patrem Lollium imitābimur.
We children will imitate our father Lollius.

Procās, rēx Albānōrum, duōs fīliōs,
Numitōrem et Amūlium, habuit.   Livy
Procas, king of the Albans, had two sons,
Numitor and Amulius.

195   4. The relative **quī, quae, quod,** agrees with its antecedent in gender, number and person; in case it takes its construction from its own clause (§ 330):

Amō tē, māter, quae mē amās.
I love you, mother, who love me.

Quis hic est homō quem ante aedēs videō?   Plautus
Who is this man whom I see before the house?

Arborēs multās serit agricola, quārum frūctūs
nōn adspiciet.   Cicero
The farmer plants many trees, of which he
will not see the fruit.

196   **Notes on the Concords**

1. The verb **est, sunt,** is often understood, not expressed:

Nihil bonum nisi quod honestum.   Cicero
Nothing is good except what is virtuous.

2. A copulative verb occasionally agrees with the complement rather than with the subject:

Amantium īrae amōris integratiō est.   Terence
The quarrels of lovers are the renewal of love.

197   3. A substantive often agrees in number and gender with the noun to which it is in apposition:

Stilus, optimus et praestantissimus dīcendī magister.   Cicero
The pen, best and chief teacher of oratory.

Philosophia, vītae magistra.   Cicero
Philosophy, the mistress of life.

4. A noun may be in apposition to a personal pronoun understood:

Hannibal petō pācem.   Livy
I, Hannibal, sue for peace.

198   Composite Subject

1. When two or more nouns are united as the subject, the verb and adjectives are usually in the plural:

> **Venēnō absūmptī sunt Hannibal et Philopoemēn.**   Livy
> Hannibal and Philopoemen were cut off by poison.
>
> **Aetās, metus, magister eum cohibēbant.**   Terence
> Age, fear, and a tutor were restraining him.

2. If the persons of a composite subject are different, the verb agrees with the first person rather than the second; with the second rather than the third:

> **Sī tū et Tullia valētis, ego et Cicerō valēmus.**   Cicero
> If you and Tullia are well, I and Cicero are well.

3. When the genders are different, adjectives agree with the masculine rather than with the feminine:

> **Rēx rēgiaque classis ūnā profectī.**   Livy
> The king and the royal fleet set out together.

4. If the things expressed are without life, the adjectives are generally neuter:

> **Rēgna, honōrēs, dīvitiae, cadūca et incerta sunt.**   Cicero
> Kingdoms, honours, riches, are frail and fickle things.

199   Notes on the Composite Subject

1. When several subjects of the third person are united, the verb is sometimes found in the singular, agreeing with one only:

> **Nunc mihi nihil librī, nihil litterae,**
> **nihil doctrīna prōdest.**   Cicero
> Now neither do books avail me, nor letters,
> nor does learning.

2. If the union of two subjects forms a single notion, the verb may be singular:

> **Senātus populusque Rōmānus intellegit.**   Cicero
> The Roman senate and people understand.

3. But sometimes when a collective noun is the subject, although it is singular in form, the verb and adjectives are plural:

Pars mīlitum captī, pars occīsī sunt. Livy
Part of the soldiers were taken captive, part were slain.

Observe that the adjectives agree in gender with the individuals of which the collective noun is made up.

The Cases

The Nominative and Vocative Cases

200 The subject of a finite verb is in the nominative case:

Annī fugiunt.	**Lābitur aetās.**	Ovid
Years flee.	Time glides away.	

Note: When an infinitive, called **historic**, is used for the imperfect of a finite verb, the nominative remains as the subject (§ 372):

Tum pius Aenēās umerīs abscindere vestem. Virgil
Then the pious Aeneas began to tear his vest from his shoulders.

201 A substantive joined to the subject by a copulative verb is in the nominative case:

Cicerō dēclārātus est cōnsul. Cicero
Cicero was declared consul.

202 The vocative stands apart from the construction of the sentence, with or without an interjection (§ 404)

Ō sōl pulcher, ō laudande! Horace
O beauteous sun, worthy of praise!
Pompēi, meōrum prīme sodālium! Horace
O Pompeius, earliest of my comrades!

Note: The nominative sometimes takes the place of the vocative:

Audī, tū, populus Albanus. Livy
Hear, thou, people of Alba.

The Accusative Case

203 The accusative case is used to express:
   A. The direct object of the verb.

B. Place to which there is motion, extent of time and place.
C. The idea contained in the verb (cognate accusative).
D. Adverbial relations.

A. Accusative of Direct Object

204 The direct object of a transitive verb is in the accusative case:

Agricola colit agrōs; uxor domum tuetur.
The farmer tills the fields; his wife takes care of the house.

Haec studia adulēscentiam alunt, senectūtem oblēctant.
These studies nurture youth, and delight old age.   Cicero

---

203 **Note 1:** Intransitive verbs when compounded with prepositions are often transitive:

Antōnius oppugnat Brūtum, Mutinam circumsedet.   Cicero
Antonius is making war on Brutus, and besieging Mutina.

Note 2: Some compounds take two accusatives:

Caesar equitēs flūmen trānsiēcit.   Caesar
Caesar threw his cavalry across the river.

---

206 Factitive verbs (verbs of making, saying, thinking) have a second accusative in agreement with the object:

Cicerōnem cōnsulem populus dēclārāvit.   Sallust
The people declared Cicero consul.

Sōcratēs tōtīus sē mundī cīvem arbitrābātur.   Cicero
Socrates considered himself a citizen of the whole world.

---

207 **Note:** The accusative is used as the subject of the infinitive to form a clause which may be the object of verbs of saying, thinking, and perceiving, or the subject of impersonal verbs (§ 414).

Sōlem fulgēre vidēmus.   We see that the sun shines.

---

208 Some verbs of *teaching, asking, concealing* (**doceō**, teach, **flāgitō**, demand, **rogō**, ask, **ōrō**, pray, **cēlō**, conceal), take two accusatives, one of the person, the other of the thing:

Racilius prīmum mē sententiam rogāvit.   Cicero
Racilius asked me first my opinion.

Quid nunc tē litterās doceam?   Cicero
Why should I now teach you letters?

Antigonus iter omnēs cēlat.   Nepos
Antigonus conceals from all his line of march.

In the passive they keep the **accusative of the thing**:

Prīmus ā Railiō sententiam rogātus sum.
I was asked my opinion first by Racilius.

Note 1: **Quaero, petō,** take ablative of the person with **ā** or **ab**: *hoc ā tē petō,* this I ask of you.

209   Note 2: Intransitive verbs which express feeling sometimes take an accusative of the object which excites the feeling:

Nōn omnia quae dolēmus querī possumus.   Cicero
We cannot complain of all things for which we grieve.

Virgās ac secūrēs dictātōris horrent et tremunt.   Livy
They shudder and tremble at the rods and axes of the dictator.

Note 3: An accusative is used in exclamations, with or without an interjection: *Mē miserum,* O wretched me! *Ō fragilem fortūnam!* O fickle fortune!

210   Note 4: Some passive verbs in poetry take an accusative, when used reflexively. Such verbs are *induor,* dress oneself, *exuor,* undress oneself, *cingor,* gird oneself:

Inūtile ferrum cingitur.   Virgil   **Exuitur cornua.**   Ovid
He girds on the useless steel.   She puts off her horns.

Note 5: A similar construction is frequently used with passive participles:

Virginēs longam indūtae vestem canentēs ībant.   Livy
Virgins marched singing, arrayed, in long robes.

Nāscuntur flōrēs īnscrīptī nōmina rēgum.   Virgil
Flowers spring up inscribed with names of kings.

This construction is analogous to that of the **Greek middle voice.**

B. Accusative Expressing Place Towards
211   Place to which motion is directed is in the accusative: *eō Rōmam,* I go to Rome (§ 269, 273).

Note: Similar are the phrases: *pessum īre,* to go to the bad; *īnfitiās īre,* to deny; *suppetiās īre,* to march in aid; *vēnum īre,* to be sold.

C. Cognate Accusative
212   Many otherwise intransitive verbs take an accusative containing the same idea as the verb, and often from the same stem:

Fortūna lūdum īnsolentem lūdit.   Horace
Fortune plays an insolent game.

Modicē et modestē melius est vītam vīvere.   Plautus
It is best to live one's life temperately and modestly.

Itque reditque viam totiēns.   Virgil
He goes and returns the same way as often.

Note: The **cognate accusative** must have some more limited meaning than that which is contained in the verb, either expressed by an adjective or implied in the noun itself: *lūdum insolentem lūdere*, to play an insolent game; *dicta dīcere*, to say witty sayings.

D. Adverbial Accusative

213 The accusative of respect is joined to verbs and adjectives, especially in poetry:

Tremit artūs.   Virgil   **Nūdae lacertōs.**   Tacitus
He trembles in his limbs.   Bare as to the arms.

Omnia Mercuriō similis vōcemque colōremque.   Virgil
In all points like Mercury, both in voice and complexion.

Note 1: Adverbial accusatives with verbs and nouns are very numerous: *multum*, much; *aliquid*, in some degree; *cētera*, in other respects; *id genus*, of that kind; *id temporis*, at that time: *multum amāre*, to love much; *quid rēfert?* what does it matter?

Note 2: Neuter adjectives and pronouns are used in the accusative by poets like adverbs:

Dulce rīdēre.   **Lūcidum fulgēre.**   Horace
To smile sweetly.   To shine brightly.

Dulce rīdentem Lalagēn amābo, dulce loquentem.   Horace
I will love the sweetly smiling, sweetly speaking Lalage.

(For the accusative of extent see time, § 278, and space, § 281–3.)

The Dative Case

214 The dative is the case of the person or thing for whose interest anything exists or is done. It expresses:

   A. The person or thing to whom or which something is done: **dative of the indirect object.**

   B. The person or thing for whom or which something is done: **dative of advantage.**

   C. Special uses are: (a) **dative of agent**, (b) **ethic dative**, (c) **dative of possessor**, (d) **dative of result**, (e) **dative of purpose.**

A. Dative of the Indirect Object.

The dative of the indirect object is used:

215 1. With transitive verbs of giving, telling, showing, promising, which take also an accusative of the direct object:

Tibi librum sollicitō damus aut fessō. Horace
We give you a book when you are anxious or weary.

Saepe tibi meum somnium nārrāvī. Cicero
I have often told you my dream.

Nōbīs spondet fortūna salūtem. Virgil
Fortune guarantees safety to us.

216 2. With intransitive verbs of pleasing, helping, sparing, pardoning, appearing, speaking, believing, obeying, and their opposites. These verbs have the dative as their only object:

Victrīx causa deīs placuit sed victa Catōni. Lucan
The conquering cause pleased the gods, but the
conquered pleased Cato.

Imperiō parent. Caesar   **Parce piō generī.** Virgil
They obey the command.   Spare a pious race.

Imperat aut servit collēcta pecūnia cuique. Horace
Money amassed rules or serves every man.

Nōn possum dolōrī tantō resistere. Cicero
I cannot withstand so great a sorrow.

Note 1: These verbs contain the ideas of being pleasing to, helpful to, obedient to, &c.

217 **Note 2:** *Dēlectō, iuvō,* delight, *laedō,* hurt, *gubernō,* govern, *regō,* rule, *iubeō,* command, take an accusative:

Multōs castra iuvant. Horace   **Animum rege.** Horace
The camp delights many.   Rule the temper.

Temperō, moderor, govern, restrain, take sometimes the accusative, sometimes the dative:

Hic moderātur equōs qui nōn moderābitur īrae. Horace
This man controls horses who will not restrain his anger.

218 3. With adjectives implying nearness, fitness, likeness, help, kindness, trust, obedience, or any opposite idea:

Hortus ubi et tēctō vīcīnus iūgis aquae fōns. Horace
Where is a garden, and near to the house a fount
of flowing water.

Quis amīcior quam frāter frātrī?   Sallust
Who [is] more friendly than a brother to a brother?

Hominī fidēlissimī sunt equus et canis.   Pliny
The horse and the dog are most faithful to man.

Turba gravis pācī, placidaeque inimīca quiētī.   Lucan
The crowd hostile to peace, unfriendly to tranquil rest.

Note: The following take genitive or dative: *commūnis*, common; *proprius*, proper. *Adfīnis*, akin, *aliēnus*, foreign; *pār*, equal; *sacer*, sacred; *superstes*, surviving, take usually dative, sometimes genitive. *Similis*, like, takes usually genitive, sometimes dative. Adjectives of fitness as *aptus*, sometimes take accusative with *ad*.

---

219   4. More rarely with substantives or adverbs:

Nūlla fidēs rēgnī sociīs.   Lucan
No reliance is to be placed on partners in government.

Iūstitia est obtemperātiō lēgibus.   Cicero
Justice is obedience to laws.

Congruenter nātūrae vīvendum est.   Cicero
We must live agreeably to nature.

Note 1: Some verbs, as *crēdō*, believe, entrust, *fīdō*, trust, *suādeō*, persuade, *minor*, threaten, *grātulor*, congratulate, are used both transitively and intransitively:

Perfidīs sē crēdidit hostibus.   Horace
He trusted himself to treacherous enemies.

Non est, crēdē mihī, sapientis dīcere: vīvam.   Martial
It is not, believe me, the part of a wise man to say, 'I will live.'

Note 2: *Nūbō*, marry (lit. take the veil for), and *vacō*, have leisure for, take the dative:

Hīs duōbus frātribus duae Tulliae nūpserant.   Livy
The two Tullias had married these two brothers.

Philosophiae semper vacō.   Cicero
I have always leisure for philosophy.

Note 3: The verbs *īrāscor*, feel angry, *pugnō*, fight, *certō*, strive, sometimes take a dative: *sibi īrāscitur*, he is angry with himself.

220 Many verbs, transitive and intransitive, are used with a dative of the indirect object when compounded with the following prepositions :

ad, ante, ab,   sub, super, ob,
in, inter, dē,   post, and prae

Also verbs compounded with **bene, male, satis.**
  (a) Transitive:

Gigantēs bellum dīs intulerunt.   Cicero
The giants waged war against the gods.

Praesentia cōnfer praeteritīs.   Lucretius
Compare present things with past.

  (b) Intransitive:

Hīs negotiīs nōn interfuit sōlum sed praefuit.   Cicero
He not only took part in these affairs, but directed them.

Nūllus in orbe sinus Baiīs praelūcet amoenīs.   Horace
No bay in the world outshines the pleasant Baiae.

Cēterīs satisfaciō semper, mihi numquam.   Cicero
I always satisfy others, myself never.

B. Dative of Advantage

221 The person or thing for whose advantage or disadvantage something is done is in the dative case:

Tibi arās, tibi seris, tibi eīdem metis.   Plautus
For yourself you plough, for yourself you sow,
for the same self you reap.

Nōn sōlum nōbīs dīvitēs esse volumus.   Cicero
We do not wish to be rich for ourselves alone.

Sīc vōs nōn vōbīs mellificātis, apēs!   Virgil
Thus you make honey not for yourselves, o bees!

C. Special Uses of the Dative

222 (a) A dative, commonly called the **dative of the agen**t, is often used with the gerundive (§ 381), and occasionally with passive participles and with adjectives in -bilis:

Ut tibi ambulandum, sīc mihi dormiendum est.   Cicero
As you have to walk, I have to sleep.

Magnus cīvis obīt et formīdātus Othōnī.   Juvenal
A great citizen and one dreaded by Otho has died.

Multīs ille bonīs flēbilis occidit.   Horace
He died a cause of weeping to many good men.

Note: Rarely, in poetry, a personal passive takes a dative:

Nōn intellegor ūllī.   Ovid
I am intelligible to none.

---

223 (b) A dative, called the **ethic dative**, is used, in familiar talk or writing, to express interest or call special attention:

Quid mihi Celsus agit?   Horace
Tell me, what is Celsus about?

Haec vōbīs per bīduum eōrum mīlitia fuit.   Livy
This, mind you, was their style of fighting for two days.

224 (c) The **dative of the possessor**, with *esse*, is used when emphasis is laid on the thing possessed, not on the possessor:

Est mihī plēnus Albānī cadus.   Horace
I have a cask full of Alban wine.

Fōns cui nōmen Arethūsa fuit.   Cicero
A fountain of which the name was Arethusa.

Note: With such phrases as *cui nomen est* a second dative is sometimes joined by attraction: *Volitāns cui nōmen asīlō Romanum est* (Virgil), an insect of which the Roman name is 'asilus'. A like attraction occurs with other factitive and copulative verbs: *Huic ego diēī nōmen Trinummō faciam* (Plautus), I will give to this day the name Trinummus. Analogous to these are the attractions: *Hoc mihi valentī est, nōn invītō*, this is with my good will, not against it. *Mihi nōn licet esse neglegentī* (Cicero), I must not be negligent.

---

225 (d) The **predicative dative**, or **dative of purpose and result**, is used in connection with the dative of the person interested (§ 221), to describe what some thing (or person) is or causes:

Exitiō est avidum mare nautīs.   Horace
The greedy sea is a destruction to sailors.

L. Cassius quaerere solēbat, 'cui bonō fuieset.'　　Cicero
Lucius Cassius used to ask who had been the gainer
(literally 'to whom had it been for a good ').

Note:　The dative of the person interested is often not expressed.

Nimia fīdūcia calamitātī solet esse.　　Nepos
Too great confidence is wont to be a calamity (to men).

Exemplō est magnī formīca labōris.　　Horace
The ant is an example of great industry.

226　(e) The **dative of purpose** expresses the purpose of action:

Equitātum auxiliō Caesarī mīsērunt.　　Caesar
They sent the cavalry as a help to Caesar.

Note:　Observe the phrases, *receptuī canere*, to give the signal for retreat; *alimentō serere*, to sow for food; *laudī vertere alicui*, to turn to the praise of someone; *vitiō vertere alicui*, to impute as a fault to someone.

227　Sometimes the dative is used in poetry for the place towards which there is motion. This is called the **dative of direction**:

It clāmor caelō.　　Virgil
A shout ascends towards heaven.

The Ablative Case

228　The ablative is the case which defines circumstances; it is rendered in English by many prepositions such as *from, with, by, in*. Its uses may be divided into:

A. **Ablative of separation** (from, of)

B. **Ablative of association** (with)

C. **Instrumental ablative** (by, with)

D. **Ablative of place and time** (locative, *in, at*)

A. Pure Ablative

229 1. The **ablative of separation** is used with verbs meaning to *remove, release, deprive;* with adjectives such as *līber,* free, *solūtus,* released, and also the adverb *procul,* far from:

> **Cēdēs coemptīs saltibus et domō. HOR.**
> You will depart from purchased glades and house.

> **Populus Athēniēnsis Phōciōnem patriā pepulit.**   Nepos
> The Athenian people drove Phocion from his country.

> **Vacāre culpā maximum est sōlācium.**   Cicero
> To be free from blame is a very great comfort.

> **Procul negōtiīs, solūtus omnī faenore.**   Horace
> Far from business, freed from all usury.

230 2. The **ablative of origin** is used with verbs, chiefly participles, implying descent or origin:

> **Atreus, Tantalō prōgnātus, Pelope nātus.**   Cicero
> Atreus, descended from Tantalus, and son of Pelops.

231 3. The **ablative of comparison** (expressing difference) is used with comparative adjectives and adverbs:

> **Nihil est amābilius virtūte.**   Cicero
> Nothing is more amiable than virtue.

> **Nēminem Lycurgō ultiōrem Sparta genuit.**   Valerius
> Sparta produced no man more serviceable than Lycurgus.

Note: This construction is equivalent to *quam,* than, with the nominative or accusative. *Virtūte* equals *quam virtus; Lycurgō* equals *quam Lycurgum.* With other cases than nom. or accus. *quam* must be used for comparison :

> **Nihilō amīcior est Phaedriae quam Antiphōnī.**   Terence
> He is in no degree more friendly to Phaedria than to Antipho.

(For 'place from where' see § 270, 274.)

B. Ablative of Association

232   **Note:** This includes the uses of an old case called the **sociative** or **instrumental** case, expressing the circumstances associated with the subject or the action of the sentence (§ 30, note 2).

233 1. The **ablative of association** is used with verbs and adjectives denoting plenty, fulness, possession: *abundō,* abound, *dōnō,* present, *praeditus,* endowed with (§ 253):

Villa abundat gallīnā, lacte, cāseō, melle.	Cicero
The farm abounds in poultry, milk, cheese, honey.	
Iuvenem praestantī mūnere dōnat.	Virgil
He presents the youth with a noble gift.	
Legiōnēs pulchrīs armīs praeditae.	Plautus
Legions furnished with splendid armor.	

Note: *Dōnō* also takes the accusative of the thing with dative of the person: *Caesar praedam mīlitibus dōnat,* Caesar gives the booty to the soldiers.

234 2. The **ablative of quality** is used with an adjective in agreement (§ 255):

Senex prōmissā barbā, horrentī capillō.	Pliny
An old man with long beard and rough hair.	
Habuit frātrem Dumnorigem summā audaciā.	Caesar
He had a brother Dumnorix of supreme audacity.	

235 3. **Ablative of respect:**

Paucī numerō.	**Natione Mēdus.**
Few in number.	By birth a Mede.

Et corde et genibus tremit.	Horace
It trembles both in heart and knees.	
Ennius, ingeniō maximus, arte rudis.	Ovid
Ennius, mighty in genius, in art (is) rude.	

Note: In the phrases *nātū māior,* older, *nātū minor,* younger, *nātū* is an ablative of respect.

236 4. The **ablative of the manner,** in which something happens or is done, has an adjective in agreement with it; or it follows the preposition **cum,** with:

Iam veniet tacitō curva senecta pede.	Ovid
Presently bent old age will come with silent foot.	
Athēniēnsēs summā vī proelium commisērunt.	Nepos
The Athenians began the battle with the greatest vigor.	

Magnā cum cūrā atque dīligentiā scrīpsit.   Cicero
He wrote with great care and attention.

Note: *More māiōrum*, in the fashion of our ancestors, *pāce tuā*, with your leave, *iūre*, by right, *iniūriā*, wrongfully, *ratiōne*, on principle, are ablatives of manner.

---

237 5. The **ablative absolute** is a phrase, consisting of a noun in the ablative case and a participle, or another noun or adjective, in agreement with it:

Rēgibus exāctīs cōnsulēs creatī sunt.	Livy
Kings having been abolished, consuls were elected.	
Pereunte obsequiō imperium intercidit.	Tacitus
Obedience failing, government falls to pieces.	
Caesare ventūrō, Phōsphore, redde diem.	Martial
Caesar being on his way, star of morn, restore the day.	
Nīl dēspērandum Teucrō duce et auspice Teucrō.	Horace
There must be no despair, Teucer being leader and Teucer omen-giver.	
Nātus est Augustus cōnsulibus Cicerōne et Antōniō.	Suet.
Augustus was born when Cicero and Antonius were consuls.	
Quid dicam hac iuventūtē?	Cicero
What can I say when our young men are of this stamp?	

Note: The ablative absolute is equivalent to a shortened adverbial clause within the sentence, serving to explain some circumstance which indirectly affects the action of the sentence. It is called absolute because it is independent in construction of the rest of the sentence. A dependent clause joined to the sentence by a conjunction may be used instead of the ablative absolute. In the above example *rēgibus exāctīs* could be replaced by *cum rēgēs exāctī essent*, when kings had been driven out.

C. Instrumental Ablative

238   **Note:** This ablative includes the uses of the old instrumental case.

239   The **agent** by whom something is done is in the ablative case, with the preposition *ā, ab*, after a passive or quasi-passive verb (§ 296, 300, 303).

240 1. The instrument by means of which something is done is in the ablative (**the ablative of instrument**) without a preposition:

> **Hī iaculīs, illī certant defendere saxīs.**   Virgil
> These strive to defend with javelins, those with stones.

> **Dente lupus, cornū taurus petit.**   Horace
> The wolf attacks with his teeth, the bull with his horns.

> **Opportūna loca armatis hominibus obsidet.**   Sallust
> He occupies convenient posts with armed men.

241 2. The **ablative of the cause** is used with adjectives, passive participles, and verbs:

> **Coeptīs immānibus effera Dīdō.**   Virgil
> Dido driven wild by her horrible designs.

> **Ōdērunt peccāre malī formīdine poenae.**   Horace
> The bad hate to sin through fear of punishment.

242 3. The deponent verbs **fungor**, perform, **fruor**, enjoy, **vēscor**, feed on, **ūtor**, use, **potior**, possess oneself of (§ 253), take an ablative:

> **Hannibal cum victōriā posset ūti fruī māluit.**   Livy
> Hannibal, when he could use his victory, preferred
> to enjoy it.

> **Numidae ferīnā carne vēscēbantur.**   Sallust
> The Numidians used to feed on the flesh of wild animals.

243 4. The adjectives **dignus**, worthy, **indignus**, unworthy, and the transitive verb **dignor**, deem worthy, also **contentus**, contented, and **fretus**, relying on, take an ablative:

> **Dignum laude virum Musa vetat morī.**   Horace
> A man worthy of praise the Muse forbids to die.

> **Haud equidem talī mē dignor honoure.**   Virgil
> I do not indeed deem myself worthy of such honour.

Note: *Opus est, ūsus est,* there is need of, take the ablative.

> **Ubī rēs adsunt, quid opus est verbīs?**   Sallust
> When things are present, what is the need of words?

---

244 5. An **ablative of the measure** of difference is joined as an adverb with comparatives and superlatives and, rarely, with verbs:

> **Sōl multīs partibus māior est quam lūna.**   Cicero
> The sun is many degrees larger than the moon.

Especially the ablatives:

> **altero, hōc, eō, quō,**   **dīmidiō, duplō, quantō, tantō,**
> **nihilō** and **nimiō,**   **paulō, multō, aliquantō**

> **Quō plūs habent, eō plūs cupiunt.**
> The more they have, the more they desire.

> **Hibernia dīmidiō minor est quam Britannia.**   Caesar
> Ireland is smaller by half than Britain.

245 6. The **ablative of price** is used with verbs and adjectives of *buying* and *selling*:

> **Vendidit hic aurō patriam.**   Virgil
> This man sold his country for gold.

> **Multōrum sanguine victōria stetit.**   Livy
> The victory cost (literally stood at) the blood of many.

Note: Ablatives of price are *magnō,* at a high price; *parvō, minimō, vīlī,* at a low price (but see also **genetive of value** § 257):

> **Parvō famēs cōnstat, magnō fastīdium.**   Seneca
> Hunger costs little, daintiness much.

D. The Ablative of Place and the Locative Case

246 Originally, Latin had a separate **locative case** to express the place at which something is or happens. Its distinct forms remain in the singular in names of towns and small islands: *Rōmae,* at Rome; *Corcȳrae,* at Corcyra; and in a few other words, as *domī,* at home. For the most part its uses have passed to the ablative, and it is often difficult to distinguish between the two cases, especially in the plural, where their forms are identical. The locative is sometimes used for a point of time: *diē septimī,* on the seventh day; *Kalendīs,* on the Kalends; *Īdibus,* on the Ides.

Note: The word *animī* in such phrases as *anxius animī,* anxious; *pendēre animī,* to waver in mind, is probably locative.

(For **place where,** see § 268, 272a.)

The Genitive Case

247 The **genitive** is used to define or complete the meaning of another noun on which it depends. It also follows certain verbs.

The uses of the genitive may be divided into:

A. **Genitive of definition**	D. **Partitive genitive**
B. **Possessive genitive**	E. **Subjective & objective genitive**
C. **Genitive of quality**	F. **Genitives with verbs**

A. Genitive of Definition

248 1. The genitive of definition follows the noun on which it depends:

Vōx voluptātis.	**Nōmen rēgis.**
The word pleasure.	The name of king.

Note: But the name of a city is always placed in apposition (and therefore shares the same case): *urbs Rōma*, the city of Rome.

---

249 2. The **attributive genitive** defines the noun on which it depends like an adjective:

Lūx sōlis	**Annī labor**
The light of the sun	A year's toil.

250 3. The **genitive of the author**:

Ea statua dīcēbātur esse Myrōnis.   Cicero
That statue was said to be Myro's.

Legendī sunt vōbīs Platōnis librī.   Cicero
You should read the works of Plato.

251 4. The genitive is often used in impersonal construction with a copulative verb (§ 187, 188), followed by an infinitive, where in English a word such as nature, part, characteristic, or mark, must be supplied to complete the meaning:

Cuiusvīs hominis est errāre.   Cicero
It is (the nature) of any man to err.

Est adulēscentis māiorēs nātū verērī.   Cicero
It is a young man's (part) to reverence his elders.

Temporī cēdere habētur sapientis.   Cicero
To yield to occasion is held (the mark) of a wise man.

Note: The word *proprium* is often used:

Sapientis est proprium nihil quod paenitēre possit facere.　　Cicero
It is the characteristic of a wise man to do nothing which
he may repent of.

---

252 5. Verbs and adjectives of accusing, condemning, convicting, or acquitting take a genitive of the fault or crime:

Alter latrōciniī reus, alter caedis convictus est.　　Cicero
The one was accused of robbery, the other was
convicted of murder.

Miltiadēs capitis absolūtus pecūniā multātus est.　　Nepos
Miltiades, acquitted of capital crime, was fined.

Note: Sometimes the ablatives *nōmine,* on the ground of, *crīmine,* on the charge of, are used:

Themistoclēs crīmine prōditiōnis absēns damnātus est.　　Nepos
Themistocles was convicted while absent on the charge of treason.

---

253 6. Verbs and adjectives implying want and fulness, especially *egeō, indigeo,* want, *impleō,* fill, *potior,* get possession of (§ 242), *plēnus,* full, often take a genitive (§ 233):

Virtūs plūrimae exercitātiōnis indiget.　　Cicero
Virtue needs very much practice.

Hanc iuventūtem speī animōrumque implēvēre.　　Livy
They filled these youths with hope and spirit.

Rōmānī signōrum et armōrum potītī sunt.　　Sallust
The Romans got possession of standards and arms.

Acerra tūris plēna.　　Horace
A pan full of incense.

254 *B. Possessive Genitive*

Rēgis cōpiae. Cicero　　**Contempsī Catilinae gladiōs**　　Cicero
The king's forces　　　　I have braved the swords of Catiline.

Singulōrum opēs dīvitiae sunt cīvitātis.　　Cicero
The means of individuals are the state's riches.

Sometimes the genitive depends on a noun understood:

Hectoris Andromachē.　　Virgi
Hector's (wife) Andromache.

Ventum erat ad Vestae.   Horace
We had come to Vesta's (temple).

C. Genitive of Quality
255 1. The **genitive of quality** has an adjective in agreement:

Ingenuī vultūs puer ingenuīque pudōris.   Juvenal
A boy of noble countenance and noble modesty.

Memoriae fēlīciōris est nōmen Appiī.   Livy
The name of Appius is of happier memory.

256 2. Number and age are expressed by the genitive:

Classis septuāgintā nāvium.   **Puer annōrum novem.**
A fleet of seventy ships.   A boy of nine years.

257 3. **Genitives of value,** *magnī, parvī, plūrimī, minimī, nihilī,* are
used with verbs of valuing; the genitives *tantī, quantī, plūris,*
minōris, are also used with verbs of buying and selling, but not
to express definite price.

Voluptātem virtūs minimī facit.
Virtue accounts pleasure of very little value.

Ēmit hortōs tantī, quantī Pȳthius voluit.   Cicero
He bought the gardens for as much as Pythius wished.

Quantī id ēmit? Vīlī.   Plautus
For how much did he buy it? For a low price.

Note: The genitives *floccī, naucī* were used in the popular speech to express
worthlessness, answering to the English expressions, not worth a straw, a
nut, &c.

Iūdicēs rempūblicam floccī nōn faciunt.   Cicero
The judges make the republic of no account.

D. Partitive Genitive or Genitive of the Whole
258 The genitive of a noun which is distributed into parts is called a
partitive genitive.

259 1. Any word denoting a definite part, whether substantive,
adjective or pronoun, is used with the genitive of the whole of
which it denotes a part.

(a) Substantives:

Sic partem māiōrem cōpiārum Antōnius āmīsit.   Cicero
Thus Antony lost the greater part of his forces.

Nēmō mortālium omnibus hōrīs sapit.   Pliny
No one of mortals is wise at all times.

(b) Pronouns or pronominal adjectives:

Incertum est quam longa nostrum cuiusque vīta futūra sit.
It is uncertain how long the life of each one of us will be.

Elephantō bēluārum nūlla est prūdentior.   Cicero
Of animals none is more sagacious than the elephant.

(c) Numerals and adjectives of number:

Sulla centum vīgintī suōrum āmīsit.   Eutropius
Bulla lost a hundred and twenty of his men.

Multae hārum arborum meā manū sunt satae.   Cicero
Many of these trees were planted by my hand.

(d) Comparatives and Superlatives:

Māior Nerōnum.   Horace
The elder of the Neros.

Hoc ad tē minimē omnium pertinet.   Cicero
This belongs to you least of all men.

Tōtīus Graeciae Platō doctissimus erat.   Cicero
Plato was the most educated man of all Greece.

Note 1: The genitives *gentium,* of nations, *terrārum,* of countries, depend on adverbs of place: *ubī,* where, *eō,* to there, *quō,* to where, *longē,* far:

Ubīnam gentium sumus?   Cicero
Where in the world are we?

Migrandum aliquō terrārum arbitror.   Cicero
I think we must migrate to some part of the world.

Note 2: A partitive genitive is found in poetry with verbs:

Scrībe tuī gregis hunc.   Horace
Enlist this man in your train.

Fīēs nōbilium tū quoque fontium.   Horace
Thou too shalt become one of famous fountains.

260 2. Any word denoting quantity may be used with the **genitive of the whole** in which such quantity is contained.

Aliquid prīstinī rōboris cōnservat.   Cicero
He keeps somewhat of his old strength.

Dīmidium factī quī coepit habet.   Horace
He has half done the work who has begun it.

Catilīnae erat satis ēloquentiae, sapientiae parum.   Sallust
Catiline had plenty of eloquence, of wisdom too little.

E. The Subjective and Objective Genitive

261 The terms **subjective** and **objective genitive** are used to express different relations of the genitive to the noun on which it depends. Thus *amor patris,* the love of a father, may mean either 'the love felt by a father' (where *patris* is a subjective genitive), or 'the love felt for a father' (where *patris* is an objective genitive).

262 An **objective genitive** is used with verbal substantives and adjectives, especially adjectives in **-āx**, and participles which have the meaning of *love, desire, hope, fear, care, knowledge, ignorance, skill, power.*

(a) With substantives:

Erat īnsitus mentī cognitiōnis amor.   Cicero
Love of knowledge had been implanted in the mind.

Difficilis est cūra rērum aliēnārum.   Cicero
The care of other people's affairs is difficult.

(b) With adjectives:

Avida est perīculī virtūs.   Seneca
Valour is greedy of danger.

Cōnscia mēns rēctī fāmae mendācia risit.   Ovid
The mind conscious of right smiled at the lies of rumor.

Homō multārum rērum perītus.   Cicero
A man skilled in many things.

Vir prōpositī tenāx.   Horace
A man holding to his purpose.

(c) With participles:

Quiā famulus amantior dominī quam canis?   Colum.
What servant is fonder of his master than the dog is?

---

263   Note: The **genitive of the gerund** is an **objective genitive**: *ars scrībendī,* the art of writing. An objective genitive also follows the ablatives *causā, grātiā,* by reason of, by favour of, for the sake of; *honōris causā,* on the ground of honour ; *exemplī grātiā,* for an example.

---

264 *Meī,* of me, *tuī,* of thee, *suī,* of him, her, them, *nostrī,* of us, *vestrī,* of you, are objective genitives:

Nīciās tuā suī memoriā dēlectātur.   Cicero
Nicias is delighted by your recollection of him.

Sī tibi cūra meī, sit tibi cūra tuī.   Ovid
If you care for me, take care of yourself.

The possessive pronouns, *meus, tuus, suus, noster, vester,* are used as adjectives: *meus liber,* my book.

Note: A genitive understood in a possessive pronoun often has a genitive agreeing with it:

Rēspūblica meā ūnīus operā salva erat.   Cicero
The state was saved by my own unaided effort.

---

265 Most verbs of remembering, forgetting, reminding, **meminī, reminīscor, oblīvīscor,** usually take the genitive, sometimes the accusative. **Recordor** almost always takes the accusative, rarely the genitive.

Animus meminit praeteritōrum.   Cicero
The mind remembers past things.

Rēs adversae admonent religiōnum.   Cicero
Adversity reminds of religious duties.

Nam modo vōs animō dulcēs reminīscor, amīcī.   Ovid
For now I remember you, o friends, dear to my soul.

The adjectives corresponding to these verbs, **memor, immemor,** always take a genitive.

Omnēs immemorem beneficī ōdērunt.   Cicero
All hate one who is forgetful of a favour.

266 Verbs of pitying, **misereor, miserēscō,** take a genitive:

> **Nīl nostrī miserēre.** Virgil
> You pity me not at all.

> **Arcadiī, quaesō, miserēscite rēgis.** Virgil
> Take pity, I entreat, on the Arcadian king.

Note 1: **Miseror, commiseror** take an accusative.

267 Note 2: Verbs of refraining and ceasing and some adjectives are used by poets with a genitive in imitation of the Greek use, especially by Horace:

> **Abstinētō īrārum.** Horace   **Fessī rērum.** Vero
> Refrain from angry words.   Weary of toil.

> **Integer vītae, scelerisque pūrus.** Horace
> Virtuous in life and pure from wrong.

PLACE, TIME AND SPACE

Place

268 Place where anything is or happens is generally in the ablative case with a preposition; sometimes without a preposition (especially in poetry), an adjective of place being attached to the substantive:

> **Castra sunt in Ītaliā contrā rempūblicam collocāta.** Cicero
> Camp has been set up in Italy against the republic.

> **Celsā sedet Aeolus arce.** Virgil
> Aeolus is seated on his high citadel.

> **Mediō sedet insula pontō.** Ovid
> The island lies in mid ocean.

269 Place to where is in the accusative with a preposition; but in poetry the preposition is sometimes omitted:

> **Caesar in Italiam magnīs itineribus contendit.** Caesar
> Caesar hastened with long marches into Italy.

> **Ītaliam fātō profugus Lāvīnaque vēnit lītora.** Virgil
> Driven by fate he came to Italy and the Lavinian shores.

270 **Place from where** is in the ablative with **ā, ab, ex,** or **dē**:

> **Ex Asiā trānsis in Eurōpam.**   Curtius
> Out of Asia you cross into Europe.

271 In **names of towns** and **small islands**, also in **domus** and **rūs**, **place where, to where,** or **from where** is expressed by the case without a preposition:

272 (a) **Place where**, by the locative (§ 246):

> **Quid Rōmae faciam?** Juvenal   **Is habitat Mīlētī.** Terence
> What am I to do at Rome?   He lives at Miletus.
>
> **Philippus Neāpolī est, Lentulus Puteolīs.**   Cicero
> Philip is at Naples, Lentulus at Puteoli.
>
> **Sī domī sum, forīs est animus; sīn forīs sum,**
> **animus est domī.**   Plautus
> If I am at home, my mind is abroad: if I am abroad,
> my mind is at home.

273 (b) **Place to where**, by the accusative:

> **Rēgulus Carthāginem rediit.**   Cicero
> Regulus returned to Carthage.
>
> **Vōs īte domum; ego rūs ībō.**
> Go home; I will go into the country.

274 (c) **Place from where**, by the ablative:

> **Videō rūre redeuntem senem.**   Terence
> I see the old man returning from the country.
>
> **Dēmarātus fūgit Tarquiniōs Corinthō.**   Cicero
> Demaratus fled from Corinth to Tarquinii.

275 The road by which one goes is in the ablative:

> **Ībam forte Viā Sacrā**   Horace
> I was going by chance along the Sacred Way

276 **Time at which**, in answer to the question *when?* is expressed by the ablative: **hieme**, in winter; **sōlis occāsū**, at sunset.

> **Ego capuam vēnī eō ipsō diē.**   Cicero
> I came to Capua on that very day.

277 Time within which, generally by the ablative:

    Quicquid est bīduō sciēmus.   Cicero
    Whatever it is, we shall know in two days.

278 Time during which, generally by the accusative:

    Periclēs quadrāgintā annōs praefuit Athēnis.   Cicero
    Pericles was leader of Athens for forty years.

> **Note1:** Often by *per* with the accusative: *per trīduum,* for three days.
>
> **Note 2:** Age is expressed by the participle *nātus,* born, used with the accusative, sometimes with the ablative:
>
>   **Catō quīnque et octōgintā annōs nātus excessit ē vītā.**   Cicero
>   Cato died aged eighty-five years.

279 How long ago, is in the accusative or ablative with **abhinc:**

    Hoc factum est fermē abhinc biennium.   Plautus
    This was done about two years ago.

    Comitia iam abhinc trīgintā diēbus habita.   Cicero
    The assembly was held thirty days ago.

280 To express **how long before, how long after,** the worde **ante,**
before, **post,** after, are used either with the ablative as adverbs,
or with the accusative as prepositions, followed by **quam:**

    Numa annīs permultīs ante fuit quam Pȳthagorās.   Cicero
    Numa lived very many years before Pythagoras.
    (or, **Numa ante permultōs annōs fuit quam Pȳthagorās.**)

    Post diem tertium gesta rēs est quam Clōdius dīxerat.   Cicero
    The affair took place three days after Clodius had spoken.
    (or, **Diē tertiō post gesta rēs est quam Clōdius dīxerat.**)

Space

281 Space over which motion takes place is in the accusative:

    Mīlia tum prānsī tria rēpimus.   Horace
    Then, having had luncheon, we crawl three miles.

282 Space which lies between, is in the accusative or in the ablative:

> **Marathon abest ab Athēnis circiter mīlia**
> **passuum decem.**   Nepos
> Marathon is distant from Athens about ten miles.

> **Aesculāpiī templum quīnque mīlia passuum**
> **ab Epidaurō distat.**   Livy
> The temple of Aesculapius is five miles distant
> from Epidaurus.

283 Space of measurement, answering the questions *how high?*
how deep? how broad ? how long? is generally in the accusative:

> **Erant mūrī Babylōnis ducēnōs pedēs altī.**   Pliny
> The walls of Babylon were two hundred feet high.

PREPOSITIONS

284 Prepositions, like the case-endings, show the relations of nouns
to other words, and they are used where these relations cannot
be clearly expressed by the case-endings alone. Almost all prepositions take the accusative or the ablative case; they are usually
placed before the noun.

285   Prepositions with Accusative

Ad, to, towards (with accusative of motion to); at: *ad urbem īre,*
to go to the city; *ad summam senectūtem,* to extreme old age;
ad octingentōs caesī, there were slain to the number of 800 ;
pugna ad Alliam, the battle at the Allia; *ad prīmam lūcem,* at
daybreak; *ad hoc,* moreover; *ad tempus,* for a time; *ad verbum,*
word for word; *nihil ad Atticum,* nothing to (in comparison
with) Atticus; *nihil ad rem,* nothing to the purpose.

Adversus, adversum, towards, against, opposite to: a*dversum
Antipolim,* opposite to Antipolis; *reverentia adversus senēs,*
respect towards the aged.

Ante, before: *ante oculōs,* before one's eyes; *ante merīdiem,*
before noon; *ante aliquem esse,* to surpass someone.

Apud, at, near (used chiefly with persons, rarely with places):
apud mē, at my house; *apud veterēs,* among the ancients;

apud Homērum, in Homer's works; but *in Īliade Homērī,* in Homer's Iliad.

Circum, circā, around, about (in place): *circum caput,* round the head; *circā forum,* around the forum.

Circā, circiter, about (in time, number): *circā prīmam lūcem,* about daybreak; *circā, circiter trīgintā,* about thirty.

Cis, citrā, on this side of: *cis Alpēs,* on this side of the Alps. **Clam,** unknown to: *clam patrem,* unknown to the father. Sometimes takes ablative (see below) and is more often used as an adverb.

Contrā, against, opposite to: *contrā hostem,* against the enemy; *contrā arcem,* opposite the citadel.

Ergā, towards (not used of place): *ergā aliquem benevolus,* feeling kindly towards someone.

Extrā, outside of, without: *extrā mūrōs,* outside the walls; *extrā culpam,* free from blame.

Intrā, within: *intrā mūrōs,* within the walls; *intrā vīgintī diēs,* within twenty days.

Inter, between (in place): during (in time), among: *inter urbem et Tiberim,* between the city and the Tiber; *inter silvās,* among the woods *inter cēnandum,* during dinner; *cōnstat inter omnēs,* all are agreed; *inter nōs,* between ourselves; *inter sē amant,* they love each other.

Infrā, under, beneath: *infrā caelum,* under the sky; *infrā dignitātem,* beneath one's dignity.

Iūxtā, adjoining to, beside: *iūxtā viam,* adjoining the road; *iūxtā deōs,* next to the gods.

Ob, over against, on account of: *mihi ob oculōs,* before my eyes; *quam ob rem,* wherefore.

Penes, in the power of: *penes mē,* in my power; *penes tē es?* are you in your senses?

Per, through (by): *per viās,* through the streets; *per vim,* by force; *per mē licet,* I give leave; *per tē deōs ōrō,* I pray you by the gods; *per explōrātōrēs certior fīō,* I ascertain through scouts.

Post, behind, after: *post terga,* behind the back; *post mortem,* after death

Pōne, behind: *pōne nōs,* behind us.

Praeter, beside, past, along: *praeter rīpam,* along the bank; *praeter omnēs,* beyond all others; *praeter mē,* except me; *praeter opīniōnem,* contrary to expectation.

Prope, near: *prope amnem,* near the river; *prope lūcem,* towards daybreak.

Propter, on account of, (rarely of place) near, close to: *propter aquam,* close to the water's edge; *propter hoc,* on that account.

Secundum, next, along, according to (following): *secundum vōs,* next to (behind) you; *secundum lītus,* along the shore; *secundum lēgem,* in accordance with the law; *secundum nōs,* in our favour.

Suprā, over, above: *suprā terram,* above the ground; *suprā mīlia vīgintī,* more than twenty thousand.

Trāns, across: *trāns Rhēnum dūcere,* to lead across the Rhine; *trāns Alpēs,* on the further side of the Alps.

Ultrā, beyond: *ultrā Euphrātem,* beyond the Euphrates; *ultrā vīrēs,* beyond their powers.

Versus, towards (following the noun): *Italiam versus,* towards Italy.

286   Prepositions with Ablative

Ā, ab, from, by: *ab eō locō,* from that place; *ab ortū ad occāsum,* from East to West; *procul ā patria,* far from one's country; *prope abesse ab,* to be near; *ā tergō,* in the rear; *ā senātū stetit,* he took the side of the senate; *hoc ā mē est,* this is in my favour; *ab urbe conditā,* from the foundation of Rome; *servus ab epistulīs,* secretary; *nōn ab rē fuerit,* it will not be irrelevant; *ab īrā facere,* to do in anger.

Absque, without (rare): *absque vōbis esset,* if it were not for you.

Clam, unknown to: *clam vōbis,* unknown to us. Sometimes takes accusative (see above).

Cōram, in the presence of: *cōram populō,* in the presence of the people.

Cum, with: *cum aliquō congruere, certare,* to agree, strive with someone, *magnō cum perīculō,* with great danger; with *mē, tē, nōbīs, vōbīs,* often with *quō, quibus, cum* follows the pronoun; *mēcum,* with me.

Dē, from (down from), concerning: *dē monte,* down from the mountain; *dē diē,* in the daytime; *dē diē in diem,* from day to

day; *ūnus dē multīs,* one out of many; *dē marmore signum,* a
marble bust; *dē pāce,* concerning peace; *quid dē nōbīs fīet,*
what will become of us? *dē industriā,* on purpose; *dē mōre,*
according to custom; *dē integrō,* anew.

Ex, Ē, out of, from: *ex urbe,* out of the city: *ē longinquō,* from far;
ex equīs pugnant, they fight on horseback; *diem ex diē,* from
day to day; *ex eō audīvī,* I heard it from him; *ūnus ex illīs,* one
of those; *ex quō,* from the time when; *ē rēpūblicā,* for the good
of the state; *ex sententiā,* satisfactorily; *ex parte,* in part; *ex
occultō,* secretly.

Palam, in sight of: *palam omnibus,* in sight of all.

Prae, before, in front of (for) (place rarely, chiefly used in
idioms): *prae sē fert speciem virī bonī,* he wears the semblance
of a good man; *prae nōbīs beātus es,* you are happy compared
with us; *prae gaudiō ubi sim nescio,* I do not know where I am
for joy.

Prō, before, for: *prō foribus,* before the door; *prō patriā mōrī,* to
die for one's country (in defence of) ; *mihi prō parente fuit,* he
was in the place of a parent to me; *prō certō hoc habuī,* I held
this for certain; *prō ratā parte,* in proportion; *prō rē,* according
to circumstances.

Sine, without: *sine rēgibus,* without kings; *sine dubiō,* without
doubt.

Note: **Prae** means in advance of; **prō,** standing for, defending.

Tenus, as far as (usually following the noun): *verbō tenus,* so far
as the word goes. Sometimes with genitive: *Corcȳrae tenus,*
as far as Corcyra; especially with a plural noun: *crūrum tenus,*
as far as the legs.

287   Prepositions with Accusative or Ablative

In, with accusative, into, to, towards, against: *Ībō in Piraeum,* I
will go into the Piraeus; *in orbem īre,* to go round; *līberālis in
mīlitēs,* liberal towards the troops; *Cicerō in Verrem dīxit,* Cicero
spoke against Verres; *in aeternum,* for ever; *in vicem,* in turn; *in
poenam dare,* to deliver to punishment; *venīre in cōnspectum,*
to come into sight.

In, with ablative, in, among, on: *in urbe Rōmā,* in the city of Rome; *in oculīs esse,* to be before one's eyes; *in tempore,* at the right time; *in dīcendō,* while speaking; *in bonīs habēre,* to count among blessings; *in Ganymēde,* in the case of Ganymede; *in eō reprehendere quod,* to blame on the score that.

Sub, with accusative, up to: *sub montem venīre,* to come close to the foot of the mountain; *sub lūcem,* towards daybreak; *sub haec dicta,* just after these things were said.

Sub, with ablative, under: *sub terrā,* underground; *sub monte esse,* to be beneath the mountain; *sub poenā,* under penalty of.

Subter, with accusative or ablative, underneath, close to: *subter mūrum venīre,* to come close to the wall; *subter lītore esse,* to be close to the shore.

Super, with accusative, over: *super terram,* over the ground; *super omnia,* above all.

Super, with ablative, upon: *super focō,* on the hearth; *super Hectore,* about Hector.

IMPERSONAL VERBS

CASE CONSTRUCTION

288 The following verbs of feeling take an accusative of the person with a **genitive of the cause**: *miseret, piget, paenitet, pudet, taedet:*

> **Miseret tē aliōrum; tuī tē nec miseret nec pudet.**   Plautus
> You pity others; for yourself you have neither pity nor shame.

> **Mē cīvitātis mōrum piget taedetque.**   Sallust
> I am sick and weary of the morals of the state.

289 **Decet, dēdecet, iuvat** take an **accusative of the person** with an infinitive:

> **Ōratōrem īrāscī minimē decet; simulāre nōn dēdecet.**   Cicero
> It by no means becomes an orator to feel anger; it is not unbecoming to feign it.

> **Si mē gemmantia dextrā scēptrā tenēre decet.**   Ovid
> If it befits me to hold in my right hand the jewelled sceptre.

290 **Libet, licet, liquet, contingit, convenit, ēvenit, expedit,** take a dative:

> **Nē libeat tibi quod nōn licet.**   Cicero
> Let not that please you which is not lawful.

> **Licet nēminī contrā patriam dūcere exercitum.**   Cicero
> It is not lawful for anyone to lead an army against his country.

291 **Interest,** it is of importance, it concerns, is used with the **genitive of the person** or thing concerned, but with the feminine ablatives *meā, tuā, suā, nostrā, vestrā* of the possessive pronouns:

> **Interest omnium rēctē facere.**   Cicero
> It is for the good of all to do right.

> **Et tuā et meā interest tē valēre.**   Cicero
> It is of importance to you and to me that you
> should be well.

292 **Rēfert,** it concerns, it matters, is also used with the feminine ablatives of the possessive pronouns:

> **Quid meā rēfert cui serviam?**   Phaedrus
> What does it matter to me whom I serve?

Note 1: Rarely with a genitive:

> **quōrum nihil rēfert**   Quintilian
> whom it does not at all concern

Note 2: The genitives of value, *magnī, parvī, tantī, quantī, pluris,* are often joined with *interest* and *refert:*

> **Illud meā magnī interest tē ut videam.**   Cicero
> It is of great importance to me that I should see you.

> **Hoc nōn pluris rēfert quam sī imbrem in crībrum gerās.**   Plautus
> This avails no more than if you pour rain-water into a sieve.

---

293 **Pertinet, attinet** take an accusative with ad:

> **Nihil ad mē attinet.**   Terence
> It does not concern me at all.

294 **Oportet** is used with the accusative and infinitive clause, or with the subjunctive alone; rarely with the prolative infinitive (§ 369):

Lēgem brevem esse oportet.   Cicero
It behoves that a law be brief.

Mē ipsum amēs oportet, nōn mea.   Cicero
You ought to love me, not my possessions.

Vīvere nātūrae sī convenienter oportet.   Horace
If it behoves to live agreeably to nature.

---

295   Note: *Coepit, dēbet, dēsinit, potest, solet* are used impersonally with an impersonal infinitive:

> **Pigēre eum factī coepit.**   Justinus
> It began to repent him of his deed.
>
> **Pervenīrī ad summa sine industriā nōn potest.**   Quintilian
> One cannot reach the highest without industry.

---

296   PASSIVE CONSTRUCTION

When a sentence is changed from the active to the passive form:

(a) The object of a transitive verb becomes the subject; the subject becomes the agent in the ablative with the preposition **ā** or **ab**:

> { **Numa lēgēs dedit.** Cicero   Numa gave laws.
> { **Ā Numā lēgēs datae sunt.**   Laws were given by Numa.

297   (b) Factitive verbs and verbs of saying and thinking become copulative (§ 187):

> { **Clōdium plēbs trībūnum**   The common people elected
> {   **creāvit.**   Clodius tribune.
> { **Clōdius ā plēbe trībūnus**   Clodius was elected tribune
> {   **creātus est.**   by the common people.

298   (c) Transitive verbs which have two objects in the accusative, the person and the thing, keep the accusative of the thing in the passive form:

> { **Rogās mē sententiam.**   You ask me my opinion.
> { **Rogor ā tē sententiam.**   I am asked my opinion by
>   you.

299 Intransitive verbs are used impersonally in the passive:

300 (a) The subject of an intransitive verb in passive construction becomes the agent in the ablative:

Nōs currimus.⎫
Ā nōbīs curritur.⎬ We run.

301 or the agent may be omitted:

Sīc īmus ad astra.⎫
Sīc ītur ad astra.⎬ Thus we go to the stars.

Ācriter utrimque usque ad vesperum pugnātum est.   Caesar
There was fierce fighting on both sides until the evening.

302 (b) Intransitive verbs which take the dative keep it in the passive:

Mihi istī nocēre nōn possunt.⎫
Mihi ab istīs nocēre nōn potest. Cicero⎬ They cannot hurt me.

Nihil facile persuādētur invītīs.   Quintilian
The unwilling are not easily persuaded of anything.

---

303 Note: The ablative of the agent is used with quasi-passive verbs (§ 128):

Mālō ā cīve spoliārī quam ab haste vēnīre.   Quintilian
I would rather be despoiled by a citizen than be sold by a foe.

ADJECTIVES

304 Some adjectives are used as substantives to express persons or things: *sapiēns,* a wise man; *bonī,* the good; *Rōmānī,* the Romans; *omnia,* all things; *multa,* many things; *bona,* goods.

Bonōs bonī dīligunt.   Cicero
The good love the good.

Aiunt multum legendum esse, nōn multa.   Cicero
They say that much should be read, not many things.

305 Neuter adjectives are used for abstract substantives: *vērum* or *vēra*, the truth.

Omne tulit pūnctum quī miscuit ūtile dulcī.   Horace
He who has combined the useful with the pleasing
has won every vote.

306 Some adjectives, when used as substantives, can be qualified by other adjectives: *amīcus*, friend; *vīcīnus*, neighbor; *dextra*, right hand; *māiōrēs*, ancestors.

Vetus vīcīnus ac necessārius.   Cicero
An old neighbor and intimate acquaintance.

307 *Medius*, middle, and superlatives of position in place and time, as *summus, īmus, prīmus, ultimus*, are used with a partitive force; *mediō pontō*, in mid ocean; *ad īmam quercum*, at the foot of the oak:

Prīmā lūce summus mōns ā Labiēnō tenēbātur.   Caesar
At dawn of day the mountain top was held by Labienus.

Note: The singular forms of **cēterī**, the rest (of which the rnasc. nom. sing. is wanting), are similarly used with collective nouns: *cētera turba*, the rest of the crowd; *ā cēterō exercitū*, by the rest of the army.

---

308 Adjectives are used adverbially when they qualify the verb rather than the substantive:

Sōcratēs laetus venēnum hausit.   Seneca
Socrates drank the poison cheerfully.

Mātūtīnus arā.   Virgil
Plough at morn.

Vespertīnus pete tēctum.   Horace
At eventide go home.

Hannibal prīmus in proelium ībat, ultimus excēdēbat.   Livy
Hannibal was the first to go into battle, the last to withdraw.

Comparative and Superlative Adjectives

309 Superlatives often express a very high degree, and not the highest:

Ego sum miserior quam tū, quae es miserrima.   Cicero.
I am more wretched than you, who are very wretched.

310 Comparatives may also express a certain degree, without special comparison: *longior*, rather long; *senior*, elderly. After a comparative with *quam*, a second comparative is often used:

Aemiliī cōntiō fuit vērior quam grātior populō.   Livy
The harangue of Aemilius was more truthful than popular.

Note: Comparatives and superlatives are often strengthened by adverbs and adverbial phrases: *multō cārior*, much dearer; *longē cārissimus*, far dearest; *vel minim us*, the very least; *quam maximus*, the greatest possible.

Numeral Adjectives

311 **Cardinals:** *ūnus*, apart from other numerals, is used only to give emphasis; it often means the one of all others:

Dēmosthenēs ūnus ēminet inter omnēs ōrātōrēs   Cicero
Demosthenes is pre-eminent among all orators.

Mīlle is used as an indeclinable adjective; sometimes as a substantive taking the genitive after it; *mīlia* is always used as a substantive, followed by a genitive:

Mīlle gregēs illī.   Ovid   **Mīlle annōrum.**   Plautus
He had a thousand flocks.   A thousand years.

Quattuor mīlia hominum Capitōlium occupāvēre.   Livy
Four thousand men seized the Capitol.

If a smaller number is added to *mīlia*, the compound number becomes adjectival: *tria mīlia et sescentī hominēs*, three thousand six hundred men.

312 **Ordinals** are used in expressing time: but in compound numbers *ūnus* is used for *prīmus*: *ūnō et octōgēnsimō annō*, in the eighty-first year:

Octāvus annus est ex quō Britanniam vīcistis.   Tacitus
It is the eighth year since you conquered Britain.

Note: *Ūnus, alter, tertius*, &c. are used for a first, a second, a third, where the order is of no importance, as distinguished from the regular ordinals, *prīmus, secundus, tertius*, which can only mean the first, the second, &c.

313 **Distributives** express how many each or at a time:

> **Mīlitibus quīnī et vīcēnī dēnāriī datī sunt.**   Livy
> Twenty-five denarii were given to each soldier.

Note 1: With a substantive of plural form distributives are used, but the plural of *ūnus* is used instead of *singulī:*

> **Ūna castra iam facta ex bīnīs vidēbantur.**   Caesar
> One camp now seemed to have been formed from two.

Note 2: *Bīnī* is used for a pair:

> **Pamphilus bīnōs habēbat scyphōs sigillātōs.**   Cicero
> Pamphilus had in use a pair of embossed cups.

314 After **plūs, amplius, minus, quam** is often left out before numerals:

> **Rōmānī paulō plūs sescentī cecidērunt.**   Livy
> Rather more than six hundred Romans fell.

PRONOUNS AND PRONOMINAL ADJECTIVES

315 The personal pronoun as subject is usually expressed only by the verb ending, but is sometimes added for emphasis:

> **Ego rēgēs ēiēcī; vōs tyrannōs intrōdūcitis.**   Cicero
> I expelled kings; you are bringing in tyrants.

Note: *Nōs* is often used for *ego,* and *noster* for *meus,* but *vōs* is not used for *tū,* nor *vester* for *tuus.*

316 The reflexive pronoun **sē, sēsē, suī, sibi,** refers to the subject in a simple sentence (§ 464):

> **Fūr telō sē dēfendit.**   Cicero
> The thief defends himself with a weapon.

> **Īra suī impotēns est.**   Seneca
> Anger is not master of itself.

> **Īrātus cum ad sē rediit, sibi tum īrāscitur.**   Syrius
> When an angry man has come to himself,
> he is angry with himself.

> **Dēforme est de sē ipse praedicāre.**   Cicero
> It is bad taste to boast of oneself.

Note 1: There is no reciprocal pronoun in Latin; *sē* with *inter* is used reciprocally: *inter sē amant,* they love each other.

Note 2: In the first and second persons, *mē, tē,* are used reflexively with *ipse; mē ipse cōnsōlor,* I console myself.

---

317 The possessive **suus,** formed from the reflexive, is used to express his own, their own, when emphasis is required, and usually refers to the subject of the verb:

> **Nēmō rem suam emit.**
> No one buys what is his own.

Sometimes to other cases if the context shows that it cannot be referred to the subject:

> **Suīs flammīs dēlēte Fīdēnās.**   Livy
> With its own flames destroy Fidenae.

Suus is especially used in combination with *quisque:*

> **Suus cuique erat locus attribūtus.**   Caesar
> To each man his own place had been assigned.

318 **Eius** is the possessive used of the third person where no emphasis is required, and does not refer to the subject.

> **Chīlius tē rogat, et ego eius rogātū.**   Cicero
> Chilius asks you, and I at his request.

Note: The possessive pronouns are often omitted when the meaning is clear without them: *frātrem amat,* he loves his brother.

---

319 **Hic, ille** are often used in contrast: *hic* usually meaning the latter, *ille* the former:

> **Quōcumque adspiciō, nihil est nisi pontus et āēr,**
> **nubibus hic tumidus, fluctibus ille minax.**   Ovid
> Wherever I look, there is nothing but sea and sky,
> the latter heaped with clouds, the former threatening
> with billows.

Note: Iste is sometimes contemptuous: *quid sibi istī miserī volunt?* What do those wretched ones want? **Ille** may imply respect: *philosophus ille,* that famous philosopher. **Is** often is the antecedent to *quī: is cuius,* he whose; *eum cui,* him to whom.

---

320 **Ipse,** self, is of all the three persons, with or without a personal pronoun: *ipse ībō,* I will go myself.

Note: Ipse sometimes means of one's own accord: *ipsī veniunt,* they come of their own accord. *Ipse, ipsa,* also stand for the chief person (master, mistress): the scholars of Pythagoras used to say *'Ipse dīxit,'* The master himself said it. Sometimes a superlative is formed: *ipsissima verba,* the very exact words.

---

321 Īdem, the same, is of all the three persons; with *quī* it expresses the same... as. It may often be translated as at the same time; also:

> **Ego, vir fortis, īdemque philosophus.**   Cicero
> I, a brave man, and also a philosopher.

322 Of the indefinite pronouns **quis, sīquis, numquis, quispiam, aliquis, quīdam,** the most definite is *quīdam,* the least so *quis.*

Quis, quī, any, cannot begin a sentence; they often follow *sī, num, nē.*

> **Sī mala condiderit in quem quis carmina iūs est.**   Horace
> If anyone has composed malicious verses on another,
> there is a remedy at law.

> **Sī quid tē volam, ubī eris?**   Plautus
> If I want anything of you, where will you be?

Aliquis means some one: *dīcat aliquis,* suppose someone to say; *sī vīs esse aliquis,* if you wish to be somebody.

Quidam means a certain person (known but not named):

> **Accurrit quīdam, nōtus mihi nōmine tantum.**   Horace
> A certain man runs up, known to me only by name.

Nescio quis, some one or other (I know not who), used as if one word, forms an indefinite pronoun:

> **Nesciō quid mihi animus praesāgit malī.**   Terence
> My mind forebodes I know not what evil.

323 Quisquam (substantive), **ūllus** (adjective), any at all, are often used after a negative word, or a question expecting a negative answer:

> **Nec amet quemquam nec ametur ab ūllō.**   Juvenal
> Let him not love anyone nor be loved by any.

> **Nōn ūllus arātrō dignus honōs.**   Virgil
> Not any due honour (is given) to the plough.

Note: *Quisquam* and *ūllus* are used after *sī* when negation is implied, or with comparatives:

Aut nēmō aut, sī quisquam, Catō sapiēns fuit.   Cicero
Either no man was wise, or, if any, Cato was.

324 Quīvīs, quīlibet, any you like:

**Quīvīs homō potest quemvīs dē quōlibet
rūmōrem prōferre.**
Any man can put forth any report of anybody.   Cicero

Nōn cuivīs hominī contingit adīre Corinthum.   Horace
It does not happen to every man to go to Corinth.

325 Quisque, each (severally), is often used with *sē, suus:*

Sibi quisque habeant quod suum est.   Plautus
Let them have each for himself what is his own.

With superlatives it expresses every, all:

Epicūrēōs doctissimus quisque contemnit.   Cicero
All the most learned men despise the Epicureans.

It also distributes ordinal numbers:

Quīntō quōque annō Sicilia tōta cēnsētur.   Cicero
A census of all Sicily is taken every fifth year.

326 Uterque, each (of two), both, can be used with the genitive of pronouns; but with substantives it agrees in case:

Uterque parēns   Ovid
Both father and mother.

Utrōque vestrum dēlēctor.   Cicero
I am delighted with both of you.

327 Uter, which (of two), is Interrogative: *uter melior?* which is the better?

Uter utrī īnsidiās fēcit?   Cicero
Which of the two laid an ambush for which?

Note: *Utrī*, plural, is used for which of two parties, *utrīque* for both parties.
So *alterī... alterī*, one party, the other party.

328 **Alter,** the one, the other (of two), the second, is the demonstrative of *uter: alter ego,* a second self.

> **Quicquid negat alter, et alter; affirmant pariter.**   Horace
> Whatever the one denies, so does the other;
> they affirm alike.

329 **Alius,** another (of any number), different:

> **Fortūna nunc mihi, nunc aliī benigna.**   Horace
> Fortune, kind now to me, now to another.

Alius, alius, repeated in two clauses, mean one… another; **aliī,
aliī** (plural), some… others:

> **Aliud est maledīcere, aliud accūsāre.**   Cicero
> It is one thing to speak evil, another to accuse.

> **Aliī Dēmosthenem laudant, aliī Cicerōnem.**
> Some praise Demosthenes, others Cicero.

Note 1: Alius repeated in different cases in the same sentence, or with one
of its derived adverbs, has an idiomatic use:

> **Aliī alia sentiunt,**
> Some think one thing, some another.

> **Illī aliās aliud īsdem dē rēbus iūdicant.**   Cicero
> They judge differently, at different times, about the same things.

Note 2: Alius expresses comparison and difference: *nīl aliud quam,* nothing
else than; *alius Lȳsippō,* Horace, other than Lysippus.

---

330 The relative **quī, quae, quod,** is of all three persons, and when
the antecedent is a noun either expressed or understood, it may
be regarded as standing between two cases of the same noun,
and agreeing with the second case.

(a) Sometimes both cases are expressed:

> **Erant itinera duo, quibus itineribus exīre possent.**   Caesar
> There were two roads by which they might go forth.

(b) usually the second is omitted:

> **Animum rege quī, nisi pāret, imperat.**   Horace
> Rule the temper, which, unless it obeys, commands.

(c) sometimes the first, in poetry:

Sīc tibi dent nymphae quae levet unda sitim,   Ovid
So may the nymphs give thee water to assuage thirst.

(d) sometimes both are omitted:

Sunt quibus in satirā videor nimis ācer.   Horace
There are some to whom I seem too keen in satire.

331 The following scheme shows this principle fully:

(1) **vir quem virum vidēs rēx est** (both cases expressed).

(2) **vir quem... vidēs rēx est** (second case omitted) (usual form).

(3) **... quem virum vidēs rēx est** (first case omitted).

(4) **... quem... vidēs rēx est** (both cases omitted).

---

332 Note 1: If the relative is the subject of a copulative verb, it often agrees in gender and number with the complement:

Thēbae, quod Boeōtiae caput est.   Livy
Thebes, which is the capital of Boeotia.

Note 2: When an adjective qualifying the antecedent is emphatic, as *ūnus, sōlus,* or is a superlative, it is often attracted to the **clause of the relative,** agreeing with it in case:

Sī veniat Caesar cum cōpiīs quās habet firmissimās.   Cicero
Should Caesar come with the very strong forces that he has.

Note 3: If the antecedent consists of two or more nouns, or is a collective noun, the rules for the agreement of the relative are the same as for the agreement of adjectives with the composite subject (see § 198, 199).

Note 4: If the relative refers to a sentence or clause, it is neuter; sometimes *id quod* is used, *id* being in apposition to the clause:

Diem cōnsūmī volēbat, id quod est factum.   Cicero
He wished the day to be wasted, which came to pass.

Note 5: The relative clause sometimes comes first:

Quam quisque nōrit artem, in hāc sē exerceat.   Cicero
Let everyone practice the art which he knows.

(For other uses of the relative see § 403, 450, 451.)

CORRELATION

333 **Pronouns and pronominal adverbs** are said to be **correlatives** when they correspond to one another as antecedent and relative (§ 102).

334 The pronoun antecedent to **quī** is usually the demonstrative **is**; sometimes **hic, ille, īdem**:

> **Is minimō eget quī minimum cupit.**   Publilius Syrus
> He wants for least who desires least.

335 **Tālis... quālis** means of such a kind... as; **tantus... quantus**, as much or as great... as; **tot... quot**, as many... as:

> **Tālis est quālem tū eum esse scrīpsistī.**   Cicero
> He is such as you wrote word that he was.

> **Tantō brevius omne, quantō fēlīcius tempus,**   Pliny
> The happier a time is, so much the shorter is it.

> **Quot hominēs, tot sententiae.**   Terence
> So many men, so many minds.

Tam... quam, so... as, as... as; **ut... ita**, as...so:

> **Tam ego ante fuī līber quam gnātus tuus.**   Plautus
> I was formerly as free as your son.

> **Ut optāstī, ita est.**   Cicero
> As you wished, so it is.

VERBS

TENSES OF THE INDICATIVE

336 The **present** expresses:

(1) What happens at the present moment: *iaciō,* I throw.

(2) What is going on at the present time: *scrībō,* I am writing.

(3) What is habitually or always: *quod semper movētur aeternum est,* that which is always in motion is eternal.

337 The **historic present** is used for a past by orators, historians, and poets, to give variety, or call up a vivid picture:

> **Dīmissō senātū decemvirī prōdeunt in cōntiōnem**
> **abdicant que sē magistrātū.**   Livy
> When the senate was dismissed, the decemvirs
> go forth to the assembled people and resign office.

338   **Note:** *Dum,* while, is used with the historic present in speaking of past time: *Dum Rōmānī cōnsultant, Saguntum oppugnabātur,* Livy. While the Romans were consulting, Saguntum was being besieged (see § 430). With *iam, iam diū (dūdum, prīdem)* the present expresses what has long been and still continues: *Iam dūdum videō,* Horace. I have seen it this long time.

339   The **perfect** expresses:

As **primary,** from the point of the present moment what has just been done: *scrīpsī,* I have written.

As **historic,** simply a past action, which happened at some indefinite time: *scrīpsī,* I wrote.

Note: The perfect is used in poetry to express past existence which has ceased: *Fuimus Trōes; fuit Īlium,* Virgil. We have been (i.e. are no longer) Trojans; Troy has been (exists no longer).

340   The **imperfect** expresses what was continued or repeated in past time, as opposed to the completed or momentary past:

Aequī sē in oppida recēpērunt mūrīsque sē tenēbant.   Livy
The Aequi retreated into their towns and remained within their walls.

Carthāgine quotannīs bīnī rēgēs creābantur.   Nepos
At Carthage two rulers were elected annually.

341   The **pluperfect** expresses an action which had already been completed prior to the (past) time of the main narrative:

Massiliēnsēs portās Caesarī clauserant.   Caesar
The Marseillais had closed the gates against Caesar.

342   The **future simple** is used in to express what will happen:

Ut volēs mē esse, ita erō.   Plautus
As you wish me to be, so I shall be.

343   The **future perfect** expresses action to be completed in the future; if two actions are spoken of, one of which will take place before the other, the prior one is in the future perfect:

Ut sēmentem fēceris, ita metēs.   Cicero
As you shall have sown, so will you reap.

Note: The Romans, in writing letters, often speak of the time of writing in a past tense, because it would be past when a letter would be received.

**Rēs, cum haec scrībēbam, erat in extrēmum
adducta discrīmen,**   Cicero
At the time I write, the affair has been brought to a crisis.

MOODS

344 The **indicative** is the mood which makes a statement with regard to a fact, or to something which is dealt with by the speaker as a fact.

345 **Note:** Verbs expressing duty, fitness, possibility, as *possum, dēbeō, decet, licet, oportet,* are often used in the indicative tenses of past time, to express that it was proper or possible at that time to do something which in fact was not done. Phrases such as *necesse est, fuit; aequum, longum, melius, satius est, fuit,* are similarly used in the indicative (§ 440 c):

Hic tamen hanc mēcum poterās requiēscere noctem.   Virgil
Yet you might have rested here with me this night.

Et vellem et fuerat melius.   Virgil
I should have wished, and it would have been better.

Longum est ea dīcere: sed hoc breve dīcam.   Cicero
It would be tedious to speak of these things, but this little I will say.

Compare with these:

Nōn Āsiae nōmen obiciendum Murenae fuit.   Cicero
Murena should not have been reproached with the mention of Asia.

346 The **imperative** is the mood of positive command or direct request:

Ī, sequere Ītaliam. Virgil   **Pergite, adulēscentēs.**   Cicero
Go, seek Italy.   Proceed, o youths.

347 Prohibitions in the second person are expressed by **nōlī, nōlīte** with the infinitive; or, more peremptorily, by **nē** with the perfect subjunctive:

Nōlīte id velle quod fierī nōn potest.   Cicero
Do not wish what cannot be.

Nē fēcerīs quod dubitās.   Pliny
Never do anything about which you are doubtful,

348 but in poetry **nē** is often used with the imperative:

> **Equō nē crēdite, Teucrī.**   Virgil
> Do not trust the horse, o Trojans.

349 The imperative forms in **-tō, -tōte** are specially used in laws; but they are also often used for emphasis.

> **Rēgiō imperiō duo suntō, iique cōnsulēs appellantor.**   Cicero
> Let there be two with royal power, and let them
> be called consuls.

---

350   **Note 1:** The following imperatives are joined with the infinitive or sub-junctive of other verbs to form imperatives; **fac, fac ut, cūrā ut,** with the Subjunctive; **mementō** with infinitive or subjunctive. In prohibitions **fac nē, cavē,** take the subjunctive; and in poetry **fuge, mitte, parce,** take the Infinitive:

> **Magnum fac animum habeās.**   Cicero
> Mind you have a lofty spirit.

Note 2 For a courteous imperative the future indicative is often used: *faciēs ut sciam,* Cicero. You will please let me know.

---

351 The **subjunctive mood** makes a statement or asks a question, not so much with regard to a fact as with regard to something thought of or imagined by the speaker, often with some condition expressed or implied. It expresses a modified or conditional command or desire.

The subjunctive has two general uses:

352 **Pure** or **independent:** *velim,* I could wish; *vellem,* I could have wished.

353 **Dependent** on another verb: *cūrā ut faciās,* take care that you do it.

354 The **pure subjunctive** must generally be rendered in English with auxiliaries, may, might, could, would, should.

Note: The subjunctive makes a statement:

355   (a) With a condition expressed or implied (**conditional use**):

Ita amicōs parēs.   Cicero
Thus you may get friends.

Crēderēs victōs.   Livy
You would have supposed them conquered
(from their appearance).

356   (b) Or in a modified tone, to avoid positiveness (**potential use**):

Dubitem haud equidem.   Virgil
For my part I should not hesitate.

The **perfect subjunctive** is especially so used:

Forsitan quispiam dīxerit.   Cicero
Perhaps someone may say.

357   (c) Conveying an admission or supposition (**concessive use**):

Haec sint falsa sāne.   Cicero   **Fuerit malus cīvis.**   Cicero
Granting this to be quite untrue.   Suppose he was a bad citizen.

358   It asks a question (**deliberative use**):

Faveās tū hostī? Cicero   **Quid facerem?**   Virgil
Would you befriend an enemy?   What was I to do?

It expresses a desire or command:

359   (a) A wish or prayer (**optative use**): often with *utinam,* Oh that!

Sīs fēlīx.   Horace   **Utinam potuissem.**
May you be happy.   Oh that I had been able.

Doceās iter et sacra ostia pandās.   Virgil
Pray show me the road and open the sacred doors.

360   (b) An exhortation (**hortative use**) chiefly in the 1st person plural:

Amēmus patriam, pāreāmus senātuī.   Cicero
Let us love our country, let us obey the senate.

361   (c) A modified command (**jussive use**) in the 3rd person:

Sit sermō lēnis.   Cicero
Let speech be calm.

Vīlicus nē sit ambulātor.   Cato
Let not a steward be a loiterer.

362   From the jussive use comes a further use of the subjunctive, by which the
expression of a wish is conveyed into past time. This use is chiefly in the
second person, but extends also to the others:

Rem tuam cūrārēs.   Terence
You should have been minding your own business.

363   The use of the 2nd pers. in the pres. subj. is often indefinite, not addressed to
anyone in particular, but expressing a general maxim:

Agēre decet quod agās consīderāte.   Cicero
Whatever you do, it is proper to do it with consideration.

THE VERB INFINITE

364 The parts of the verb infinite have some of the uses of verbs, some of the uses of nouns.

THE INFINITIVE

365 The infinitive as a verb has tenses, present, past, or future, it governs cases and is qualified by adverbs; as a noun it is neuter, indeclinable, used only as nominative or accusative.

366 The **infinitive** in the nominative may be the subject of impersonal verbs, or of verbs used impersonally:

Iuvat īre et Dōrica castra vidēre. It is pleasant to go and view the Doric camp.	Virgil
Ipsum philosophārī nunc displicet, The very study of philosophy now displeases,	Cicero
Dulce et decōrum est prō patriā morī. To die for one's country is sweet and seemly.	Horace
Non vīvere bonum est sed bene vīvere. It is not living which is a good, but living well.	Seneca

Note: Occasionally the infinitive is the complement:

Homō cui vīvere est cōgitāre. Man to whom to live is to think.	Cicero

367 The **infinitive** is often one of the two accusatives depending on an active verb of saying or thinking:

Errāre, nescīre, dēcipī et malum et turpe dūcimus. To err, to be ignorant, to be deceived, we deem both unfortunate and disgraceful,	Cicero

368 **Note:** Sometimes, though rarely, it is a simple object:

Hoc rīdēre meum nūllā tibi vēndō Īliade. This laughter of mine I won't sell you for an Iliad.	Persius

369 The **prolative infinitive** is used to carry on the construction of indeterminate and some other verbs (§ 190):

Verbs of possibility, duty, habit: *possum, queō, dēbeō*, etc.;

Verbs of wishing, purposing: *volō, nōlō, mālō, optō*, etc.;

Verbs of beginning, ceasing, endeavoring, continuing, hastening: *coepī*, begin; *dēsinō*, cease; *cōnor*, try; *pergō*, proceed, etc.;

Verbs of knowing, teaching, learning: *scio, discō, doceō*.

Ego plūs quam fēcī facere nōn possum.   Cicero
I cannot do more than I have none.

Solent diū cōgitāre quī magna volunt gerere.   Cicero
They are wont to reflect long who wish to do great things.

Praecēdere coepit.	Horace	**Sapere audē.**	Horace
He begins to walk on.		Dare to be wise.	

Note: The infinitive of a copulative verb used prolatively is followed by a complement in the nominative:

Sōcratēs parēns philosophiae iūre dīcī potest.   Cicero
Socrates may rightly be called the parent of philosophy.

Vīs formōsa vidērī.   Horace
You wish to seem beautiful.

370   The **prolative infinitive** is also used with the passives of verbs of saying and thinking:

Barbara nārrātur vēnisse venēfica tēcum.   Ovid
A barbarian sorceress is said to have come with thee.

Aristīdēs ūnus omnium iūstissimus fuisse trāditur.   Cicero
Aristides is recorded to have been the one man of all most just.

Note: This construction is called the **nominative with infinitive**, and is used with most passive verbs of saying and thinking. A few, however, *nārror*, *nūntior*, *trādor*, are used impersonally – always when in the perfect, and often in the present and imperfect:

Galbam et Āfricānum doctōs fuisse trāditum est.   Cicero
It has been handed down that Galba and Africanus were learned.

371   With an infinitive perfect passive *esse* is often omitted:

Pōns in Ībērō prope effectus nūntiābātur.   Caesar
The bridge over the Ebro was announced to be nearly finished.

Titus Manlius ita locūtus fertur.   Livy
Titus Manlius is reported to have spoken thus.

372   The **historic infinitive** is the present infinitive used by historians in vivid description for the imperfect indicative:

> **Multī sequī, fugere, occīdī, capī**   Sallust
> Many were following, fleeing, being slain, being captured.

373   An infinitive often follows an adjective prolatively, chiefly in poetry:

> **Audāx omnia perpetī.**   Horace   **Īnsuētus vincī.**   Livy
> Bold to endure all things.   Unused to be conquered.

> **Fīgere doctus erat sed tendere doctior arcūs.**   Ovid
> He was skilled in piercing (with a dart), but more skilled in bending the bow.

GERUND AND GERUNDIVE

374   The **gerund** is a verbal noun, the **gerundive** a verbal adjective. The genitive, dative, and ablative of the gerund, and the accusative with a preposition, are used as cases of the infinitive.

375   The **accusative** of the **gerund** follows some prepositions, especially *ad, oh, inter*:

> **Ad bene vīvendum breve tempus satis est longum.**   Cicero
> For living well a short time is long enough.

> **Mōrēs puerōrum sē inter lūdendum dētegunt.**   Quint.
> The characters of boys show themselves in their play.

376   The **genitive** of the **gerund** depends on some abstract substantives, and adjectives which take a genitive:

> **Ars scrībendī discitur.**   **Cupidus tē audiendī sum.**   Cicero
> The art of writing is learnt.   I am desirous of hearing you.

377   The **dative** of the **gerund** follows a few verbs, adjectives, and substantives implying help, use, fitness:

> **Pār est disserendō.**   Cicero   **Dat operam legendō.**
> He is equal to arguing.   He gives attention to reading.

Note: Observe the phrase: *solvendō nōn est,* he is insolvent.

378 The **ablative** of the **gerund** is of cause or manner, or it follows one of the prepositions *ab, dē, ex, in, cum:*

Fugiendō vincimus.   We conquer by flying.

Dē pugnandō dēlīberant.   They deliberate about fighting.

379 If the verb is transitive, the **gerundive** is more often used than the gerund, agreeing with the object as an adjective. It takes the gender and number of the object, but the object is drawn into the case of the gerundive.

The following examples show how the gerundive takes the place of the gerund.

Gerund	Gerundive	
Ad petendum pācem	**ad petendam pācem**	in order to seek peace
Petendī pācem	**petendae pācis**	of seeking peace
Petendō pācem	**petendae pācī**	for seeking peace
Petendō pācem	**petendā pāce**	by seeking peace
Ad mutandum lēgēs	**ad mutandās lēgēs**	in order to change laws
Mutandī lēgēs	**mutandārum lēgum**	of changing laws
Mutandō lēgēs	**mutandīs lēgibus**	for or by changing laws

Note 1: In order to seek peace may also be rendered by the genitive of the gerund or gerundive with *causā or grātiā: pācem petendī causā* or *petendae pācis causā* (see § 423, note 3).

380   **Note 2:** The dative of the gerundive is used with names of office to show the purpose of the office:

Comitia rēgī creandō.   Livy
An assembly for electing a king.

Trēsvirī agrīs dīvidendīs.   Florus
Three commissioners for dividing lands.

---

381 The gerund and gerundive are often used to express that something ought or is to be done, the **dative of the agent** being expressed or understood (§ 222).

382 If the verb is **intransitive** the gerund is used impersonally:

Eundum est.
One must go.

Mihi eundum est.
I must go.

Suō cuique iūdiciō est ūtendum.   Cicero
Each must use his own judgment.

383 If the verb is **transitive** the **gerundive** is used in agreement:

Caesarī omnia ūnō tempore erant agenda.   Caesar
All things had to be done by Caesar at one time.

Prīncipiō sēdēs apibus statiōque petenda.   Virgil
First of all a site and station must be sought for the bees.

Note 1: If an intransitive verb has an object in the dative, the agent is in the ablative with the preposition *ā* or *ab: patriae est ā tē cōnsulendum,* you must consult for your country.

384 Note 2 After some verbs, as *dō, trādō, cūrō,* the gerundive is used in the accusative to express that something is caused to be done:

Caesar pontem faciendum cūrat.   Caesar
Caesar causes a bridge to be made.

SUPINES

385 The supines are also used as cases of the infinitive:

386 The **supine** in **-um** is an accusative after verbs of motion, expressing the purpose:

Lūsum it Maecēnās, dormītum ego.   Horace
Maecenas goes to play, I to sleep.

Athēniēnsēs mīserunt Delphōs consultum.   Nepos
The Athenians sent to Delphi to consult.

387 With the infinitive **īrī**, used impersonally, the supine forms a future passive infinitive:

Aiunt urbem captum īrī.
They say that the city will be taken.

Note: Literally, they say there is a going to take the city.

388 The **supine** in **-ū** (dative and ablative) is used with some adjectives, such as facilis, dulcis, turpis, and the Substantives *fās, nefās: turpe factū,* disgraceful to do.

Hoc fās est dictū.
It is lawful to say this.

Lībertās, dulce audītū nōmen.   Livy
Freedom, a name sweet to hear.

Nec vīsū facilis, nec dictū adfābilis ūllī.   Virgil
One not easy for any to gaze on, or to address.

PARTICIPLES

389 The present and perfect participles of some verbs are used as adjectives:

Homō frūgī ac dīligēns.   Cicero
A thrifty and industrious man.

Odōrāta cedrus.   Virgil
The fragrant cedar.

390 Most participles which can be used as adjectives have comparison: *pietāte praestantior,* more excellent in piety; *nocentissima victōria,* a very hurtful victory.

391 A participle, agreeing with a noun in any case, often expresses within one sentence what might be expressed by a dependent or a co-ordinate clause:

Saepe sequens agnam lupus est a vōce retentus.   Ovid
Often, when following a lamb, the wolf has been
held back by his voice.

Elephantēs, amnem trānsitūrī, minimōs praemittunt.   Pliny
Elephants, intending to cross a river, send forward the
smallest ones.

Tīmotheus ā patre acceptam glōriam multīs auxit
virtūtibus.
Timotheus increased by many virtues the glory which
he had received from his father.

Sacrās iaculātus arcēs terruit urbem.   Horace
He has smitten the sacred towers and terrified the city.

Caesar mīlitēs hortātus castra mōvit.   Caesar
Caesar addressed the soldiers, and moved his camp.

392 **Note 1:** Only deponent verbs have an active perfect participle; in other verbs its place is supplied either by a finite active verb with the relative or a particle, or by the **ablative absolute** passive:

The enemy, having thrown away their arms, fled, can be expressed in Latin by

Hostēs
| qui arma abiēcerant |
| cum arma abiēcissent | terga vertērunt.
| armīs abiēctīs |

393 **Note 2:** Sometimes when a substantive has a perfect participle in agreement, the substantive must be rendered in English by a genitive, the participle by a substantive: *ademptus Hector,* the removal of Hector; *ante urbem conditam,* before the foundation of the city.

Terra mūtāta nōn mūtat mōrēs.   Livy
Change of country does not change character.

Note on the Verb Infinite

394 The infinitive, the gerund, the supine in -*um* and the participles govern the same cases as the finite verbs to which they belong.

Ingenuās didicisse fidēliter artēs ēmollit mōrēs.   Ovid
To have truly learned the liberal arts refines the character.

Cupiō satisfacere reīpūblicae.   Cicero
I desire to do my duty to the republic.

Rōmae prīvātīs iūs nōn erat vocandī senātum.   Livy
At Rome private persons did not have the right of summoning the senate.

Ast ego nōn Graiīs servītum mātribus ībō.   Virgil
But I will not go to be a slave to Greek matrons.

Ausī omnēs immane nefās, ausōque potītī.   Virgil
All having dared monstrous impiety and having accomplished what they dared.

ADVERBS

395 Adverbs show how, when, and where the action of the verb takes place; they also qualify adjectives or other adverbs: *rēctē facere,* to do rightly; *hūc nunc venīre,* to come hither now; *facile prīmus,* easily first; *valdē celeriter,* very swiftly.

Many words are both adverbs and prepositions, as *ante,* before, *post,* after:

Adverbs: *multō ante,* long before; *paulō post,* shortly after.

Prepositions: *ante oculōs,* before one's eyes; *post tergum,* behind one's back.

Joined with quam they form conjunctions: *antequam,* before that... *postquam,* after that... (see § 428, 431).

396 Negative adverbs are **nōn, haud, nē. Nōn,** not, is simply negative:

Nivēs in altō marī nōn cadunt.   Pliny
No snow falls on the high seas.

Haud, not, is used with adjectives, with other adverbs, and a few verbs of knowing and thinking: *haud aliter, haud secus,* not otherwise; *rēs haud dubia,* no doubtful matter; *haud scio an vērum sit,* I am inclined to think it is true.

Nē is used with the second person of the perfect subjunctive for prohibitions (§ 347): *nē trānsierīs Hibērum,* Livy. Do not cross the Ebro. With the second person of the present subjunctive **nē** often means lest: *nē forte crēdās,* Horace. Lest by chance you believe, *or* that you may not by chance believe.

397 Two negatives make an affirmative, as in English: *nōn sum nescius,* I am not unaware, that is I am aware. *Nōn nēmō* means, somebody; *nēmō nōn,* everybody; *nōn nihil,* something; *nihil nōn,* everything.

In ipsā cūriā nōn nēmō hostis est.   Cicero
In the very senate-house there is some enemy.

Nēmō Arpīnās nōn Plranciō studuit.   Cicero
Every citizen of Arpinum was zealous for Plancius.

Note 1: Neque, nec, nor, (conjunction) is used for 'and not':

Rapimur in errōrem, neque vēra cernimus.   Cicero
We are hurried into error, and do not perceive truth.

So also are generally rendered:

and no one,	**nec quisquam, nec ūllus;**
and nothing,	**nec quidquam;**
and never, nowhere,	**nec umquam, nec ūsquam.**

398   Note 2: **Nē** is used with **quidem** to express *not even*, and the word or words on which emphasis is laid comes between them:

> **Nē ad Catōnem quidem prōvocābō.**   Cicero
> Not to Cato even will I appeal.

'Not only not... , but not even' is *nōn modo nōn...sed nē... quidem* (or *nē... quidem, nōn modo nōn*).

> **Nōn modo tibi nōn īrāscor, sed nē reprehendō quidem factum tuum.**
> I am not only not angry with you, but do not even blame your act.   Cicero

If the predicate of both clauses is the same, it is often expressed only in the second clause with *nē... quidem*, and also the negative is omitted in the first clause – i.e. *nōn modo* is used rather than *nōn modo nōn*.

> **Adsentātiō nōn modo amīcō, sed nē līberō quidem digna est.**   Cicero
> Flattering is unworthy, not only of a friend, but even of a free man.

CONJUNCTIONS

399   Conjunctions connect words, sentences, and clauses.

400   (1) **Co-ordinative conjunctions** connect two or more nouns in the same case:

> **Mīrātur portās strepitumque et strāta viārum.**   Virgil
> He marvels at the gates and the noise and the pavements.

> **Et nostra rēspūblica et omnia rēgna.**   Cicero
> Both our own republic and all kingdoms.

> **Sine imperiō nec domus ūlla nec cīvitās stāre potest,**   Cicero
> Without governrnent neither any house nor any state
> can be stable.

Or they join two or more simple sentences (§ 402).

Note 1: *Aut... aut* are used to mark an emphatic distinction; *vel... vel* where the distinction is of little importance:

> **Aut Caesar aut nūllus.**
> Either Caesar or nobody.

> **Vel magna, vel potius maxima.**   Cicero
> Great, or rather very great.

Note 2: **Sed** distinguishes with more or less opposition, or passes to a fresh point; while **autem** corrects slightly or continues:

> **Non scholae sed vitae discimus.**   Seneca
> We learn not from the school but for life.

Note 3: Autem, enim, quidem, vērō, never begin a sentence:

Neque enim tū is es quī quid sīs nesciās.   Cicero
For you are not the man to be ignorant of your own nature.

---

401 (2) **Subordinative conjunctions** join dependent clauses to the
principal sentence (see compound sentence, § 410 ff.).

Co-ordination

402 When two or more sentences are joined together by co-ordinative conjunctions, so as to form part of one sentence, they are
said to be **co-ordinate sentences**, and each is independent in
its construction.

Et mihi sunt vīrēs et mea tēla nocent.   Ovid
I too am not powerless, and my weapons hurt.

Gȳgēs ā nūllō vidēbātur, ipse autem omnia vidēbat.   Cicero
Gyges was seen by no-one, but he himself saw all things.

403 The **relative pronoun** with a verb in the indicative often forms
a co-ordinate sentence:

Rēs loquitur ipsa, qua esemper valet plūrimum.   Cicero
The fact itself speaks, and this always avails most.

Cōnstantēs amīcī sunt ēligendī, cuius
generis magna est pēnūria.   Cicero
Firm friends are to be chosen, but of such there is great scarcity.

INTERJECTIONS

404 Interjections are apart from the construction of the sentence.
Ō, ah, eheu, heu, prō, are used with the vocative, nominative, or
accusative; *ēn, ecce,* with the nominative or accusative; *ei, vae,*
with the dative only:

Ō fōrmōse puer, nimium nē crēde colōrī.   Virgil
O beautiful boy, trust not too much to complexion.

Ō fortūnātam Rōmam!   Cicero
O fortunate Rome!

Ēn ego vester Ascānius!   Virgil
Lo here am I your Ascanius!

Ei miserō mihi!
Alas! wretched me.

Vae victīs!   Livy
Woe to the vanquished!

QUESTION AND ANSWER

405 (a) Single questions are asked by:

nōnne, expecting the answer yes.

num, expecting the answer no.

-ne, expecting either answer.

an, expressing surprise and expecting answer no.

Canis nōnne similis lupō est?   Cicero
Is not a dog like a wolf?

Num negāre audēs?   Cicero
Do you venture to deny?

Potēsne dīcere?   Cicero
Can you say?

An tū mē tristem esse putās?   Platus
Do you think I am sad?

Note: Questions are also asked by **interrogative pronouns** (§ 95, 100,102, 327) and **adverbs** (§ 167, 168).

406 (b) Alternative questions are asked by:

utrum... an (or).

num... an (or).

-ne... an (or).

... an, anne (or).

Haec utrum abundantis an egentis sīgna sunt?   Cicero
Are these the tokens of one who abounds or lacks?

Num duās habētis patriās an est illa patria commūnis? Cicero
Have you two countries, or is that your common country?

Rōmamne veniō, an hīc maneō, an Arpīnum fugiō?   Cicero
Do I come to Rome, or stay here, or flee to Arpinum?

Note: A single question is sometimes asked without any particle:

Înfēlīx est Fabricius quod rūs suum fodit?   Seneca
Is Fabricius unhappy because he digs his land?

407 For **deliberative questions** the present or imperfect subjunctive is used:

Quid faciam? roger anne rogem?   Ovid
What shall I do? Shall I be asked or ask?

Tibi ego īrāscerer, mī frater? tibi ego possem īrāscī?   Cicero
Should I be angry with you, my brother? Could I
be angry with you?

408 **Answer in the affirmative** is expressed:
(a) By repeating the emphatic word of the question, sometimes with **vērō, sānē, inquam:**

Estne?...est.   Livy   **Dasne?... Dō sānē.**   Cicero
Is it? It is.   Do you grant? I grant indeed.

(b) By **ita, ita est, etiam, sānē, sānē quidem...** :

Vīsne potiōra tantum interrogem?... Sānē.   Cicero
Would you have me ask only the principal matters?... Certainly.

409 **Answer in the negative** is expressed:
(a) By repeating the emphatic verb with **nōn.**

Estne frāter intus?... Nōn est.   Terence
Is my brother within?... No.

(b) By **nōn, nōn ita, minimē, minimē vērō:**

Vēnitne?... Nōn.   Plautus
Did he come?... No.

Nōn pudet vānitātis?... Minimē.
Are you not ashamed of your folly?... Not at all.

Note: **Immō,** nay rather, yes even, is used in answers to correct or modify, either by contradicting, or by strengthening:

Ubī fuit Sulla, num Rōmae?... Immō longē āfuit.   Cicero
Where was Sulla? at Rome?... Nay, he was far away from it.

Tenāxne est?... Immō pertināx.   Plautus
Is he tenacious?... Yes, even pertinacious.

410 ## THE COMPOUND SENTENCE

A compound sentence consists of a principal sentence with one or more subordinate clauses.

Subordinate Clauses depend in their construction on the Principal Sentence. They are divided into:

1. Substantival   2. Adverbial   3. Adjectival

1. A **substantival clause** stands, like a substantive, as subject or object of a verb, or in apposition.
2. An **adverbial clause** qualifies the principal sentence like an adverb, answering the questions *how? why? when?* Adverbial clauses are introduced by subordinative conjunctions, and are (1) consecutive (so that); (2) final (in order that); (3) causal (because, since); (4) temporal (when, while, until); (5) conditional (if, unless); (6) clauses of proviso (provided that); (7) concessive (although, even if); (8) comparative (as if, as though).
3. An **adjectival clause** qualifies the principal sentence like an adjective. It is introduced by the relative **quī** or by a relative particle, as **ubī** (where), **unde** (from where), **quō** (to where).

411 ## SEQUENCE OF TENSES

The general rule for the sequence of tenses is that a primary tense in the principal sentence is followed by a primary tense in the clause, a historic tense by a historic tense.

PRIMARY

Simple Pres.	**rogō**, I ask	Act.	**quid agās**	what you are doing
Pres. Perf.	**rogāvī**, I have asked	Pass.	**quid ā tē agātur**	
		Act.	**quid ēgerīs**	what you have done
Simple Fut.	**rogābō**	Pass.	**quid ā tē āctum sit**	
Fut. Perf.	**rogāvero**	Act.	**quid āctūrus sīs**	what you are going to do

HISTORIC

Imperf.	rogābam	Act.	quid agerēs	what you were doing
Perf.	rogāvī, I asked	Pass.	quid ā tē agerētur	
		Act.	quid ēgissēs	what you had done
Pluperf.	rogāveram	Pass.	quid ā tē āctum esset	
		Act.	quid āctūrus essēs	what you were going to do

Note: The historic present and historic infinitive are generally used with historic sequence. The primary perfect indicative has primary sequence in most writers, but Cicero often gives it historic sequence. The perfect subjunctive in its pure use is always primary; in its dependent use, it is generally primary, sometimes historic.

---

412 TENSES OF THE INFINITIVE IN INDIRECT SPEECH

If the time of the clause is the same as that of the principal verb, the present infinitive is used.

If the time is before that of the principal verb, the perfect infinitive. If the time follows that of the principal verb, the future infinitive.

Dīcō I say	**eum amāre** that he is loving	**amāvisse** has loved	**amātūrum esse** will love
	cōpiās mittī that forces are being sent	**missās esse** have been sent	**missum īrī** will be sent
Dīxī I said	**eum amāre** that he was loving	**amāvisse** had loved	**amātūrum esse** would love
	cōpiās mittī that forces were being sent	**missās esse** had been sent	**missum īrī** would be sent

---

Note: For the supine in **-um** with **īrī**, may be substituted **fore ut** or **futūrum ut** with the subjunctive: *fore (futūrum esse), ut cōpiae mittantur ut cōpiae mitterentur.*

I. Substantival Clauses

413 Substantival clauses are indirect statements, commands, requests or questions. Their forms correspond to the three direct forms of the simple sentence.

1	DIRECT STATEMENT	1	INDIRECT STATEMENT
	Valeō		**Scis mē valēre**
	I am well		You know that I am well
	Calet ignis		**Sentimus calēre ignem**
	Fire is hot		We feel that fire is hot
2	DIRECT POSITIVE COMMAND OR REQUEST	2	INDIRECT COMMAND OR REQUEST
	Valē		**Curā ut valeās**
	Farewell		Take care that you keep well
	Manē in sententiā		**Ōrō maneās in sententiā**
	Keep firm in your opinion		I beg that you keep firm in your opinion
3	DIRECT QUESTION	3	INDIRECT QUESTION
	Valēsne?		**Quaero an valeā**
	Are you well?		I ask whether you are welL
	Quis est?		**Incertum est quis sit**
	Who is he?		It is doubtful who he is

1. Indirect Statement

414 The accusative with infinitive is the most usual form of indirect statement. It may stand:

(a) As the subject of an impersonal verb, or of *est* with an abstract substantive or neuter adjective:

Cōnstat lēgēs ad salūtem cīvium inventās esse.   Cicero
It is agreed that laws were devised for the safety of citizens.

Nūntiātum est Scīpiōnem ad esse.   Caesar
It was announced that Scipio was at hand.

Rem tē valdē bene gessisse rūmor erat.   Cicero
There was a report that you had conducted the affair very well.

Vērum est amīcitiam nisi inter bonōs esse nōn posse.   Cicero
It is true that friendship cannot exist except between
the good.

(b) As object, after verbs of saying, thinking, feeling, perceiving,
knowing, believing, denying:

Dēmocritus dīcit innumerābīlēs esse mundōs.   Cicero
Democritus says that there are countless worlds.

Pompeiōs dēsēdisse terrae mōtū audīvimus.   Seneca
We have heard that Pompeii has perished in an earthquake.

(c) In apposition:

Illud temerē dictum, sapientēs omnēs esse bonōs.   Cicero
It was rashly said that all wise men are good.

Note: Verbs of hoping, promising, swearing, threatening generally take the
accusative with future infinitive:

Spērābam id mē assecūtūrum.   Cicero
I hoped to attain this.

Pollicēbātur pecūniam sē esse redditūrum.   Cicero
He promised that he would return the money.

---

415 A clause formed by **ut** with the subjunctive is used as subject
with impersonal verbs or phrases which express fact or occur-
rence; it is also used in apposition, but it seldom stands asob-
ject:

Expedit ut cīvitātes sua iūra habeant.   Livy
That states should have their own laws is expedient.

Mōs erat ut in pāce Ianī templum claudērētur.   Livy.
It was the custom that in time of peace the temple
of Janus was shut.

Extrēmum illud est ut tē obsecrem.   Cicero
The last thing is for me to beseech you.

Note: The accusative with infinitive, or the *ut* clause, used interrogatively,
sometimes expresses indignation:

Mēne inceptō dēsistere victam?   Virgil
What! I to be vanquished and abandon my design?

Tē ut ulla rēs frangat?   Cicero
Can anything break your pride?

416 A clause formed by **quod** with the indicative is used as subject, or in apposition, where a fact is to be dwelt on:

> **Accēdit hūc quod postrīdiē ille vēnit.**   Cicero
> Add to this that he came the next day.

> **Hōc praestāmus maximē ferīs, quod loquimur.**   Cicero
> We excel beasts most in this respect, that we speak.

Rarely as object, after verbs such as *addō, mittō, omittō, praetereō:*

> **Adde quod īdem nōn hōram tēcum esse potes.**   Horace
> Add moreover that you cannot keep your own
> company for an hour.

It is also used with verbs of rejoicing and grieving:

> **Dolet mihi quod tū stomachāris.**   Cicero
> It grieves me that you are angry.

> **Gaudē, quod spectant oculī tē mīlle loquentem.**   Horace
> Rejoice, that a thousand eyes behold you speaking.

Note: With verbs of rejoicing and grieving, the accusative with Infinitive or the *quod* clause may be used: *Salvum tē advenīre gaudeō* (Plautus). I rejoice that you arrive in health; might be, *Gaudeō quod salvus advenīs.*

---

2. Indirect Command, Request or Prohibition

417 A clause depending on a verb of commanding, wishing, exhorting, entreating, is in the subjunctive: if positive, with **ut**; If negative, with **nē**. The clause may stand:

(a) as **subject**;   (b) as **object**;   (c) **in apposition**:

> **(a) Postulātur ab amīcō ut sit sincērus.**   Cicero
> It is required of a friend that he be sincere.

> **Nūntiātum est Antōniō nē Brūtum obsideret.**   Cicero
> An order was sent to Antony that he should not
> besiege Brutus.

> **(b) Etiam atque etiam tē rogō atque ōrō ut eum iuvēs.**   Cicero
> I urgently beg and pray you to help him.

> **Mihi nē abscēdam imperat.**   Terence
> He commands me not to go away.

(c) Hoc tē rogō, nē dīmittās animum.   Cicero
This I beg you, not to lose heart.

Note 1: With *ōrō, rogō, moneō, suādeō, sinō, imperō, cūrō, volō, nōlō, mālō,* and some other verbs, *ut* is often omitted. With *licet oportet* it is not used. *Idque sinās ōrō;* and I pray that you grant that.

Haec omnia praetermittās licet.   Cicero
It is allowable to omit all these things.

Note 2: Verbs of willing and desiring, *volō, nōlō, cupiō,* also *iubeō* and many others, frequently take the accusative with infinitive:

Eās rēs iactārī nōlēbat.   Caesar
He was unwilling to have those things discussed.

Eōs suum adventum exspectāre iussit.   Caesar
He desired them to await his arrival.

Note 3: Verbs of taking care, effecting, causing, are used with *ut;* verbs of guarding against, with *nē:*

Cūrā et prōvidē ut nē quid eī dēsit.   Cicero
Take care and provide that nothing be wanting to him.

Sōl efficit ut omnia flōreant,   Cicero
The sun causes all things to bloom.

Cavē, beware lest, with *nē* without a conjunction; *cavē,* take care that, is used with *ut:*

Cavē ne portus occupet alter.   Horace
Beware, lest another forestall you in occupying, the harbor.

Note 4: Verbs of fearing take the subjunctive: with **nē** to express fear that something will happen; with **ut** or **nē nōn** to express fear that something will not happen:

Metuō nē faciat.	**Metuō ut faciat** (*or* **nē nōn faciat**).
I fear he may do it	I fear he may not do it.

418 Quōminus, that not (literally 'by which the less'), with the subjunctive, forms a clause depending on a verb or phrase which expresses hindrance or prevention:

Senectūs nōn impedit quōminus litterārum studia teneāmus.   Cicero
Age does not prevent our continuing literary pursuits.

Neque repugnābō quōminus omnia legant.   Cicero
Nor will I oppose their reading all things.

Per Afrānium stetit quōminus proelium dīmicārētur.   Caesar
It was owing to Afranius that no battle was fought.

419 **Quīn**, that not, with the subjunctive, follows many of the same verbs, and phrases of similar meaning:

> **Nihil abest quīn sim miserrimus.**   Cicero
> Nothing is wanting to my being most miserable.

> **Aegrē sunt retentī quīn oppidum irrrumperent.**   Caesar
> They were hardly withheld from bursting into the city.

Note 1: The sentence on which *quōminus* depends is generally negative or interrogative, but it may be positive; the sentence on which *quīn* depends is always negative, or virtually negative.

Note 2: Many of these verbs take nē:

> **Atticus, nē qua sibi statua pōnerētur, restitit.**   Nepos
> Atticus opposed having any statue raised to him.

Prohibeō takes *quōminus* or *nē, vetō* more often *nē*, and both take accusative with infinitive.

---

3. Indirect Question

420 An indirect question is formed by a dependent interrogative pronoun or particle with a verb in the subjunctive.

The clause of the indirect question may be (a) subject or (b) object or (c) in apposition, and the question may be single or alternative:

(a) Videndum est, quandō, et cui, et quemadmodum, et quārē dēmus.   Cicero
Care must be taken, when, to whom, how, and why we give.

> **Dēmus, necne dēmus, in nostrā potestāte est.**   Cicero
> Whether we give or do not give is in our own power.

(b) Fac mē certiōrem quandō adfutūrus sīs.   Cicero
Let me know when you will be here.

> **Haud scio an quae dīxit sint vēra omnia.**   Terence
> I am inclined to think that all he has said is the truth.

(c) Ipse quis sit, utrum sit, an nōn sit, id quoque nescit.   Catullus
He knows not even this, who he himself is, whether he is or is not.

II. Adverbial Clauses

1. Consecutive Clauses

421 Consecutive clauses define the consequence of what is stated in the principal sentence. They are introduced by **ut**, with a verb in the subjunctive; if negative, by **nōn, ut nōn, ut nihil**, &c.

    Ut, in consecutive clauses, usually follows a demonstrative, **adeō, eō, hūc, ita, tam, sīc, tantus, tālis, tot**:

> **Nōn sum ita hebes ut istud dīcam.**   Cicero
> I am not so stupid as to say that.

> **Quis tam dēmēns est ut suā voluntāte maereat?**   Cicero
> Who is so mad as to mourn of his own free will?

> **Nēmō adeō ferus est ut nōn mītēscere possit.**   Horace
> No one is so savage that he cannot soften.

Note: Sometimes the demonstrative is omitted:

> **Arboribus cōnsita Ītalia est, ut tōta pōmārium videātur.**   Varro
> Italy is planted with trees, so as to seem one orchard.

> **Clārē et ut audiat hospes**   Persius
> Aloud, and so that a bystander may hear.

    Ut is used in a restrictive sense after **ita**:

> **Litterārum ita studiōsus erat ut poētās omnīnō neglegeret.**
> He was fond of literature, with the reservation that
> he cared nothing for poetry.   Cicero

    Ut consecutive sometimes follows **quam** with a comparative:

> **Īsocratēs māiōre ingeniō est quam ut cum Lysiā comparētur.**
> Isocrates is too great genius to be compared with Lysias.   Cicero

422 **Quīn,** but that, with the subjunctive, follows phrases and questions such as **nōn**, or **haud dubium est; quīs dubitat?**

> **Nōn dubium erat quīn tōtius Galliae plūrimum**
> **Helvetiī possent.**   Caesar
> There was no doubt that in the whole of Gaul
> the Helvetii were the most powerful.

> **Quis dubitet quīn in virtūte divitiae positae sint ?**   Cicero
> Who would doubt that riches consist in virtue?

Note 1: A **consecutive ut clause** sometimes depends on the phrase *tantum abest* followed by a substantival *ut* clause, the meaning being so far from... that...

**Tantum abest ut nostra mīrēmur, ut nōbīs nōn
satisfaciat ipse Dēmosthenēs.**   Cicero
So far am I from admiring my own productions, that
Demosthenes himself does not satisfy me.

Note 2: In consecutive clauses the sequence of tenses sometimes varies from the general rule. If it is intended to mark the consequence as something exceptional, the primary perfect in the clause may follow the imperfect or historic perfect in the principal sentence.

**Nōn adeō virtūtum sterile erat saeculum ut nōn et
bona exempla prōdiderit.**   Tacitus
The age was not so bare of virtues that it has not furnished
some good examples.

(For consecutive clauses with **quī**, see § 452.)

2. Final Clauses

423   Final clauses express the aim or purpose of the action of the principal sentence. They are formed by **ut**, or, if negative, by **nē ut nē,** with the subjunctive:

Veniō ut videam.   **Abiī nē vidērem.**
I come that I may see.   I went away that I might not see.

Ut iugulent hominēs surgunt dē nocte latrōnēs.   Juvenal
Robbers rise by night that they may kill men.

Scīpiō rūs abiit nē ad causam dīcendam adesset.   Cicero
Scipio went into the country that he might not be
present to defend his cause.

Ut, with a **final clause**, often corresponds to the demonstratives **eō, ideō, idcircō, proptereā, ob eam rem**:

Lēgum idcircō servī sumus ut līberī esse possīmus.   Cicero
We are the bondmen of the law in order that we may be free.

Note 1: A final clause with **ut** or **nē** is used parenthetically in such phrases as: *ut ita dīcam*, so to say; *nē longus sim*, not to be tedious.

Note 2: Nēdum, much less (not to say), may take a verb in the subjunctive:

**Mortālia facta peribunt,
Nēdum sermōnum stet honōs et grātia vīvāx.**   Horace
Mortal deeds will perish, much less can the honour and
popularity of words be lasting.

Note 3: The purpose of action is expressed in many ways, all equivalent to *ut* with a final clause. He sent ambassadors to seek peace may be rendered:

Lēgātoō mīsit ut pācem peterent.
"   "   quī pācem peterent.
"   "   ad petendam pācem.
"   "   petendī pācem causā.
"   "   petendae pācis causā.
"   "   petītum pācem.

Note 4: The sequence of tenses in final clauses always follows the general rule.

(For final clauses with **quī,** see § 453.)

3. Causal Clauses

424 **Causal clauses** assign a reason for the statement made in the principal sentence.

425 When an actual reason for a fact is given, **quod, quia, quoniam, quandō, quandō quidem, quātenus, sīquidem,** are used with the indicative (clauses in **ōrātiō oblīqua**, indirect speech, must be understood to be excepted from this and all following rules for the use of the indicative):

> Adsunt intereā quod officium sequuntur;
> tacent quia perīculum metuunt.   Cicero
> They are present because they follow duty; they are
> silent because they fear danger.

> Vōs, Quirītēs, quoniam iam nox est, in vestrā tēctā
> discēdite.   Livy
> Since it is already night, depart, you, Quirites,
> to your tents.

> Gerāmus, dīs bene iuvantibus, quandō ita
> vidētur, bellum.   Livy
> Let us wage war, the gods helping us, since so
> it seems good.

Note: **Quod, quia, quoniam** correspond to **eō, ideō, idcircō, proptereā:** *ideō quia uxor rūrī est,* Terence; for the reason that my wife is in the country.

426 **Cum**, since, with a causal clause takes the subjunctive:

> **Quae cum ita sint, ab Iove pācem ac veniam petō.**   Cicero
> Since these things are so, I ask of Jupiter peace
> and pardon.

Note 1: After *grātulor, laudō, gaudeō, doleō,* **cum**, for the reason that, takes the indicative, if the verb is in the first person:

> **Grātulor tibi cum tantum valēs apud Dōlabellam.**   Cicero
> I congratulate you that you have so much weight with Dolabella.

Note 2: **Nōn quod, nōn quia** take the indicative when they refer to the actual cause of a fact; if they refer to a cause thought of, not actual, they take the subjunctive, and a following clause, with **sed**, gives the true reason:

> **Nōn quia salvōs vellet, sed quia perīre causā indictā nōlebat.**   Livy
> Not because he wished them to be saved, but because he did
> not wish them to die without trial.

(For causal clauses with **quī**, see § 464.)

---

4. Temporal Clauses

427 **Temporal clauses** define the time when anything has happened, is happening, or will happen.

    The mood of a temporal clause is indicative if its connection with the principal sentence is one of time only, and if the time of each is independent of the other; but, if the time of the clause is thought of as depending on the time of the principal sentence, the mood of the clause is subjunctive.

428 **Ubī, ut** (when), **postquam, simulae, quandō, quotiēns, cum prīmum** are generally used with the indicative:

> **Olea ubī mātūra erit quam prīmum cōgī oportet.**   Cato
> When the olive is (shall be) ripe, it must be gathered in
> as soon as possible.

> **Ut Hostus cecidit, cōnfestim Rōmāna inclīnātur aciēs.**   Livy
> When Hostus fell, immediately the Roman line gave way.

> **Eō postquam Caesar pervēnit, obsidēs,**
> **arma poposcit.**   Caesar
> After Caesar had arrived there, he demanded
> hostages and arms.

429　Dum, dōnec, quoad, while, as long as, take the indicative:

> **Hominēs dum docent discunt.**　　　　　　Seneca
> Men learn while they teach.

> **Dum haec Veiīs agēbantur, interim Capitōlium**
> **in ingentī perīculō fuit.**　　　　　　Livy
> While these things were being done at Veii, the
> Capitol was meanwhile in dire peril.

> **Catō, quoad vīxit, virtūtum laude crēvit.**　　　　Nepos
> Cato increased in the renown of virtue as long
> as he lived.

430　Dum, while, is used with the historic present, the verb of the
principal sentence being in a historic tense:

> **Dum haec in colloquiō geruntur, Caesarī nūntiātum**
> **est equitēs accēdere.**　　　　　　Caesar
> While this parley was being carried on, it was announced
> to Caesar that the cavalry were approaching.

431　Dum, dōnec, quoad, until, and **antequam, priusquam,** before
that, take the indicative when the only idea conveyed is that of
time:

> **Milō in senātū fuit eō diē, quoad senātus**
> **dīmissus est.**　　　　　　Cicero
> On that day Milo was in the Senate until the Senate
> was dismissed.

> **Priusquam dē cēterīs rēbus respondeō, dē amīcitiā**
> **pauca dīcam.**　　　　　　Cicero
> Before I answer about other matters, I will say a few
> things about friendship.

432　But when the idea of expecting or waiting for something comes
in, they take the subjunctive:

> **Exspectāte dum cōnsul aut dictātor fīat Kaeso.**　　Livy
> Wait till Kaeso become consul or dictator.

433　Cum, if it expresses only the time when something happens,
　　is used with the indicative:

Dē tē cum quiēscunt probant; cum tacent clāmant. Cicero
Concerning you, when they are quiet they approve;
when they are silent they cry aloud.

**Cum Caesar in Galliam vēnit, alterīus factiōnis
prīncipēs erant Haeduī, alterīus Sēquānī.** Caesar
When Caesar came into Gaul, the Haedui were chiefs
of one faction, the Sequani of another.

The addition of the demonstratives **tum, tunc,** marks that
the times of the principal sentence and clause correspond more
exactly:

**Lituō Rōmulus regiōnēs dīrēxit tum cum urbem
condidit.** Cicero
Romulus marked out the districts with a staff at the time
when he founded the city.

**Tum cum in Āsiā rēs āmiserant, scīmus Rōmae
fidem concidisse.** Cicero
At the time when they had lost their power in Asia,
we know that credit sank at Rome.

434 If the action of the clause with **cum** takes place while that of
the principal sentence is continuing, or if it quickly follows it,
the clause sometimes contains the main statement, while the
principal sentence defines the time (**inverse cum**):

Iam vēr appetēbat cum Hannibal ex hībernīs mōvit. Livy
Spring was already approaching when Hannibal moved
out of his winter quarters.

Commodum discesserat Hilarus cum vēnit tabellārius. Cicero
Hilarus had just departed, when the letter-carrier came.

Note: **Cum** with the indicative sometimes expresses what has long been
and still continues:

Multī annī sunt cum Fabius in aere meō est. Cicero
For many years past Fabius has been in my debt.

435 Cum is used in narrative with the imperfect or pluperfect subjunctive, the verb of the principal sentence being in the perfect
or the historic present (**historic cum**).

Note: It is used with the Imperfect for contemporary time, with the pluperfect for prior time.

Cum trīgintā tyrannī oppressās tenērent Athēnās,
Thrasybūlus hīs bellum indīxit.   Nepos
When the thirty tyrants were oppressing Athens,
Thrasybulus declared war against them.

Cum Pausaniās dē templō ēlātus esset, cōnfestim
animam efflāvit.   Nepos
When Pausanias had been carried down from the temple,
he immediately expired.

Cum hostēs adessent, in urbem prō sē quisque
ex agrīs dēmigrant.   Livy
On the approach of the enemy, they move, each as he
best can, from the country into the city,

---

436   **Note:** In and after the Augustan age the subjunctive is used in temporal
clauses for repeated action like the Greek optative:

Id fētiālis ubī dīxisset, hastam in fīnēs hostium mittēbat.   Livy
As soon as a fetial (priest) had thus spoken, he used to fling
a spear within the enemies' boundaries.

Saepe cum aliquem vidēret minus bene vestītum,
suum amīculum dedit.   Nepos
Often when he saw someone ill dressed, he gave him
his own cloak.

But **cum is** used down to the time of Cicero and Caesar (inclusive) with the
indicative for repeated action; in reference to present time with the perfect,
in reference to past time with the pluperfect:

Verrēs cum rosam viderat, tum vēr esse arbitrabātur.   Cicero
Whenever Verres had seen a rose, he considered that it was spring.

---

5. Conditional Clauses

437   **Conditional statements** consist of a clause introduced by **sī,**
nisī, containing the preliminary condition, which is called the
protasis, and a principal sentence, containing that which follows
from the condition, which is called the apodosis. They have two
chief forms:

(1) where the indicative is used in both protasis and
apodosis;
(2) where the subjunctive is used in both.

A primary tense in the protasis is usually followed by a primary
in the apodosis, and a historic by a historic.

438 (1) The indicative is used in the **sī**-clause and in the principal sentence when the truth of the one statement depends on the truth of the other; if one is a fact, the other is also a fact:

Sī valēs, bene est.   Cicero
If you are in good health, all is well.

Parvī sunt forīs arma, nisi est cōnsilium domī.   Cicero
Arms are of little avail abroad, unless there is
counsel at home.

Sī fēceris id quod ostendis, magnam habēbō grātiam.   Cicero
If you do what you offer, I shall be very grateful.

Sī quod erat grande vās, laetī adferēbant.   Cicero
If there was any large vessel, they gladly produced it.

Sī licuit, patris pecūniam rēctē abstulit fīlius.   Cicero
If it was lawful, the son rightly took his father's money.

Note 1: A sī-clause with the indicative is often used with the imperative:

Sī mē amās, paullum hīc ades.   Horace
If you love me, stand by me here a short time.

Causam investīgātō, sī poteris.   Cicero
Search out the cause if you can.

Note 2: A sī-clause with the indicative also follows a subjunctive (optative use):

Moriar, sī vēra nōn loquor.   Cicero
May I die if I am not speaking the truth.

---

439 (2) The **subjunctive** is used both in the **sī**-clause and in the principal sentence when the condition is imaginary:

(a) The **present subjunctive** is used when the statements are thought of as possible, more or less probable:

Sexcenta memorem, sī sit ōtium.   Plautus
I could mention endless things, had I leisure.

Sī ā corōnā relictus sim, nōn queam dīcere.   Cicero
If I were forsaken by my circle of hearers, I
should not be able to speak.

(b) The **historic subjunctive** is used when the statements are purely imaginary; when there is no possibility of their becoming actual:

Sī foret in terrīs, rīdēret Dēmocritus.   Horace
Democritus would be laughing, if he were upon earth.

Sī id scīssem, numquam hūc tulissem pedem.　　　Terence
If I had known that, I should never have come hither.

Magis id dīcerēs, sī adfuissēs.　　　Cicero
You would have said so all the more, had you
been present.

440　Note 1: The indicative may be used in the principal sentence with a
sī-clause in the subjunctive,

(a) When the truth of the statement in the principal sentence is less closely
dependent on the sī-clause:

Tē neque dēbent adiuvāre sī possint, neque possunt sī velint. Cicero
They neither ought to help you if they could, nor can if they would.

(b) When the principal sentence expresses action begun, but hindered by
the condition in the sī-clause:

Numerōs meminī sī verba tenērem.　　　Virgil
I remember the measure if I could recall the words.

(c) With the past tenses of verbs of duty and possibility:

**Poterat utrumque praeclārē fierī, sī esset fidēs in
hominibus cōnsulāribus.**　　　Cicero
Both might have been done admirably if there had been
honour in men of consular rank.

(d) With the past tenses of *esse,* especially in periphrastic conjugation:

Sī ūnum diem morātī essētis, moriendum omnibus fuit.　　　Livy
If you had delayed a single day, you must all have died.

Et factūra fuit, pactus nisi Iuppiter esset.　　　Ovid
And she would have done it, if Jupiter had not agreed...

441　Note 2: Sī is sometimes omitted:

Ait quis, aiō; negat, negō.　　　Terence
If anyone affirms, I affirm; if anyone denies, I deny.

Note 3: **Nisi forte, nisi vērō** are ironical. **Sī nōn** throws the emphasis of the
negative on a single word:

Sī nōn feceris, ignōscam.
If you have not done it, I will pardon.

Note 4: **Sīve... sīve, seu... seu,** whether... or, or whether... if, are used for
alternative conditions:

Sīve retractābis, sīve properābis.
Whether you delay or hasten (it).

442 **Note 1:** The following table shows how to convert conditional sentences into ōrātio oblīqua when the apodosis become an infinitive clause, and the protasis is subordinate to it.

after a primary tense

1. Sī peccās (peccāstī), dolēs		1. sī peccēs (peccāveris), dolēre
2. Sī peccābis, dolēbis		2. sī peccēs, ⎫
3. Sī peccāveris, dolueris	⎫	3. sī peccāveris, ⎬ dolitūrum
4. Sī peccēs, doleās	⎬ Āiō tē,	4. sī peccātūrus sis, ⎭ esse
5. Sī peccārēs, dolērēs	⎭	5. sī peccarēs, dolitūrum esse
6. Sī peccāvissēs ⎫		6. sī peccāvissēs, ⎫ dolitūrum
7. Sī peccārēs ⎬ doluissēs		7. sī peccārēs, ⎭ fuisse
8. Sī peccāvissēs, dolērēs		8. sī pecāvissēs, dolitūrum fore

after a historic tense

Āiebam tē,
⎧ 1. sī peccārēs (pecāvissēs), dolēre
⎪ 2. ⎧ peccārēs, ⎫ dolitūrum
⎨ 3. sī ⎨ peccāvissēs, ⎬
⎪ 4. ⎩ peccātūrus essēs, ⎭ esse

The other four forms remain unchanged.

Note 2: Sī peccāvissēs, doluissēs is equivalent to sī peccāvissēs, dolitūrus fuistī; and this may either be converted, as above, into the infinitive clause, or into the subjunctive:

Āiō tē, sī peccāvissēs, dolitūrum fuisse.
Haec talia sunt ut, sī peccāvissēs, dolitūrus fueris.

6. Clauses of Proviso

443 **Dum, dummodo, modo,** if only, provided that, take the subjunctive:

Ōderint dum metuant.   Sueton.
Let them hate provided they fear.

Modo nē laudārent iracundiam.   Cicero
If only they did not praise wrath.

7. Concessive Clauses

444 **Concessive clauses** are introduced by **etsī, etiamsī, tametsī, quamquam, quamvīs, licet.**

Note: A concessive clause is so called because it concedes, or allows, an objection to the statement in the principal sentence. The rule for mood is the same as in conditional clauses.

445 **Etsī, etiamsī, tametsī** are used (a) with the indicative, (b) with
the subjunctive:

 (a) **Etiamsī tacent, satis dīcunt.**   Cicero
    Even if they are silent, they say enough.

 (b) **Etiamsī nōn is esset Caesar quī est, tamen**
    ōrnandus vidērētur,   Cicero
    Even if Caesar were not what he is, yet he
    would be considered worthy of honour.

446 **Quamquam** is used with the indicative:

  Quamquam festīnās, nōn est mora longa. Horace
  Although you are in haste, the delay is not long.

447 **Quamvīs, licet** are used with the subjunctive:

  Quamvīs nōn fuerīs suāsor, approbātor fuistī. Cicero
  Although you did not make the suggestion, you
  have given your approval.

  Licet vitium sit ambitiō, frequenter tamen
  causa virtūtum est.   Quintus
  Granted that ambition be a fault, yet often it is a
  cause of virtues.

---

448 Note 1: **Quamquam** is used by later writers with the subjunctive, and
quamvīs is often found in poets with the indicative.

Note 2: **Ut, nē, cum** are occasionally used in a concessive sense, and take
the subjunctive:

  Ut dēsint vīrēs, tamen est laudanda voluntās. Ovid
  Though strength be wanting, yet must the will be praised.

  Nē sit summum malum dolor, malum certē est. Cicero
  Granted that pain be not the greatest evil, is is surely an evil.

  Hīs cum facere nōn possent, loquī tamen et scrībere
  honestē et magnificē licēbat.   Cicero
  These, though they could not so act, were yet at liberty
  to speak and write virtuously and loftily.

Note 3: Concessive clauses are sometimes formed without conjunctions:

  Nātūram expellās furcā, tamen ūsque recurret. Horace
  Though you. drive out Nature with a pitchfork,
  yet she will always come back.

449 ## 8. Comparative Clauses

In **comparative clauses** the action or fact of the principal sentence is compared with a supposed condition; they are formed by **quasi (quam sī), tamquam, tamquam sī, ut sī, velut sī, ac sī** with the subjunctive:

Assimulābō quasi nunc exeam.   Terence
I will pretend to be just going out.

Tamquam dē rēgnō dīmicārētur ita concurrērunt.   Livy
They joined battle as if it were a struggle for the kingdom..

Tamquam sī claudus sim, cum fūstī est ambulandum. Plautus
I must walk with a stick as if I were lame.

Eius negōtium sīc velim cūrēs, ut sī esset rēs mea. Cicero
I would wish you to care for his business just as if
it were my affair.

Note: The demonstratives are **ita, lio, perinde, preinde, aequē, similiter.**

III. Adjectival Clauses

450 The **relative quī** in its simple use takes the indicative:

Est in Britanniā flūmen, quod appellātur Tāmesis. Caesar
There is in Britain a river which is called the Thames.

Quis fuit horrendōs prīmus quī prōtulit ēnsēs? Ovid
Who was (the man) who first invented terrible swords?

Note: This rule applies to correlatives, *quālis, quantus, quot,* and to universals, *quisquis, quīcumque,* &c.

Nōn sum quālis eram.   Horace
I am not what I was.

Quidquid erit, tibi erit.   Cicero
Whatever there is will be for you.

---

451 But the relative often introduces a **consecutive clause**, final or causal, with the subjunctive, corresponding to the adverbial clauses with similar meaning.

452 **Quī** with the subjunctive forms a **consecutive clause** with the meaning of such a kind that:

(a) After a demonstrative:

Nōn sum is quī hīs rēbus dēlēcter.   Cicero
I am not one to delight in these things.

Ea est Rōmāna gēns quae victa quiēscere nesciat.   Livy
The Roman race is such that it knows not how to rest
quiet under defeat.

Nihil tantī fuit quō vēnderēmus fidem nostram
et libertātem   Cicero
Nothing was of such value that we should sell for it
our faith and freedom.

(b) After indefinite and interrogative pronouns, or negatives,
nēmō, nihil, nūllus, etc.:

Est aliquid quod nōn oporteat, etiamsī licet.   Cicero
There is something which is not fitting, even if it is lawful.

Quis est cui nōn possit malum ēvenīre?   Cicero
Who is there to whom evil may not happen?

Nihil est quod tam deceat quam cōnstantia.   Cicero
Nothing is so becoming as consistency.

Note: Quīn for *quī nōn* is similarly used:

Nēmō est quīn audierit quemadmodum captae sint
Syrācūsae.   Cicero
There is no one who has not heard how Syracuse was taken.

(c) After **impersonal est**, there is, **sunt**, there are:

Sunt qui duōs tantum in sacrō monte creātōs
tribunōs esse dīcant.   Livy
There are who say that only two tribunes were elected
on the sacred mount.

but **est quī, sunt quī** take the indicative if they refer to definite antecedents:

Sunt item quae appellantur alcēs   Caesar
There are also (some animals) which are called elks.

(d) After **comparatives with quam**:

Māiōra dēlīquerant quam quibus ignōsci posset.   Livy
They had committed greater offences than could be pardoned.

(e) After **dignus, indignus**:

Dignus est quī imperet.   Cicero
He is worthy to govern.

453   Quī with the subjunctive forms a **final clause**, in order that:

Clūsīnī lēgātōs Rōmam, quī auxilium ā senātū
peterent, mīsēre.   Livy
The Clusini sent ambassadors to Rome to seek aid
from the senate.

Quō with a comparative introduces a **final clause**, and takes
the subjunctive:

Solōn furere se simulāvit, quō tūtior eius vīta esset.   Cicero
Solon pretended to be mad in order that his life might
be the safer.

454   Quī introduces a **causal clause**, and usually takes the subjunctive:

Miseret tui mē quī hunc faciās inimīcum tibi.   Terence
I pity you for making this man your enemy.

Note 1:   Quī causal is sometimes strengthened by **quippe, ut, utpote.**

Note 2:   Nōn quō is sometimes used for *nōn quod*:

Nōn quō quemquam plūs amem, eō fēcī.   Terence
I have not done it because I love anyone more.

Note 3:   Quī with the indicative forms a causal clause as a parenthesis:

Quā es prūdentiā, nihil tē fugiet.   Cicero
Such is your prudence, nothing will escape you.

---

455   The rules for the use of quī with indicative or subjunctive apply
also to the relative particles **quō** (to where, to which), **quā**
(where, in what way), **ubī** (where), **unde** (from where).

Locus, quō exercituī aditus nōn erat.   Caesar
A place to which there was no approach for the army.

Collēs, unde erat dēspectus in mare.   Caesar
The hills, from which there was a view over the sea.

Quā dūcitis, adsum.   Virgil
Where you lead, I am present.

Nē illī sit cēra, ubī facere possit litterās.   Plautus
Let him have no wax on which to write.

A clause introduced by a relative particle may be adverbial, unless the clause distinctly qualifies a noun in the principal sentence:

Antōnius quō sē verteret nōn habēbat.   Cicero
Antony had no place to which he could turn.

---

456   **Note: Quī** with the subjunctive sometimes limits a statement: *quod sciam*, so far as I know; *omnium quōs quidem cognōverim*, of all those at least whom I have known.

457   **Note:** The **relative** is often used at the beginning of a principal sentence to show the connection with something which has gone before; *quō factō*, this being done; *quā dē causā*, for which reason; *quod dīcis*, as to that which you say.

ŌRĀTIŌ OBLĪQUA

458   **Ōrātiō oblīqua** (indirect speech) is used in reports, whether short or long, of speeches, letters, &c. Indirect statement, command, and question are often contained in the report of one speech by historians, especially by Caesar, Livy, and Tacitus.

459   In **indirect statement** the principal verbs are changed from the Indicative to the infinitive in the same tense:

Direct	Indirect
Rōmulus urbem condidit.	**Narrant Rōmulum urbem condidisse.**
Romulus founded the city.	They say that Romulus founded the city.

---

460   **Note:** If the actual words of the speaker or writer are quoted, they are often introduced with **Inquit**, he says, following the first word:

**Rōmulus haec precātus, 'hinc,' inquit, 'Rōmānī, Iuppiter
iterāre pugnam iubet.'**   Livy
When Romulus had thus prayed, 'Hence,' he says, 'Romans,
Jupiter commands (you) to renew the battle.'

---

461   In **indirect commands**, the subjunctive (usually in the imperfect, but sometimes in the present tense) takes the place of the imperative of direct commands:

Direct	Indirect
Īte, inquit, creāte cōnsulēs ex plēbe.	**(Hortātus est:) īrent**
Go, he says, elect consuls from the people.	**creārent cōnsulēs ex plēbe.**

462 In **indirect questions in the second person,** the verbs are in the subjunctive (usually in the imperfect or pluperfect tense, but sometimes in the present or perfect):

Direct	Indirect
Quid agis? inquit. Cūr nōn anteā pugnam commīsistī?	**Quid ageret? Cūr nōn anteā pugnam commīsisset?**
What are you about? he says. Why have you not joined battle before?	

463 **Indirect questions** in the first or third person are generally expressed by the accusative and infinitive:

Direct	Indirect
Cūr ego prō hominibus ignāvīs sanguinem profūdī? Num semper hostēs ad pugnam cessābunt?	**Cūr sē prō hominibus ignāvīs sanguinem profūdisse? Num semper hostēs ad pugnam cessātūrōs?**
Why have I shed my blood for cowards? Will the enemy always be slow to fight?	

Note: Such questions are really statements put for rhetorical effect in an interrogative form. 'Why have I shed my blood for cowards?' means, 'I have shed my blood for cowards – why?' i.e. 'I have shed my blood for cowards to no purpose.' 'Will the enemy always be slow to fight? means 'The enemy will not always be slow to fight.'

---

464 The pronouns **ego, mē, nōs, meus, noster** of **ōrātiō rēcta** (direct speech) are converted in **ōrātiō oblīqua** into **sē, suus.**
    Tu, te, vos, tuus, vester, are converted into **ille, illum, illī, illōs, illīus, illōrum:**

Direct	Indirect
Ego tē prō hoste habēbō; sociī quoque nostrī amīcitiam tuam exuent.	**Dixit sē illum prō hoste habitūrum; sociōs quoque suōs illīus amīcitiam exūtūrōs.**
I shall regard you as an enemy; our allies also will throw off your friendship.	

465 The reflexive pronoun, **sē, suus,** in compound sentences is often used to refer, not to the subject of the principal sentence (§ 316), but to the subject of the clause in which it stands:

> **Nerviōs hortātur nē suī līberandī occāsiōnem dīmittant.** Caesar
> He urges the Nervii that they should not lose the
> opportunity of freeing themselves.

> **Rēx supplicem monuit ut cōnsuleret sibi.**
> The king warned the suppliant that he should take
> heed to himself.

466 Sometimes **ipse** is used for the sake of clear distinction.

> [Caesar asked the soldiers:]
> **Quid tandem verērentur aut cūr dē suā**
> **virtūte aut dē ipsīus dīligentiā dēspērārent?**   Caesar
> What cause had they to fear, why did they despair either
> of their own bravery or of his carefulness?

SUBORDINATE CLAUSES IN ŌRĀTIŌ OBLĪQUA

467 **Substantival clauses** may have clauses subordinate to them; if the verb in such clauses is finite, it is generally in the subjunctive mood, and the construction is called **suboblique.** This construction is seen in the following examples:

> **Caesar ad mē scrīpsit gratīssimum sibi esse**
> **quod quiēverim.**   Cicero
> Caesar has written to me that it is very pleasing to him
> that I have remained quiet.

> **Ais, quōniam sit nātūra mortālis, immortālem**
> **etiam esse oportēre.**   Cicero
> You say that, since there is a mortal nature, there must
> also be an immortal one.

> **Quotiēns patriam vidēret, totiēns sē beneficium**
> **meum vidēre dīxit.**   Cicero
> He said that, as often as he saw his country, so often
> did he see my service.

Sapientissimum esse dīcunt eum, cui, quod opus sit,
ipsī veniat in mentem; proximē accēdere illum,
quī alterīus bene inventīs obtemperet.   Cicero
They say that the wisest man is he to whose mind
whatever is needful occurs; that the next to him is he
who turns to account the useful discoveries of another.

Note 1: A relative clause in *ōrātiō oblīqua*, if added merely by way of explanation, may be in the indicative:

Xerxem certiōrem fēcī id agī ut pōns, quem in Hellēspontō
fēcerat, dissolverētur,   Nepos
I sent Xerxes word that a plot was being arranged that the bridge
(which he had made over the Hellespont) might be broken down.

The words 'which he had made over the Hellespont' were not part of the
message to Xerxes, but are added by the writer for explanation.

Note 2: Dum, while, is used with the indicative, even in *ōrātiō oblīqua:*

Vident sē, dum lībertātem sectantur, in servitūtem prōlāpsōs.
They see that, while striving for liberty, they have themselves fallen
into slavery.

---

468 A finite verb subordinate to a subjunctive is usually in the subjunctive :

Mirāris sī nēmō praestet quem nōn mereāris amōrem? Horace
Are you surprised if no one shows you the love which
you do not deserve?

Utinam tunc essem nātus quandō Rōmānī dōna
accipere coepissent.   Sallust
Would that I had been born when the Romans began
to receive gifts.

469 A clause may be virtually oblique, with the verb in the subjunctive (**virtual ōrātiō oblīqua**), when it contains the speaker's
statement of another person's words or opinions, for which he
does not make himself responsible. If the speaker made the
statement his own, as being one of fact, the verb would be in
the indicative:

Laudat Āfricānum Panaetius quod fuerit abstinēns.   Cicero
Panaetius praises Africanus because (as he says) he was
temperate.

Caesar Haeduōs frūmentum, quod pollicitī essent, flāgitābat.   Caesar
Caesar demanded of the Haedui the corn which (he reminded them) they had promised.

Themistoclēs noctū ambulābat, quod somnum capere nōn posset.   Cicero
Themistocles used to walk at night because (as he said) he could not sleep.

Alium rogantēs rēgem misēre ad Iovem, Inūtilis quōniam esset quī fuerat datus.   Phaedr.
They (the frogs) sent envoys to Jupiter to ask for another king, since (as they complained) the one who had been given was useless.

NARRATIVE IN ŌRĀTIŌ OBLĪQUA

470 Direct Statement

(1) Ars eārum rērum est quae sciuntur; ōrātōris autem omnis āctiō opīniōnibus, nōn scientiā, continētur; nam et apud eōs dīcimus quī nesciunt, et ea dīcimus quae nescīmus ipsī. Cicero

Art belongs to the things which are known; but the whole sphere of an orator is in opinion, not in knowledge; for we both speak in the presence of those who know not, and speak of that which we ourselves know not.

Indirect Statement

(Antonius apud Ciceronem docet:) Artem eārum rērum esse quae sciantur; ōrātōris autem omnem āctiōnem opiniōne, nōn scientiā, continērī; quia apud eōs dīcat quī nesciant: et ea dīcat quae ipse nesciat.

(Antonius teaches in Cicero:) That art belongs to the things which are known; but that the whole sphere of an orator is in opinion, not in knowledge; because he both speaks before those who know not; and speaks of that which he himself knows not.

(2) Cum Germānīs Haeduī semel atque iterum armīs contendērunt; magnam calamitātem pulsī accēpērunt, omnem nōbilitātem, omnem equitātum āmīsērunt. Sed peius victōribus Sēquanīs quam Haeduīs victīs accidit; proptereā quod Ariovistus, rēx Germānōrum, in eōrum finibus cōnsēdit, tertiamque partēm agrī Sēquanī, quī est optimus tōtīus Galliae, occupāvit. Ariovistus barbarus, īrācundus, temerārius est, nōn possunt eius imperia diūtius sustinērī.

Locūtus est prō Haeduīs Divitiacus: Cum Germanīs Haeduōs semel atque iterum armīs contendisse; magnam calamitātem pulsōs accēpisse, omnem nōbilitātem, omnem equitātum āmīsisse. Sed peius victōribus Sēquanīs quam Haeduīs victīs accidisse; proptereā quod Ariovistus, rēx Germānōrum, in eōrum finibus cōnsēdisset, tertiamque partem agrī Sēquanī, qui esset optimus tōtīus Galliae, occupavisset. Ariovistum esse barbarum, īrācundum, temerārium, non posse eius imperia diūtius sustinērī.

The Haedui have repeatedly fought with the Germans; they have been defeated and have suffered great misfortune; they have lost all their nobles and all their cavalry. But worse has befallen the conquering Sequani than the conquered Haedui, for Ariovistus, king of the Germans, has settled in their dominions and occupied a third part of their territory, which is the best in all Gaul. Ariovistus is barbarous, passionate and violent; his commands can no longer be endured.

Divitiacus said on behalf of the Haedui that the Haedui had fought repeatedly with the Germans; that, having been defeated, they had suffered great misfortune (and) had lost all their nobles, all their cavalry. But that worse had befallen the conquering Sequani than the conquered Haedui, for Ariovistus, king of the Germans, had settled in their dominions and had occupied a third part of their territory, which was the best in all Gaul. Ariovistus was barbarous, passionate and violent; his commands could no longer be endured.

(3) Cōnsulēs scrīpta ad Caesarem mandāta remittunt, quōrum haec erat summa:
'In Galliam revertere, Arīminō excēde, exercitūs dīmitte; quae sī fēceris, Pompeius in Hispāniās ībit.'

In Galliam reverterētur, Arīminō excēderet, exercitūs dīmitteret; quae sī fēcisset, Pompeium in Hispāniās itūrum.

The Consuls sent back to Caesar written instructions, of which this was the sum total: 'Return into Gaul, quit Ariminum, and disband your armies; when you have done these things, Pompey will go into Spain.'

(4) Thrasybūlus, cum exercitus
trīgintā tyrannōrum fugeret, magnā
vōce exclamat:

'Cūr mē victōrem fugitis? Cīvium	Cūr sē victōrem fugiant? Cīvium
hanc mementōte aciem, nōn	illam meminerint aciem, nōn
hostium esse; trīgintā ego dominīs,	hostium esse; trīgintā sē dominīs,
nōn cīvitātī, bellum īnferō.'	non cīvitātī, bellum inferre.

*Thrasybulus, when the army of the thirty tyrants was in flight, cried aloud:
'Why do you fly from me as your conqueror? Remember that this is an army of
fellow-citizens, not of foreign enemies; I am waging war on the thirty tyrants,
not on the community.'*

(5) Ōrō vōs, Veientēs (inquit), nē me	Orat Tarquinius Veientēs nē sē
extorrem egentem, ex tantō modo	extorrem egentem ex tantō modo
rēgnō cum līberīs adolescēntibus	rēgnō cum līberīs adolēscentibus
ante oculōs vestrōs perīre sinātis.	ante oculōs suōs perīre sinerent:
Aliī peregrē in rēgnum Rōmam	aliōs peregrē in rēgnum Rōmam
accītī sunt; ego rēx, augēns bellō	accītōs; sē rēgem augentem bellō
Rōmānum imperium, ā proximīs	Rōmōnum imperium, ā proximīs
scelerātā coniūrātiōne pulsus	scelerātā coniūrātiōne pulsum...
sum. Patriam rēgnumque meum	patriam sē rēgnumque suum
repetere, et persequī ingrātōs cīvēs	repetere et persequī ingrātōs cīvēs
volō. Ferte opem, adiuvāte; vestrās	velle: ferrent opem, adīuvārent; suās
quoque veterēs iniūriās ultum īte,	quoque veterēs iniuriās ultum īrent,
totiēns caesās legiōnēs, agrum	totiēns caesās legiōnēs, agrum
adēmptum.	adēmptum. Livy

I entreat you, men of Veii (said Tarquin), not to let me with my young
children die before your eyes, banished in destitution from a kingdom
lately so great. Others were fetched to Rome from abroad to reign. I,
their king, while enlarging by war the Roman empire, was expelled by a
wicked conspiracy of my nearest kinsmen. I wish to reclaim my country
and my kingdom, and to punish ungrateful citizens. Give me help, assist
me; hasten to avenge also your own old wrongs, your legions so often
slaughtered, your land taken from you.

PROSODY

471 Prosody treats of the quantity of syllables and the laws of metre. We shall use the terms **light** and **heavy** for syllables in preference to **short** and **long** avoid confusion with vowel length.

I. GENERAL RULES OF QUANTITY

1. A syllable is **light** when it contains a short vowel followed by a simple consonant or by another vowel: as *păter, dĕus.*

2. A syllable is **heavy** when it contains a long vowel or diphthong: *frāter, caedēs, nēmō*

3. A syllable containing a short vowel is **heavy** when it is followed by two consonants, or by **x** or **z**: *canto, simplex, oryza.*

Exception: A syllable containing a short vowel before a stop followed by a liquid becomes doubtful: *lugubre, tenebrae, triplex.*

---

4. A syllable containing a long vowel or diphthong becomes light before another vowel, or before *h* followed by a vowel: *prŏavus, trăho, præesse.* But in Greek words the syllable reamins heavy: *āēr, Aenēas, Enȳo.*

Exceptions: In *fīō, Gāius, dīus, diēī, Rhēa (Silvia),* the syllable remains heavy. Also note that *prae* in compounds is the only Latin word in which a diphthong occurs before a vowel.

---

5. A syllable is called **doubtful** when it is found in poetry to be sometimes heavy, sometimes light: *Diāna, fideī, reī,* and genitives in *-ius.*

6. The quantity of a stem syllable is kept, as a rule, in compounds and derivatives: *cădō occĭdō, rătus irrĭtus, flūmen flūmineus.* Exceptions to this rule are numerous, *lūceo, lŭcerna.*

472   II. RULE FOR MONOSYLLABLES

Most monosyllables are **heavy:** *dā, dēs, mē, vēr, sī, sīs, sōl, nōs, tū, vīs, mūs.* However, there are many exceptions.

473   ## III. RULES FOR FINAL SYLLABLES

1. Final a is short, and thus the syllable is light.

Exceptions: Ablatives of first declension: *mēnsā, bonā;* vocative of Greek names in *ās, Aenēā;* and of some in *ēs, Anchīsā;* indeclinable numerals, *trīgintā;*. imperatives of first conjugation: *amā* (but *pută*); most particles in -a; *frūstrā, intereā.* (but *ita, quia,* short).

2. Final e is short and the syllable is light: *lege, timēte, carēre.*

Exceptions: Ablatives of the fifth declension: *rē, diē,* with the derivatives *quārē, hodiē.* Cases of many Greek nouns; also *famē.* Adverbs formed from adjectives: *miserē;* also *ferē, fermē* (but *bene, male, facile, impūne, temere,* short). Imperatives of the second conjugation: *monē* (but *cave* is doubtful). Also the interjection *ohē.*

3. Final i is long and the syllable is heavy: *dīcī, plēbī, dolī.*

Exceptions: Vocatives and datives of Greek nouns; *Chlōri, Thyrsidi;* but datives sometimes long: *Paridī.* Particles; *sīcubi, nēcubi, nisi, quasī. Mihi, tibi, sibi, ubi,* and *ibi* are doubtful.

4. Final o is long and the syllable is heavy: *virgō, multō, iuvō.*

Exceptions: *Duo, ego, modo, cito,* and a few velbs: *puto, scio, nescio.* In the Silver Age (approximately the first and second centuries of the Christian era) **ō** was often shortened in verbs and nouns.

5. Final u is long and the syllable is heavy: *cantū, dictū, diū.*

6. Finals in c are long and the syllable is heavy: *illīc;* except *nec* and *dōnec.*

7. Finals in l, d, t are short, the syllables light: *Hannibal, illud, amāvit.*

8. Finals in n are short and the syllables are light: *Īlion, agmen.*

Exceptions: Many Greek words: *Hymēn, Ammōn.*

9. Finals in r are short, the syllables light: *calcar, amābitur, Hector.*

Exceptions: Many Greek words: *āēr, crātēr;* and compounds of *pār: dispār, impār.*

10. **Finals in as** are long, the syllables heavy: *terrās, Menalcās.*

Exceptions: Greek nouns of third declension: *Arcas* (gen. *-adis*) and accusative plural *lampadas; anas,* a duck.

11. **Finals in es** are long, syllables heavy: *nūbēs, pariēs, vidērēs.*

Exceptions: Cases of Greek nouns: *Arcades, Nāiades.* Nominatives of a few substantives and adjectives with dental stems in **et, it,** or **id:** *seges, pedes, obses, dīves;* also *penes.* Compounds of *es: ades, potes.*

12. **Finals in is** are short, the syllables light: *dīceris, ūtilis, ēnsis.*

Exceptions: Datives and ablatives in **īs,** including *grātīs, forīs.* Accusatives in **īs:** *navīs;* some Greek nouns in **īs:** *Salamis. Sanguis, pulvis,* are doubtful. 2nd Pers. sing. pres. ind. 4th conj. *audīs;* compounds of *vīs, sīs;* also *velīs, mālīs, nōlīs.* In 2nd pers. sing. fut. perf. the ending is doubtful: *dixeris.*

13. **Finals in os** are long, syllables heavy: *ventōs, custōs, sacerdōs.*

Exceptions: Greek words in **os** (ος): *Dēlos, Arcados;* also *compos, impus, exos.*

14. **Finals in us** are light: *holus, intus, amāmus.*

Exceptions: Nominatives from long stems of third declension are long: *virtūs, tellūs, incūs, iuventūs;* the contracted cases of the fourth declension: *artūs, gradūs;* and a few Greek words: *Dīdūs, Sapphūs* (genitive).

15. The Greek words *chelys, Tiphys, Erīnys* have the final syllable light and the vocative ending **y.**

474   IV. ON THE LAWS OF METRE

A verse (*versus,* line) is composed of a certain number of feet. A foot consists of two or more syllables, of which one has the

ictus or principal accent, said to be in **arsis** (rise); the other syllable or syllables are said to be in **thesis** (fall). The principal feet in Latin poetry are the following:

Iambus, one light and one heavy syllable (⏑ -), *carō.*

Trochee, one heavy and one light syllable (- ⏑), *arma.*

Dactyl, one heavy and two light syllables (- ⏑ ⏑), *lītora.*

Anapaest, two light and one heavy syllable (⏑ ⏑ -), *patulae.*

Spondee, two heavy syllables (- -), *fātō.*

Tribrach, light short syllables (⏑ ⏑ ⏑), *temere.*

The spondee often takes the place of the dactyl in dactylic verse. It may also take the place of the iambus or trochee in certain parts of an iambic or trochaic verse.

The tribrach can take the place of the iambus or the trochee in any place but the last, but is more rarely used.

A light syllable in versification constitutes one **mora** or 'time.' A heavy syllable (= two light) constitutes two morae, or 'times.'

The iambus, trochee, tribrach are feet of three morae; dactyl, anapaest, spondee, are feet of four morae.

A vowel is dropped at the end of a word if there be a vowel at the beginning of the next word: *Phyllid' am' ant' aliās,* for' *Phyllida amō ante aliās;*, this is called **elision** (*synaloepha*).

A vowel and **m** are cut off at the end of a word if there be a vowel at the beginning of the next word: *Ō cūras homin' Ō quant' est in rēbus ināne,* for *Ō cūras hominum Ō quantum est in rēbus ināne* This is called **ecthlipsis**.

A vowel unelided in such a position is said to be in **hiatus**:

Ter sunt | cōnā|tī īm|pōnere | Pēlio | Ossam.

475

V. METRE AND RHYTHM.

(a) Metre

Metre (*metrum,* measure) is used in two different senses:

1. It means any system of versification: which may take its name either (a) from the foot which prevails in it: dactylic, iambic, trochaic, anapaestic, metre; or (b) from the subjects of which it treats: heroic (elegiac) metre; or (c) from the musical instrument to which it was sung: lyric metres; or (d) from the poet who is said to have invented or chiefly used it: Alcaic metre (from Alcaeus), Sapphic (from Sappho), etc.
2. Some part of a verse is called a metre. In dactylic and some other verses each foot constitutes a metre. In iambic, trochaic, and anapaestic verses, two feet constitute a metre.

Note: Hence a verse gains a name from the number of such metres.

A verse with two metres is called dimeter.

A verse with two metres is called trimeter.

A verse with two metres is called tetrameter.

A verse with two metres is called pentameter.

A verse with two metres is called hexameter.

A verse which has its metres complete is said to be acatalectic (unclipped). If its metres are incomplete, it is catalectic (clipped).

476   **(b) Rythm**

Harmonious order of words is called rhythm. Prose has rhythm as well as verse; but that of verse is called poetic rhythm. The dividing of a verse according to rhythm is called scanning or scansion. The method of scansion may be shown by two dactylic hexameters of Virgil :

1	2	3	4	5	6

(a) Tītyre | tū ‖ patu | lae ‖ recu | bāns ‖ sub | tegmine | fāgī

(b) Fōrmō | sam ‖ reso | nāre ‖ do | cēs ‖ Ama | ryllida | silvās.

Note: The numerals and single strokes show the six feet or metres of the hexameter.

Caesura means the division of a word before the ending of a foot. There are three caesuras in each of the verses (a), (b), marked by a short double stroke. A verse without caesura is unrhythmical and inadmissible. Caesura after a long syllable is called strong, and is most frequent. Caesura after a short syllable is called weak, as that in the third foot of (b) after -nāre (see dactylic hexameter below). The ending of word and foot together is called **diaeresis**, as in *Tityre* and *tegmine* in line (a) above.

VI. DACTYLIC, IAMBIC AND SOME LYRIC SYSTEMS OF VERSE

477

(a) Dactylic Hexameter:

This metre has six feet. The first four may be dactyls or spondees. The fifth must be a dactyl (rarely a spondee). The sixth a spondee or trochee (the last syllable in a verse heavy or light).

Scheme

1	2	3	4	5	6
– ∪ ∪	– ∪ ∪	– ∪ ∪	– ∪ ∪	– ∪ ∪	– ∪
– –	– –	– –	– –	– ∪ ∪	– –

(See the examples, a, b, § 476)

Note: A verse called **hypermeter** (a syllable over-measure) is occasionally found, the syllable in excess being elided before the initial vowel of the next line:

Aerea | cui gradi|bus sur|gēbant | līmina nexae|qu[e]
Aere tra|bēs...

The caesura by far most common in dactylic hexameters is that in the third foot (called **penthemimeral**), which is generally strong, as in (a) after *patulae,* but occasionally weak, as in (b) after *resonāre.*

Next in importance is that in the fourth foot, called hephthemimeral, which is sometimes the chief caesura of the verse, as:

(c) clāmōr|ēs simul | horren|dōs ‖ ad | siīdera | tollit.

The **trihemimeral caesura** in the second foot often contributes to the rhythm usefully, as after *clāmōrēs* (c).

Note: *Hemimeris* means 'a half.' Hence, *Trihemimeral* means 'after three half-feet': clā-mōr-ēs; *Penthemimeral* means 'after five half-feet': hīc il-lum vī-dī; *Hephthemimeral* means 'after seven half-feet': quam lūnō fertur terrīs. This notation counts two short syllables as one half-foot: Tīt**yre** tū patu-*lae* recu-bāns.

The **heroic measure** of epic poets, Virgil, Lucan, &c., consists of dactylic hexameters only.

478 (b) Dactylic Pentameter

This verse consists of two parts, called **penthemimers**, which are kept distinct. The first penthemimer contains two feet (dactyls or spondees) and a long syllable. The second contains also two feet (both dactyls) and a long syllable.

Scheme

Example: **tū domi|nus tū | vir‖tū mihi | frāter e|rās.**

This verse is not used alone, but follows a hexameter in the elegiac distich:

> **Dōnec eris fēlīx, multōs numerābis amīcōs,**
> **Tempora sī fuerint nūbrla, sōlus eris.**

The chief Elegiac poets are Ovid, Tibullus, and Propertius.

479 (c) Iambic Trimeter or Sēnārius

This metre has six feet. Each may be an iambus:

> **Suīs | et i|psa Rō|ma vīribus | ruit.**

But a spondee may stand in the first, third, and fifth foot; and (rarely) a dactyl or anapaest in the first. A tribrach sometimes takes the place of an iambus, except in the two last feet.

Scheme

1	2	3	4	5	6
◡ –	◡ –	◡ –	◡ –	◡ –	◡ –
– –		– –		– –	
◡ ◡ ◡	◡ ◡ ◡	◡ ◡ ◡	◡ ◡ ◡		
– ◡ ◡					
◡ ◡ –					

Examples

(a) lābun|tur al|tīs ‖ in|terim | rīpīs | aquae.
(b) Cānid|a brevi|bus ‖ im|plicā|ta vī|perīs.
(c) positōs|que ver|nās ‖ dī|tis ex|āmen | domūs.

The usual caesura is after the first syllable of the third foot. Another less usual, is after the first syllable of the fourth foot; as,

Ībē|ricīs | perūs|te ‖ fū|nibus | latus.

The trimeter may form a distinct measure.

480   ## (d) Iambic Dimeter

This verse leaves out the third and fourth feet of the trimeter, with which it is used to form an iambic distich:

pater|na rū|ra bō|bus ex|ercet | suis,
solū|ltus om|ni fae|nore.

Horace uses this distich more often in his Epodes than any other measure.

481   ## (e) Strophic Metres

The lyric poets Horace and Catullus used more than twenty metres. But we shall notice here only the **Sapphic** and **Alcaic** stanzas, each of four lines.

Note: Anacrusis is a short or long syllable, which introduces the scansion of a verse. **Base** is a foot of two syllables (spondee, iambus or trochee) which introduces the scansion. These may be represented in English:

Anacrusls   1   2   3
                     O | Mari|on's a | bonnie | lass
Base   1   2   3
                     O my | Mari|on's a | bonnie | lass

A double base means two feet, each of two syllables, introducing the scansion.

---

482 1. The Sapphic Stanza

The stanza is scientifically scanned in Latin by three verses of this form:

Double Base		Dactyl		Trochee		Trochee or spondee
– ◡ – –	‖	– – ◡	|	– ◡	|	– ◡ *or* – –

followed by a verse called Adonius,

Dactyl		Trochee or spondee
– ◡	|	– ◡ *or* – –

1. Terruit gen|tēs grave | nē re|dīret

2. Saecu|lum Pyr|rhae novia | mōnstra | questae

3. Omne | cum Prō|tus peciis | egit | altōs

4. Visere | montes.

Sappho used two trochees as the double base; but Latin poets always lengthened the fourth syllable.

The strong caesura after the fifth syllable is most frequent, but the weak caesura after the sixth is occasionally used for variety.

Nōn semel dīcēmus || Iō triumphe.

The Adonian verse is so closely united with the third line that hiatus at the close of this line is unusual, and words are sometimes divided between the two:

Thrāciō bacchante magis sub inter-
lūnia ventō.

Note: A hypermeter also occurs (§ 471, note).

Dissidēns plēbī numerō beātō | r(um)
Eximit virtūs.

483 2. The Alcaic Stanza

	Anacrusis		Double Base		Dactyl		Trochee		
1 2	⏒	|	– ◡ – –	‖	– ◡ ◡	|	– ◡	|	⏓
	Anacrusis		Trochee		Spondee		Trochee		Trochee
3	⏓	|	– ◡	|	– –	|	– ◡	|	– ⏓
4	– ◡ ◡		|		– ◡ ◡	|	– ◡	|	– ⏓

1. Quī | rōre pūrō | Castali|ae la|vit.
2. Crī|nēs so||lūtōs | quī Lyci|ae te|net
S. Dū|mēta | nātā|lemque | silvam
4. Dēlius | et Pata|reus A|pollō.

Rules for the Rhythm of the Alcaic Stanza

(a) First and Second Lines

(1) A short syllable at the beginning is rare.

(2) The fifth syllable generally ends a word; but an elision often occurs after it, as:

Quō Styx et invīs|(ī) horrida Taenarī.

(3) The fifth and the last syllables are rarely monosyllables.

(b) Third Line

(1) The first syllable is seldom short.

(2) The line rarely begins with a word of four syllables, and only when elision follows, as:

Fūnāli(a) et vectēs et arcūs.

It never begins with two dissyllables.

(3) The line should not end with a word of four syllables, rarely with two dissyllables.

(4) No monosyllable should end the line except (rarely) *et* or *in*, with an elision:

Cum flōre Maecēnās rosār(um), et
Incūde diffingās retūs(um) in

(c) Fourth Line.

(1) If the first dactyl ends a word, the second should end in the middle of a word.

(2) A weak caesura in the second dactyl should be avoided, but is sometimes justified by the sense of the passage:

Iuppiter ipse ruēns tumultū.
Stēsichorīque gravēs Camēnae.

Note: Hypermeters occur only twice in Horace:

Sors exitūra, et nōs in aeter|n(um)
Exsili(um) impositūra cymbae.

Cum pāce dēlābentis Etrus|c(um)
In mare.

But in his third and fourth books he avoids ending a verse with a vowel or **m** before a verse in the same stanza beginning with a vowel.

DERIVED AND COMPOUNDED WORDS

Many **substantives** are derived from verbs, adjectives and other substantives. The chief classes of substantives derived from verbs are the following:

484   SUBSTANTIVES FROM THE VERB STEM

-a, denoting the agent: *scrība*, notary (*scrībō*) ; *advena*, new-comer (*advenio*) ; *convīva*, guest (*convīvō*).

-or, abstract words denoting action or feeling: *amor*, love (*amō*); *timor*, fear (*timeō*); *clamor*, outcry (*clāmō*); *terror*, terror (*terreō*).

-ium, denoting action or effect: *gaudium*, joy (*gaudeō*); *ingenium*, mind (*ingignō*); *iūdicium*, judgment (*iudicō*, for *iūs-dicō*); *naufragium*, shipwreck (*naufragiō*, formed from the stems of *nāvis*, ship, and *frangō*, break).

-iēs, denoting a thing formed: *aciēs*, line of battle (*aceō*); *faciēs*, face, form (*faciō*); *effigiēs*, likeness (*effingō*); *speciēs*, appearance (*speciō*); *seriēs*, order (*serō*).

-es: *sēdēs*, seat (*sedeō*) ; *nubēs*, cloud (*nūbō*).

-iō, denoting the thing acted on: *regiō*, region (*regō*); *legiō*, legion (*legō*); *opīniō*, opinion (*opīnor*).

-men, denoting the instrument or the thing done: *agmen*, column (*agō*); *tegmen*, covering (*tegō*).

-mentum: *documentum*, document (*doceō*); *īnstrūmentum*, instrument (*īnstruō*).

-bulum, -brum, denoting the instrument or object: *vocābulum*, name (*vocō*); *vēnābulum*, hunting-spear (*vēnor*); *flābrum*, blast (*flō*, stem *flā-*).

-culum, -crum: curriculum, course (*currō*); *spectāculum*, spectacle (*spectō*); sepulcrum, tomb (*sepeliō*).

-īle, denoting the instrument: *sedīle*, seat (*sedeō*); *cubīle*, couch (*cubō*).

485　　　　　　FROM THE SUPINE STEM

-tor, -sor, denoting the agent: *arātor*, ploughman (*arō*); *auctor*, author (*augeō*); *victor*, victor (*vincō*) ; *auditor*, hearer (*audiō*); *dictātor*, dictator (*dictō*); *spōnsor*, surety (*spondeō*); *cursor*, runner (*currō*). A few nouns in **-tor** form a feminine in **-trīx**, as *victrīx*.

-tus, -sus, denoting action: *ēventus*, event (*ē-veniō*); *mōtus*, motion, (*moveō*); *sonitus*, sound (*sonō*); *cursus*, running (*currō*); *plausus*, clapping (*plaudō*) ; *lūsus*, game (*lūdō*).

-tūra, -sūra, denoting function or result of action: *dictātūra*, dictatorship (*dictō*); *cultūra*, culture (*colō*); *pictūra*, picture (*pingō*); *tōnsūra*, tonsure (*tondeō*) ; *caesūra*, dividing (*caedō*).

-tiō, -siō, abstract: *āctio*, action (*agō*) ; *cōgitātiō*, thought (*cōgitō*); *relātiō*, relation (*referō*); *vīsiō*, sight (*videō*); *pēnsiō*, payment (*pendō*).

486　　SUBSTANTIVES DERIVED FROM ADJECTIVES

-ia: *memoria*, memory (*memor*); *concordia*, peace (*concors*); *sapientia*, wisdom (*sapiēns*); *dīvitiae*, pl., riches (*dīves*).

-itia: *laetitia*, joyfulness (*laetus*); *amīcitia*, friendship (*amīcus*); *mollitia*, also *mollitiēs*, softness (*mollis*).

-tās: *lībertās*, freedom (*līber*); *vēritās*, truth (*vērus*); *fēlīcitās*, happiness (*fēlīx*).

-tūdō: *fortitūdō*, valour (*fortis*); *multitūdō*, multitude (*multus*).

-mōnia: *ācrimōnia*, sharpness (*ācer*); *sānctimōnia*, sanctity (*sānctus*); *parcimōnia*, parsimony (*parcus*).

487   SUBSTANTIVES DERIVED FROM SUBSTANTIVES

-tor: *viātor*, traveller (*via*); *iānitor*, doorkeeper (*iānua*); *balneātor*, bath-keeper (*balneum*). The feminines *iānitrix, balneātrix* are used.

-ātus: *senātus*, senate (*senex*); *magistrātus*, magistracy (*magister*) ; *cōnsulātus*, consulship (*cōnsul*).

-iō, -ō: *lūdiō*, player (*lūdus*); *pelliō*, furrier (*pellis*); *centuriō*, captain of a hundred (*centum, centuria*); *praedō*, robber (*praeda*).

-ārius: *aquārius*, water-carrier (*aqua*); *tabulārius*, registrary (*tabula*). A secondary derivative is *tabellārius*, letter-carrier (*tabella*).

-ārium: *grānārium*, granary (*grānum*); *tabulārium*, archives (*tabula*).

-ētum, -tum: *olīvētum*, olive-grove (*olīva*); *rosētum*, rose-garden (*rosa*); *pīnētum*, a pine-wood (*pīnus*); *arbustum*, shrubbery; also the later form *arborētum* (stem *arbos-, arbor-*); *salictum*, willow-ground (*salix*).

-īna, -īnum: *textrīna*, weaver's shop (*textor*); *pistrīnum*, bakehouse (*pistor*).

-ulus -olus, (-a, -um): *ānulus*, little ring (*annus*); *gladiolus*, little sword (*gladius*); *fōrmula*, little form (*fōrma*); *līneola*, little line (*līnea*); *scūtulum*, little shield (*scūtum*); *palliolum*, little cloak (*pallium*).

-ellus, (-a, -um): *agellus*, small field (*ager*); *fābella*, short story (*fābula*); *flagellum*, little whip (*flagrum*); *corōlla*, chaplet (*corōna*).

-culus, (-a, um): *versiculus*, little verse (*versus*); *mātercula*, little mother (*māter*); *rēticulum*, little net (*rēte*).

488   ADJECTIVES DERIVED FROM VERBS

-āx: *audāx*, daring (*audeō*); *rapāx*, grasping (*rapiō*); *tenāx*, tenacious (*teneō*) ; *ferāx*, fruitful (*ferō*).

-bundus, -cundus: *furibundus*, raging (*furō*); *moribundus*, dying (*morior*); *iūcundus*, pleasant (*iuvō*).

-uus: *continuus*, continuous (*con-tineō*) ; *vacuus*, empty (*vacuō*); *assiduus*, persevering (*assideō*).

-ulus: *tremulus,* trembling (*tremō*); *querulus,* complaining (*queror*); *crēdulus,* trustful (*crēdō*).

-idus, -idis: *calidus,* hot (*caleō*); *pavidus,* timid (*paveō*); *viridis,* green (*vireō*).

-ilis: *ūtilis,* useful (*ūtor*) ; *facilis,* easy (*faciō*); *docilis,* teachable (*doceō*).

-bilis: *penetrābilis,* penetrable (*penetrō*); *flēbilis,* lamentable (*fleō*); but sometimes active: *penetrābile frīgus,* penetrating cold.

-īvus, joined to the supine stem: *captīvus,* captive (*capiō*); *natīvus,* native (*nāscor*); *fugitīvus,* fugitive (*fugiō*).

489   ADJECTIVES DERIVED FROM NOUNS

-ius: *rēgius,* royal (*rēx*); *plēbēius,* plebeian (*plēbs*); *ēgregius,* out of the common (*grex*).

-icus: *bellicus,* warlike (*bellum*); *barbaricus,* barbarous (*barbarus*); *Gallicus,* Gaulish (*Gallia*); *cīvicus,* civic (*cīvis*).

-ticus: *rūsticus,* belonging to the country (*rūs*); *domesticus,* domestic (*domus*).

-ānus, -iānus: *humānus,* human (*homō*); *urbānus,* urban (*urbs*); *Rōmānus,* Roman (*Rōma*); *Āfricānus,* African; *praetōriānus,* praetorian (*praetor*).

-nus: *frāternus,* fraternal (*frāter*); *aeternus,* eternal (*aetās*); *externus,* external (*exter*); *alternus,* alternate (*alter*).

-īnus: *marīnus,* marine (*mare*); *Latīnus,* Latin (Latium); *palātīnus,* belonging to the palace (*palātium*).

-estis: *caelestis,* heavenly (*caelum*); *agrestis,* rural (*ager*).

-ēnsis: *forēnsis,* belonging to the forum; *castrēnsis,* belonging to the camp (*castra*).

-ālis, -āris: *nātūrālis,* natural (*nātūra*); *generālis,* general (*genus*); *rēgālis,* kingly (*rēx*); *vulgāris,* common (*vulgus*); *salūtāris,* healthful (*salūs*) (see § 20).

-ōsus: *fōrmōsus,* beautiful (*fōrma*); *glōriōsus,* glorious (*glōria*).

-lentus: *fraudulentus,* deceitful (*fraus*); *turbulentus,* noisy (*turba*).

-bris, -cris: *fūnebris,* funereal (*fūnus*), *mediocris,* middling (*medius*).

-eus: *aureus*, golden (*aurum*); *ferreus*, iron (*ferrum*).
-ulus: *parvulus* very small (*parvus*).
-ellus: *misellus* poor (*miser*).
-tus: *modestus*, moderate (*modus*); *rōbustus*, strong (*rōbur*); *vetustus*, aged (*vetus*).
-tinus: *crāstinus*, of tomorrow (*crās*); *diūtinus*, lasting (*diū*).

490   VERBS DERIVED FROM NOUNS, ADJECTIVES

ā-stems: *cūrō*, take care (*cūra*); *onerō*, burden (*onus*); *pācō*, pacify (*pāx*). **Deponents**: *moror*, delay (*mora*); *dignor*, deem worthy (*dignus*); *miseror*, pity (*miser*).
ē-stems: *flōreō*, bloom (*flōs*); *lūceō*, shine (*lūx*); *flāveō*, am yellow (*flāvus*).
u-stems: *metuō*, fear (*metus*) ; *minuō*, diminish (*minus*).
ī-stems: *fīniō*, limit (*fīnis*); *serviō*, am a slave (*servus*); *largior*, bestow (*largus*).

491   VERBS COMPOUNDED WITH PREPOSITIONS

ā, ab, abs: *āvertō*, turn away; *absum*, am absent; *absterreō*, frighten away.
ad: *adeō*, go to; *adspiciō*, look at; *accipiō*, accept; *adferrō* or *afferō*, carry to; *adloquor*, address; *appōnō*, place near; *arripiō*, seize; *assentior*, agree; *attrahō*, attract.
ambi-: *ambiō*, go around.
con: *contrahō*, contract; *compōnō*, compose; *committō*, commit; *colligō*, collect; *corripiō*, seize violently; *cōnfīdō*, rely on.
dē: *dēcēdō*, depart; *dēcipiō*, deceive; *dēscendō*, come down.
ē, ex: *ēdūcō*, lead forth; *ēloquor*, utter; *ēvocō*, evoke; *ēffundō*, pour out; *exeō*, go forth; *expellō*, expel.
in: *īnferō*, bring into; *imperō*, command; *immineō*, overhang; *inligō* or *illigō*, bind on; *irrigō*, water; *indūrō*, make hard.
inter: *intersum*, am among; *interrogō*, question; *intellegō*, understand.
ob: *obtineō*, maintain; *offerō*, offer; *oppōnō*, oppose; *occurrō*, meet, occur.

per: *permittō*, let go, permit; *pereō*, perish; *pellūceō*, shine through, am transparent; *perterreō*, frighten greatly.

post: *postpōnō*, put after.

prae: *praecēdō*, go before; *praeferō*, prefer; *praesto*, excel.

praeter: *praetereō*, pass by.

prō, prōd-: *prōdeō*, go or come forth; *prōcēdō*, proceed; *prōpōnō*, propose; *prōmō*, produce.

red, re: *redeō*, return; *recordor*, remember; *referō*, refer; *restituō*, restore.

sē: *sēcernō*, separate; *sēparō*, separate; *sēcludō*, shut up, seclude.

sub: *subdō*, subdue; *submergō*, submerge; *subcurrō* or *succurrō*, succor; *sufferō*, suffer; *suggerō*, suggest; *supplicō*, supplicate; *surripiō*, steal; *suspiciō*, look up at, suspect.

trāns, trā: *trānsmittō*, transmit; *trānsportō*, transport; *trādūcō*, lead across; *trāiciō*, throw across.

Note: A few verbs are compounded with adverbs, as: *benedīcō*, commend (*bene dīcō*); *benefaciō*, benefit (*bene faciō*) *maledīcō*, speak ill (of) (*male dīcō*); *malefaciō*, do evil (to) (*male faciō*); *satisfaciō*, satisfy (*satis faciō*) ; *satisdō*, give bail (*satis dō*).

---

492 SPECIMENS OF COMPOUND WORDS: NOUN + VERB

auceps, birdcatcher (*avis, avi-capiō*).

agricola, husbandman (*ager, agro-colō*).

fidicen, lute-player (*fidēs-canō*)

tībīcen, flute-player (*tibia, tibi- canō*)

tubicen, trumpeter (*tuba, tubi-canō*)

artifex, artisan (*ars, arti-faciō*).

Lūcifer, morning star (*lūx, lūc-ferō*),

frūgifer, -a, -um, fruit-bearing (*frūx, frūg-ferō*).

Graiugena, Greek (*Graius, Graio-gignō*).

armiger, armor-bearer (*arma, armo-gerō*).

iūsiūrandum, oath (*iūs-iūrō*).

senātūscōnsultum, decree of the senate (*senātūs-cōnsultum*, from *cōnsulō*).

493 TWO SUBSTANTIVES, OR SUBSTANTIVE + ADJECTIVE

paterfamiliās, father of a family (*pater, familiās,* an old genitive).

rēspūblica, state, republic (*rēs-pūblicus*).

bipēs, two-footed (*bis-pēs*).

tridēns, three-pronged, trident (*trēs-dēns*).

ROMAN MONEY, WEIGHTS, MEASURES, AND TIME

494   MONEY

(a) The **ās** (primary unit) of money was the **lībra,** or pound of 12 ounces (**ūnciae**), and was thus divided:

ūncia = 1 oz. or ¹⁄₁₂ of the **ās.**	**septūnx** = 7 oz. or ⁷⁄₁₂ of the **ās.**
sextāns = 2 oz. or ⅙ of the **ās.**	**bēs** = 8 oz. or ⅔ of the **ās.**
quadrāns = 3 oz. or ¼ of the **ās.**	**dōdrāns** = 9 oz. or ¾ of the **ās.**
triēns = 4 oz. or ⅓ of the **ās.**	**dēxtāns** = 10 oz. or ⅚ of the **ās.**
quīncūnx = 5 oz. or ⁵⁄₁₂ of the **ās.**	**deūnx** = 11 oz. or ¹¹⁄₁₂ of the **ās.**
sēmissis = 6 oz. or ½ of the **ās.**	

(b) Interest rates were expressed in **ūnciae ūsūrae** =¹⁄₁₂% per month = 1% per annum. **Sextantēs ūsūrae** = ⅙% per month, etc.

Assēs ūsūrae = 1%. per month = 12% per annum. **Assēs ūsūrae** were also called **centēsimae: bīnae centēsimae** = 2% per month = 24 % per year. **Ūnciārium faenus** was 1 *ūncia* yearly per *ās* = 8⅓% per annum.

(c) **Hērēs ex asse**   means heir to the whole estate

Hērēs ex sēmisse, or }
Hērēs ex dīmidiā parte } means heir to half the estate

etc.   etc.

(d) The **sēstertius** (or **nummus**), was a silver coin equal to 2½ *assēs,* being ¼ of the **dēnārius** (coin of 10 *assēs*). Its symbol is **HS** (for **IIS,** *duo et sēmis,* 2½ *assēs*).

The **sēstertium** (= 1,000 *sēstertiī*) was not a coin, but a sum, and is only used in the plural number, *sēstertia.*

Sēstertia (also represented by **HS**) joined with the cardinal or distributive numbers, denotes so many 1,000 sēstertiī.

The numeral adverbs, joined with (or understanding) *sēstertiī* (gen. sing.), *sēstertium*, or *HS*, denote so many 100,000 *sestertiī*:

Thus   **HS.X** = sēstertiī decem, 10 sesterces

         HS.X̄ = *sēstertia dēna*, 10,000 sesterces

         H̄S̄.X̄ = *sēstertium deciēns*, 1,000,000 sesterces

(e) Fractions might also be expressed by the ordinals as denominators and the cardinals for numerators (above 1). Thus, ½ is *dīmidia pars;* ⅓ *tertia pars*, etc.; ⅙ *sexta* or *dīmidia tertia* (½ × ⅓); ⅛ *octāva pars* or *dīmidia quārta* (½ × ¼), etc. So ¹⁄₂₁ was *tertia septima* (⅓ × ⅐). Again, ⅔ was *duae tertiae*, or *duae partēs*, or *dīmidia et sexta* (½ + ⅙ = ⁴⁄₆ = ⅔). And ¾ is *trēs quārtae*, or *trēs partēs*, or *dīmidia et quārta*.

495   WEIGHT

The unit or *ās* of weight was the **lībra**, or Roman pound (the supposed weight which a man could support on his hand horizontally extended). It was divided duodecimally, the **ūncia** (ounce) being its 12th part; the **scrīpulum** (scruple) the 24th part of an *ūncia*. The *ūncia* was approximated 96% of the modern ounce, at about 27.3 g, the *lībra* at 328 g, only about 72% of the modern pound (which, of course, has 16 ounces).

496   LENGTH

The unit or *ās* of length was **pēs** (foot), also divided duodecimally, the **ūncia** (inch) being its 12th part.

Cubitum (cubit) was 1½ *pedēs*. The **ulna** (ell) was variously measured, sometimes = cubit. Land was measured out by the *decempeda* (rod of 10 feet). In roads the unit was the *passus*, pace or double step (5 *pedēs*). *Mille passūs* (5,000 feet) were the Roman mile, ⅛ of which was called a **stadium** (furlong). The exact measure of the *pēs* is a difficult point, but it seems to have been rather shorter than a foot avoirdupois.

497   SURFACE

The *ās* of surface was the **iūgerum** (the Roman acre), about ⅝ of an US or English acre (approx. 0.25 hectares). The **scrīpulum**, or **decempeda quadrāta** (ten square feet) was the most important subdivision of the *iūgerum*.

498   CAPACITY

1. Liquid measure

The *ās* was the **sextārius** (less than a pint), divided into 12 **cyathī** (wine ladles), one of which (its *ūncia*) was not quite half an ordinary wine-glass. 24 *sextāriī* were 1 **urna** (water jar), and 2 *urnae* were an **amphora**, a vessel of 10 cubic Roman feet.

2. Dry measure

Here too the *ās* was the **sextārius** and the **cyathus** its *ūncia;* 16 *sextāriī* made the **modius**, which was about 2.4 US gallons (approx. 9 litres).

499   TIME: THE ROMAN CALENDAR

Every Roman month had three chief days: **Kalendae** (Calends) **Nōnae** (Nones), **Īdūs** (Ides). The Calends were always the 1st day of the month; the Nones were usually on the 5th; the Ides on the 13th; but in four months the Nones were on the 7th, the Ides on the 15th:

> March, May, July, October; these are they
> Make Nones the 7th, Ides the 15th day.

These three days, the Calends, Nones, and Ides, were taken as points, from which the other days were counted backwards. That is, the Romans did not say, such and such a day after, etc., but such and such a day before the Calends, or Nones, or Ides. They reckoned inclusively, counting in the days at both ends; therefore the rules are: (1) For days before the Calends subtract the day of the month from the number of days in the month increased by two. (2) For days before the Nones or Ides subtract from the day on which they fall, increased by one.

Examples: May 31 **Prīdiē Kalendās Iūniās.**
May 30 **Ante diem tertium (a.d. III) Kal. Iūn**
May 11 **Ante diem quīntum (a.d. V) Īd. Māi.**
May 2 **Ante diem sextum (a.d. VI) Nōn. Māi.**

THE JULIAN CALENDAR

day of month	MĀRTIUS, MĀIUS, IŪLIUS, OCTOBER. 31 days			IĀNUĀRIUS, AUGUSTUS, DECEMBER, 31 days			APRĪLIS, IŪNIUS, SEPTEMBER, NOVEMBER, 30 days			FEBRUĀRIUS, 28 days, 29 days in every fourth year		
1	Kalendīs			Kalendīs		Dec.	Kalendīs		Nov.	Kalendīs		
2	a.d. VI		Oct.	a.d. IV			a.d. IV			a.d. IV		
3	a.d. V			a.d. III	Nōnās		a.d. III	Nōnās		a.d. III	Nōnās	
4	a.d. IV	Nōnās		Prīdiē			Prīdiē			Prīdiē		
5	a.d. III			Nōnīs			Nōnīs		Sept.	Nōnīs		
6	Prīdiē		Iūl.	a.d. VIII			a.d. VIII			a.d. VIII		
7	Nōnīs			a.d. VII		Aug.	a.d. VII			a.d. VII		Feb.
8	a.d. VIII			a.d. VI			a.d. VI			a.d. VI		
9	a.d. VII			a.d. V	Īdūs		a.d. V	Īdūs	Iūn.	a.d. V	Īdūs	
10	a.d. VI		Māi.	a.d. IV			a.d. IV			a.d. IV		
11	a.d. V			a.d. III			a.d. III			a.d. III		
12	a.d. IV	Īdūs		Prīdiē		Iān.	Prīdiē			Prīdiē		
13	a.d. III			Īdibus			Īdibus		Apr.	Īdibus		
14	Prīdiē		Mārt.	a.d. XIX			a.d. XVIII			a.d. XVI		
15	Īdibus			a.d. XVIII			a.d. XVII		Dec.	a.d. XV		
16	a.d. XVII			a.d. XVII		Iaān.	a.d. XVI			a.d. XIV		
17	a.d. XVI		Nov.	a.d. XVI			a.d. XV			a.d. XIII		
18	a.d. XV			a.d. XV			a.d. XIV			a.d. XII		
19	a.d. XIV			a.d. XIV			a.d. XIII			a.d. XI		
20	a.d. XIII			a.d. XIII			a.d. XII		Oct.	a.d. X		
21	a.d. XII			a.d. XII			a.d. XI	Kalendāas		a.d. IX	Kalendāas	Mārt.
22	a.d. XI		Aug.	a.d. XI			a.d. X			a.d. VIII		
23	a.d. X			a.d. X	Kalendāas	Sept.	a.d. IX			a.d. VII		
24	a.d. IX	Kalendāas		a.d. IX			a.d. VIII			a.d. VI		
25	a.d. VIII			a.d. VIII			a.d. VII		Iūl.	a.d. V		
26	a.d. VII		Iūn.	a.d. VII			a.d. VI			a.d. IV		
27	a.d. VI			a.d. VI			a.d. V			a.d. III		
28	a.d. V			a.d. V			a.d. IV			Prīdiē		
29	a.d. IV			a.d. IV		Feb.	a.d. III		Māi.			
30	a.d. III		Apr.	a.d. III			Prīdiē					
31	Prīdiē			Prīdiē								

In leap-years, February 24 (a.d. VI Kal. Mārt.) was reckoned twice – hence this day was called **diēs bissextus**, and the leap-year itself **annus bissextus**.

Note 1: *Ante diem tertium (a.d. III) Kal. Iūn.,* means 'on the third day before the Kalends of June,' or 'before the Kalends of June by three days.' *Diem tertium,* being placed between *ante* and *Kalendās,* is attracted to the accusative case. This mode of expression became so purely idiomatic that it was used with prepositions: *ex ante diem tertium, ex ante diem sextum,* &c.

Note 2: The names of the months are adjectives used in agreement with *mēnsis, m.* expressed or understood, *Iānuārius, Aprīlis, September,* &c. The old names of July and August were *Quintīlis, Sextīlis* (see next note), but later they were called Julius and Augustus after the two Caesars.

Note 3: The Roman calendar originally contained only ten months: *Mārtius* (31 days), *Aprīlis* (30 days), *Māius* (31 days), *Iūnius* (30 days), *Quintīlis* (31 days), *Sextīlis* (30 days), *September* (30 days), *October* (31 days), *November* (30 days) and *December* (30 days). This meant that there were only 304 calendar days in the year, leaving sixty-odd winter days 'off-calendar'. In about 713 B.C. the introduction (attributed to Numa Pompilius) of *Iānuārius* and *Februārius* brought the tally up to 355 days. The Julian Calendar, introduced by Julius Caesar in 45 B.C., consisted of 365 days and a leap-day every fourth year. It was not until 1582 that Pope Gregory introduced a minor revision to the Julian Calendar. Great Britain and its colonies (including those in North America) did not adopt the Gregorian Calendar until 1752.

Note 4: The Romans usually distinguished the year by the two consuls holding office, and sometimes by the regnal year of the emperor. The year was also expressed *ab urbe conditā,* from the founding of the city of Rome (traditionally identified as 753 B.C.).

500

ABBREVIATIONS

(1) Praenomina

A. Aulus	**M.** Mārcus	**Ser.** Servius
C. Gaius	**M'.** Mānius	**Sp.** Spurius
Cn. Gnaeus	**Mam.** Māmercus	**T.** Titus
D. Decimus	**P.** Pūblius	**Ti. (Tib.)** Tiberius
K. Kaesō	**Q.** Quīntus	
L. Lūcius	**S. (Sex.)** Sextus	

Note: A Roman of distinction had at least three names: the **praenōmen,** individual name; the **nōmen,** name showing the **gēns** or clan; and the **cognōmen,** surname showing the **familia** or family. Thus, *Lūcius Iūnius Brūtus*

expressed *Lūcius* of the *gēns Iūnia* and *Familia Brūtōrum*. To these were sometimes added one or more **agnōmina**, titles either of honour (as *Āfricānus,*
Macedonicus, Magnus, etc.), or expressing that a person had been adopted
from another *gēns*: as *Aemiliānus,* applied to the younger *Scīpiō Āfricānus,*
who was the son of *L. Paulus Aemilius,* but adopted by a *Scīpiō.* The full name
of the emperor *Augustus* (originally an *Octāvius*) after he had been adopted
by his uncle's will and adorned by the Senate with a title of honour, was
Gaius Iūlius Caesar Octāviānus Augustus.

---

(2) Varia

A. D. Ante diem
A. U. C. Annō urbis
  conditae *or* ab urbe conditā
Aed. Aedīlis
Cal. (Kal.) Calendae
Cos. Cōnsul
Coss. Cōnsulēs
D. Dīvus
Des. Dēsignātus
Eq. Rom. Eques Rōmānus
F. Fīlius
HS. Sēstertius,
  Sēstertium
Id. Īdus
Imp. Imperātor
Kal. (Cal.) Kalendae

L. Lībra
LL. Dupondius
Non. Nōnae
O. M. Optimus Maximus
P. C. Patrēs Cōnscrīptī
P. M. Pontifex Maximus
P. R. Populus Rōmānus
Pl. Plēbis
Proc. Prōcōnsul
S. Senātus
S. P. Q. R. Senātus
  Populusque Rōmānus
S. C. Senātūscōnsultum
S. D. P. Salūtem
  dīcit plūrimam
Tr. Tribūnus

FIGURES OF SPEECH

501   FIGURES OF SYNTAX

Asyndeton: omission of conjunctions: *Abiit, excessit, ēvāsit,*
ērūpit. Cicero.

Attraction: words are drawn by the influence of others to take
irregular constructions: (1) attraction of copulative verb
(§ 196); (2) attraction of relative and of adjective to relative

clause (§ 332). Attraction of case happens after copulative verbs, especially the dative (§ 224), and especially with *licet esse*: *Vōbīs licet esse beātis.* Horace. *Licuit esse ōtiōsō Themistoclī.* Cicero.

Ellipsis (omission): words are left out which can be supplied from the sense. Thus are used:

(1) An adjective without its substantive: *gelida, calida (aqua); dextra, sinistra (manus).*

(2) A genitive without the word on which it depends: *Caecilia Metellī (fīlia), Faustus Sullae (fīlius).*

(3) A verb without its object: *obīre (mortem); movēre (castra).*

(4) A sentence without its verb: *Suus cuique mōs. Quid multa?* (*dīcam*).

Enallage: use of one word for another:
(1) One part of speech for another: *aliud crās (alius diēs crāstinus).*
(2) One case for another: *Mātūtīne pater, seu Iāne libentius audīs.* HOR. (for *Iānus.*)
(3) One number for another: *nōs* for *ego; mīles* for *mīlitēs.*

Hendiadys: use of two substantives coupled by a conjunction for a substantive and adjective: *Paterīs lībāmus et aurō* (for *paterīs aureīs*). Virgil.

Hypallage: interchange of cases: *Dare classibus Austrōs.* Virgil. (for *dare classēs Austrīs.*) Also attraction of adjectives to substantives to which they do not properly belong: *Fontium gelidae perennitātēs.* Cicero. (for *fontium gelidōrum perennitātēs.*)

Hyperbaton: alteration of natural order of words: *Per tē deōs ōrō* (for *per deōs tē ōrō*). The four following figures belong to hyperbaton :
(1) **Anacoluthon**: passing from one construction to another before the former is completed: *Si, ut Graecī dīcunt, omnēs aut Graiōs esse aut barbarōs, vereor nē Rōmulus barbarōrum rēx fuerit.* Cicero.

(2) **Hysteron-proteron**: when, of two things, that which naturally comes first is placed last: *Moriāmur et in media arma ruāmus.* Virgil.

(3) **Anastrophe**: placing a preposition after its case: *quōs inter* for *inter quōs.* Horace.

(4) **Parenthesis**: interpolation of one sentence within another: *At tū (nam dīvum servat tūtēla poētās), praemoneō, vātī parce, puella, sacrō.* Tibullus.

Pleonasmus (redundance): use of needless words: *Sīc ōre locūta est.* Virgil

Polysyndeton: redundance of conjunctions: *Ūnā Eurusque Notusque ruunt crēberque procellīs Āfricus.* Virgil.

Syllepsis: Connection of a verb or adjective with a composite subject.

Synesis: Agreement with meaning not with form:

1 Gender: *Capita coniūrātiōnis virgīs caesī sunt.* Livy. *Capita*, though neuter in form, is masculine in meaning, therefore *caesī.*

2. Number: A collective noun or a phrase implying more than one, though singular in form, may take a plural verb: *Cētera classis… fūgērunt.* Livy. *Optimus quisque iussīs pāruēre.* Tacitus.

Tmesis: separation of the parts of a compound word: *Quae mē cumque vocant terrae.* Virgil. (for *quaecumque*).

Zeugma: connection of a verb or adjective with two words or clauses to both of which it does not equally belong; therefore zeugma is a sort of ellipsis: *Ex spoliīs et torquem et cognōmen induit;* put on the necklace and assumed the surname. Agreement with one only of two or more subjects is also called zeugma.

502   **FIGURES OF RHETORIC**

Allegoria: a chain of metaphors:

Claudite iam rīvōs, puerī, sat prāta bibērunt.   Virgil.
Cease to sing, shepherds, recreation enough has been taken.

Antithesis: contrast of opposites: *Urbis amātōrem Fuscum salvēre iubēmus rūris amātōres.* Horace.

Aposiopesis: the conclusion of a thought is suppressed: *Quos ego... sed mōtōs praestat compōnere flūctūs.* Virgil.

Apostrophe: an appeal to some person or thing: *Quid nōn mortālia pectora cōgis, auri sacra famēs?* Virgil. **Climax:** a high point of effect led up to gradually: *Quod libet iīs, licet; quod licet, possunt; quod possunt, audent.* Cicero.

Hyperbole: exaggeration.

Ironia: one thing is said while the contrary is meant, but so that the real meaning may be understood: *Ēgregiam vērō laudem et spolia ampla refertis tūque puerque tuus.* Virgil. (ignoble praise and paltry spoils).

Litotes: less is said than is meant: *nōn laudō* for *culpō.*

Metaphora: one expression put for another which has some resemblance to it in a different kind, generally a concrete for an abstract; *portus* for *refugium; sentīna* (dregs) *reīpūblicae* for *turpissimī cīvēs; exsultō* for *gaudeō.* A strong metaphor is often qualified by *quasi, tamquam, quīdam,* or *ut ita dīcam: In ūnā philosophiā quasi tabernāculum vītae suae allocārunt.* Cicero. *Scōpās, ut ita dīcam, mihi videntur dissolvere.* Cicero.

Metonymia: a related word conveying the same idea is put for another. *Mārs* for *bellum; cēdant arma togae.* Cicero. (for *cēdat bellum pācī*); *iuventūs* for *iuvenēs; Graecia* for *Graecī; aurum* for *vāsa aurea.*

Oxymoron: union of seeming contraries: *Temporis angustī mānsit concordia discors.* Lucan.

Paronomasia: a play upon the sound of words: *Tibi parāta sunt verba, huic verbera.* Terence.

Periphrasis: description of a simple fact by various attending circumstances. Instead of 'Now night is approaching,' Virgil says *Etiam summa procul vīllārum culmina fūmant, māiōrēsque* *cadunt altīs dē montibus umbrae.* See the beautiful periphrases of old age and death in *Ecclesiastes,* ch. xii.

Polyptoton: cases of the same noun are brought together: *Iam clipeus clipeīs, umbōne repellitur umbō; ēnse mināx ēnsis, pede pēs et cuspide cuspis.* Statius.

Prosopopoeia: personification. An abstract idea, as faith, hope, youth, memory, fortune, is addressed or spoken of as a person: *Tē Spēs et albō rāra Fidēs colit vēlāta pannō.* Horace.

Simile: illustration of a statement by an apt comparison, as: *Per urbēs Hannibal Ītalās ceu flamma per taedās vel Eurus per Siculās equitāvit undās.* Horace.

Synecdoche: the part stands for the whole: *caput* for *homō; tēctum* for *domus; carīna* for *nāvis.*

MEMORIAL LINES ON THE GENDER OF LATIN SUBSTANTIVES

The following verses are mostly of antiquarian interest. Not only do they rely on unreformed, anglicised pronunciations to make, for instance, *Athēnae* rhyme with *tree,* they also rely on obsolete English rhymes, such as *noun* with *shown.*

503   I. GENERAL RULES

The gender of a Latin noun
by meaning, form, or use is shown.

1.   A man, month, mountain, river, wind,
      and people masculine we find:
      Rōmulus, Octōber, Pindus, Padus, Eurus, Achīvī.

2.   A woman, island, country, tree,
      and city, feminine we see:
      Pēnelopē, Cyprus, Germānia, laurus, Athenae.

3   To nouns that cannot be declined
      The neuter gender is assigned:
      Examples fās and nefās give

And the verb-noun infinitive:
Est summum nefâs fallere:
Deceit is gross impiety.

Common are: sacerdos, dux,	*priest (priestess), leader*
vatēs, parēns et coniunx,	*seer, parent, wife (husband)*
cīvis, comes, custōs, vindex,	*citizen, companion, guard, avenger*
adolēscēns, infāns, index,	*youth (maid), infant, informer*
iūdex, testis, artifex	*judge, witness, artist*
praesul, exsul, opifex,	*director, exile, worker*
nērēs, mīles, incola,	*heir (heiress), soldier, inhabitant*
auctor, augur, advena,	*author, augur, newcomer*
hostis, obses, praeses, āles,	*enemy, hostage, president, bird*
patruēlis et satelles,	*cousin, attendant*
mūniceps et interpres,	*burgess, interpreter*
iuvenis et antistes,	*young person, overseer*
aurīga, prīnceps: add to these	*charioteer, chief*
bōs, damma, talpa, serpēns, sūs,	*ox (cow), deer, mole, serpent, swine*
camēlus, canis, tigris, perdix, grūs.	*camel, dog, tiger, partridge, crane*
(For exceptions see § 31)	

504   ## II. SPECIAL RULES FOR THE DECLENSIONS

First Declension (a-stems)

Rule   Feminine in First **a, ē,**
       Masculine **ās, ēs** will be.

Exc   Nouns denoting males in **a**
       are by meaning māscula:
       and masculine is found to be
       Hadria, the Adriatic Sea.

Second Declension (o-stems)

Rule   **O**-nouns in **us** and **er** become
       Masculine, but neuter **um.**

Exc Feminine are found in **us,**	
alvus, Arctus, carbasus,	*paunch, Great Bear, linen*
colus, humus, pampinus,	*distaff, ground, vine-leaf*
vannus: also trees, as pirus;	*winnowing-fan, pear-tree*
with some jewels, as sapphīrus;	*sapphire*
neuter pelagus and vīrus.	*sea, poison*
Vulgus neuter commonly,	*common people*
rarely masculine we see.	

Third Declension (consonant and i-stems)

Rule 1 Third-nouns masculine prefer
    endings ō, or, ōs, and **er**;
    add to which the ending **ēs**,
    if its cases have increase.

Exc.(a) Feminine exceptions show
    Substantives in **dō** and **gō**.
    But ligō, ōrdō, praedō, cardō,   *spade, order, pirate, hinge*
    masculine, and common margō.   *margin*

Exc.(b) Abstract Nouns in **iō** call
    feminine, one and all:
    masculine will only be
    things that you may touch or see,
    (as curculiō, vespertīliō,   *weevil, bat*
    pugiō, scīpio, and pāpiliō)   *dagger, staff, butterfly*
    with the nouns that number show,
    such as terniō, sēniō.   *3, 6*

Exc.(c) Echo feminine we name: *echo*
    carō (carnis) is the same.   *flesh*

Exc.(d) Aequor, marmor, cor decline   *sea, marble, heart*
    neuter; arbor feminine.   *tree*

Exc.(e) Of the substantives in **os**,
    feminine are cōs and dōs;   *whetstone, dowry*
    while, of Latin nouns, alone
    neuter are os (ossis), *bone*
    and ōs (ōris), *mouth*: a few
    Greek in **os** are neuter too.*

Exc.(f) Many neuters end in **er**,
    siler, acer, verber, vēr,   *withy, maple, stripe, spring*
    tūber, über, and cadāver,   *hump, udder, carcase*
    piper, iter, and papāver.   *pepper, journey, poppy*

Exc.(g) Feminine are compēs, teges,   *fetter, mat*
    mercēs, merges, quiēs, seges,   *fee, sheaf, rest, com.*
    though their cases have increase:
    with the neuters reckon aes.   *copper*

Rule 2 Third-nouns feminine we class
    ending **is, x, aus**, and **ās**,
    s to consonant appended,
    ēs in flection unextended.

Exc.(a) Many nouns in **is** we find
to the masculine assigned:

amnis, axis, caulis, collis,	*river, axle, stalk, hill*
clūnis, crīnis, fascis, follis,	*buttock, hair, bundle, bellows*
fūstis, ignis, orbis, ēnsis,	*bludgeon, fire, orb, sword*
pānis, piscis, postis, mēnsis,	*bread, fish, post, month*
torris, unguis, and canālis,	*stake, nail, canal*
vectis, vermis, and nātālis,	*lever, worm, birthday*
sanguis, pulvis, cucumis,	*blood, dust, cucumber*
lapis, assēs, mānēs, glīs.	*stone, nets, ghosts, dormouse*

Exc.(b) Chiefly masculine we find,
sometimes feminine declined,

callis, sentis, fūnis, fīnis,	*path, thorn, rope, end*
and in poets torquis, cinis.	*necklace, cinder*

Exc.(c) Masculine are most in **ex**:

feminine are forfex, lēx,	*shears, law*
nex, supellex; common, pūmex,	*death, furniture, pumice*
imbrex, ōbex, silex, rumex.	*tile, bolt, flint, sorrel*

Exc.(d) Add to masculines in **ix**,

fornix, phoenix, and calix.	*arch, phoenix, cup*

Exc.(e) Masculine are adamās,

elephās, mās, gigās, ās:	*adamant*
	elephant, male, giant, as [weight &c.]
vas (vadls) masculine is known,	*surety*
vas (vasis) is a neuter noun.	*vessel*

Exc.(f) Masculine are fons and mōns,

chalybs, hydrōps, gryps, and pōns,	*iron, dropsy, griffin, bridge*
rudens, torrēns, dēns, and cliens,	*cable, torrent, tooth, client*
fractions of the ās, as triēns.	*four ounces*
Add to masculines tridēns,	*trident*
oriēns, and occidēns,	*east, west*
bidēns (*fork*); but bidēns (*sheep*),	
with the feminines we keep.	

Exc.(g) Masculine are found in **ēs**

verrēs and acīnacēs.	*boar, scimetar*

Rule 3 Third-nouns neuter end **a, e,**
ar, ur, us, c, l, n, and **t**.

Exc.(a) Masculine are found in **ur**

furfur, turtur, vultur, fūr.	*bran, turtle-dove, vulture, thief*

Exc.(b) Feminine in **ūs** a few
    keep, as virtūs, the long **ū**:   *virtue*
    servitūs, iuventūs, salūs,   *slavery, youth, safety*
    senectūs, tellūs, incūs, palūs.   *old-age, earth, anvil, marsh*

Exc.(c) Also pecus (pecudis)   *beast*
    feminine in gender is.

Exc.(d) Masculine appear in **us**
    lepus (leporis) and mūs.   *hare, mouse*

Exc.(e) Masculines in **l** are mūgil,   *mullet*
    cōnsul, sal, and sōl, with pugil.   *consul, salt, sun, boxer*

Exc.(f) Masculine are rēn and splēn,   *kidney, spleen*
    pecten, delphīn, attagēn.   *comb, dolphin, grouse*
Exc.(g) Feminine are found in **ōn**
    Gorgōn, sindōn, halcyōn.   *Gorgon, muslin, kingfisher*

Fourth Declension (u-stems)

Rule   Masculines end in **us;** a few
    are neuter nouns, that end in **ū**.

Exc.   Women and trees are feminine,
    with acus, domus, and manus,   *needle, house, hand,*
    tribus, Īdūs, porticus.   *tribe, the Ides, porch*

Fifth Declension (e-stems)

Rule   Feminine are fifth in **ēs**,
    except merīdiēs and diēs.   *noon, day*

Exc.   Dies in the singular
    common we define;
    but its plural cases are
    always masculine.

List of Prepositions

With Accusative
ante, apud, ad, adversus,   prope, propter, per, secundum,
circum, circā, citrā, cis,   suprā, versus, ultrā, trāns;
contrā, inter, ergā, extrā,   Add super, subter, sub and in,

---

* As *melos*, melody, epos, *epic*, poem.

īnfrā, intrā, iuxtā, ob,
penes, pōne, post, and praeter,

when *motion* 'tis, not *state*,
they mean.

With Ablative

ā, a.b, absque, cōram, de,
palam, clam, cum, ex, and ē,
sine, tenus, prō, and prae.

Add super, subter, sub and in,
when state, not motion 'tis they
mean.

Subject Index

[Note: reference is to sections, not page numbers]

abbreviations, 500
ablative case, definition of, 30; uses of, 228
et seq.
  absolute, 237
  of agent, 239, 298, 300
  of association, 233
  of cause, 241
  of comparison, 231
  English rendering of, 30 (n. 2)
  in -ī .and -e (3rd decl.), 45, 46, 74, (adj.);
  in -ubus (4th decl.), 55 (n.1)
  of instrument, 240
  locative, 246
  of manner, 236
  of measure, 244
  of origin, 230
  of place where, 268; from where, 270,
  271, 274
  of price, 245
  of quality, 234
  of respect, 235
  of the road by which, 275
  of separation, 229
  of space, 282
  of Time, 276, 277,279, 280
  with contentus, dignus (indignus),
  fretus, opus est, ūsus est. 243
  with fruor, fungor, potior, ūtor, vescor,
  242; dignor, 243
abstract substantives, 27
accent, 9
accusative case
  definition of, 30
  uses of, 203 et seq.
  adverbial, 213
  cognate, 212
  double, 206, 208, 298
  in exclamations, 209 (n.)
  of extent, 278, 281–3
  in -im (3rd decl.),45 (nn.); in -is or
  -ēs (pl.), 45–47, 49 (n. 1)
  of direct object, 204 et seq., 215
  of neuter adjectives and pronouns, as
  adverbs, 213 (n. 2)
  after passive verbs, 210, 296
  of place to where, 211, 269, 271, 273
  with infinitive, 201, 414
accusative case
  with prepositions, 286, 287
  of respect, 213
active voice, definition of, 108
adjectival clauses, 410, 450 et seq.

adjectives
  definition of, 25
  used adverbially, 308
  agreement of, 193
  comparative, 310
  comparison of, 76 et seq.; irregular, 83
  declension of, 70 et seq.
  taking genitive or dative, 218 (n.)
  numeral, 88 et seq.
  used as substantives, 304–8
  superlative, 307, 309, 310 (n.)
Adonius (versus), 482
advantage, dative of, 221
adverbial clauses, 410, 421 et seq.
adverbs
  of affirmation, 170
  of cause, 166
  comparison of, 85 et seq.
  of degree, 166
  of doubt, 170
  formation of, 163
  of limitation, 110
  of manner, 164
  of negation, 170
  numeral, 88, 90
  of order, 169
  of place, 167
  of question, 170
  of time, 168
  use of, 395–398
adversative conjunctions, 177
affirmation, adverbs of, 170
age: how expressed, 278 (n. 2);
  genitive of, 256
agent, ablative of, 239, 296, 300; dative of,
  222, 381
agnomen, 500
agreement (the four concords), 192 et seq.
Alcaic stanza, 483
allegoria, 502
alphabet, the Latin, 2
anacoluthon, 501
anacrusis, definition of, 481 (n.)
analytic languages, meaning of, 24 (n. 1)
anapaest, 474, 479
anastrophe, 501
answers: affirmative, 408; negative,409
antecedent, 195, 330 et seq.
antithesis, 502
aorist, Greek: no corresponding separate
  tense in Latin, 105 (n.)

Index of Latin Words

[Note: reference is to sections, not page numbers]

Typeset in the United Kingdom
of Great Britain & Northern Ireland
by Tiger of the Stripe,
Richmond, Surrey.
The typeface is
Adobe Myriad Pro.

Printed in the United Kingdom
by Lightning Source UK Ltd.
131893UK00001B/42/P